Praise for *A Jewish Trinity*

The work of theological reflection in Jewish-Christian dialogue too often has been lop-sided, with Christian theological perspectives dominating. In this book, Alan Brill offers a Jewish counterweight, indicating new pathways for Jewish comparative theological reflections on core Christian doctrines. Such work is needed in order to propel the dialogue further.

Daniel Joslyn-Siemiatkoski, Kraft Family Professor and director of the Center for Christian-Jewish Learning at Boston College, and author of *The More Torah, the More Life: A Christian Commentary on Mishnah Avot*

A Jewish Trinity: Contemporary Christian Theology through Jewish Eyes is a groundbreaking study that signifies a new development in the relation of Jews to Christianity. Alan Brill should be commended for the breadth and depth of his scholarship, as well as for his openness of mind and respectful approach to Christian tenets of faith. This is a unique achievement, and both Jews and Christians will greatly benefit from reading it.

Yaakov Ariel, professor of religious studies, University of North Carolina–Chapel Hill

This book brims with generosity to Brill's Christian interlocutors, grounded in his lifelong serious study of Christian texts and theologies and in his mastery of Jewish traditions. That such a book exists is a cause for rejoicing. Too often, Jewish and Christian thinkers avoid talking together in a constructively comparative way, due to a paralyzing fear of getting things wrong or being criticized by the other. This book is a treasure trove for future conversation, undertaken in a spirit of respect while avoiding a false syncretism.

Matthew Levering, James N. Jr. and Mary D. Perry Chair of Theology, Mundelein Seminary, and author of *Engaging the Doctrine of Israel*

Alan Brill is central to the new age of Christian-Jewish theological dialogue and cooperation. Here, he shows his unique mastery of the greats of modern Christian theology. Brill reviews traditional Jewish and Christian background materials to modern positions to reveal fascinating parallels and important differences between Christian and Jewish theology. The book will be of great interest to Christians interested in comparisons between Jewish and Christian theology. In addition, it holds deep resources for work in constructive Jewish theology and contemporary Christian theology.

Steven Kepnes, professor of world religions
and Jewish studies, Colgate University

Alan Brill is a master of Jewish and Christian sources, and this is a breakthrough book. He examines key Christian doctrines, showing commonality, difference, and intriguing unanswered questions arising from his comparative exercise. Brill keeps the conversation open and avoids any facile assimilation.

Gavin D'Costa, professor of interreligious theology, Pontifical
University of St Thomas Aquinas, Rome, and emeritus
professor of Catholic theology, University of Bristol

Alan Brill's direct engagement of Christian systematic theology helps advance the profoundly important but neglected area of theological study in the dialogue called for by the Second Vatican Council. The book significantly deepens the theological dimension of contemporary Christian-Jewish dialogue.

Matthew Tapie, associate professor of theology,
and director of the Center for Catholic-Jewish
Studies, Saint Leo University

Brill's approach to Christian and Jewish theologies as two vibrant, diverse, and constantly evolving traditions makes this book a true tour de force in comparative theology. Brill compellingly demonstrates that these two traditions coexist in a shared theological "neighborhood," at times intersecting and at times diverging, without ever renouncing their common intellectual and spiritual milieu. *A Jewish Trinity* offers an inspiring, illustrative, and delightful journey into the multidimensional relationship between Christian and Jewish theologies, through which one can learn much about both oneself and the other.

Karma Ben Johanan, Department of Comparative Religion, The Hebrew University of Jerusalem, and author of *Jacob's Younger Brother: Christian-Jewish Relations after Vatican II*

A JEWISH TRINITY

A JEWISH TRINITY

CONTEMPORARY CHRISTIAN THEOLOGY THROUGH JEWISH EYES

ALAN BRILL

FORTRESS PRESS
Minneapolis

A JEWISH TRINITY
Contemporary Christian Theology through Jewish Eyes

30 29 28 27 26 25 1 2 3 4 5 6 7 8 9

Library of Congress Cataloging-in-Publication Data

Names: Brill, Alan, author.
Title: A Jewish trinity : contemporary Christian theology through Jewish eyes / Alan Brill.
Description: Minneapolis : Fortress Press, [2025] | Includes bibliographical references and index.
Identifiers: LCCN 2024055041 (print) | LCCN 2024055042 (ebook) | ISBN 9781506484235 (paperback) | ISBN 9781506484242 (ebook)
Subjects: LCSH: Judaism--Relations--Christianity. | Christianity and other religions--Judaism. | Judaism--Doctrines--Comparative studies.
Classification: LCC BM535 .B7325 2025 (print) | LCC BM535 (ebook) | DDC 230--dc23/eng/20250209
LC record available at https://lccn.loc.gov/2024055041
LC ebook record available at https://lccn.loc.gov/2024055042

Cover image: A general view of the ceiling of Prague's Spanish Synagogue is pictured on December 30, 2014 in Prague, Czech Republic, sourced from rysos/Getty Images
Cover design: Kris E. Miller

Print ISBN: 978-1-5064-8423-5
eBook ISBN: 978-1-5064-8424-2

CONTENTS

PREFACE

In 1943, Trude Weiss-Rosmarin wrote her widely influential work *Judaism and Christianity: The Differences*, where she sets out to show that the two religions are fundamentally irreconcilable and contradictory. For many Jews and Christians, Weiss-Rosmarin's basic unbridgeable theological divide between the religions remains a truism.[1] This book rejects Weiss-Rosmarin's simple zero-sum declaration by asking whether the Jewish theological vision and the Christian theological vision are fundamentally irreconcilable, or can the positions be conceptually bridged? This book reopens the question from a contemporary perspective situated in our current historical and theological understandings of Judaism and Christianity.

I have been thinking about this project for decades. As heir of the Jewish-Christian reconciliation of the latter half of the twentieth century, I attended Fordham University, a Jesuit University, where I obtained a doctorate in Catholic theology. I learned Christian theology firsthand, having read as part of my training Augustine of Hippo, Richard of Saint Victor, Thomas Aquinas, Bonaventure, Karl Rahner, and Jürgen Moltmann. My field was comparative mysticism, where I absorbed the medieval classics and learned how to make productive comparisons between the texts of different religious traditions.

Consequently, instead of tentatively learning to understand Christianity, I became the one helping Christians understand Christian theology, teaching them to catch allusions to Christian classics, and how to compare church documents. I am the one explaining contemporary Christian theology including Christology and ecclesiology to Christians, rather than the one to whom it needs to be explained.

The Christians I encounter teaching in New Jersey in a Catholic diocesan university are comfortable with Jewish instructors and knowledgeable about Jews; most have attended a synagogue service, and many go out of their way to wish me greetings before Jewish holidays. The original obstacles to a Jewish-Christian encounter seem remote when one teaches in a department of Jewish-Christian studies that situates early Christianity in a Jewish context, teaches Christian students to read classical Hebrew, and grants certificates in Jewish and Holocaust studies to Christian students. My experience is part of a growing trend in twenty-first century theological education of numerous programs and centers of Jewish-Christian studies and many institutions where Jewish studies is integrated into theological studies.

In 2011, I was invited to give a lecture at the Boston Theological Institute, a consortium of nine Christian theological schools whose members include institutions of every major Christian church or denomination. The event was to celebrate the membership of the Hebrew College into the consortium, the first non-Christian institution to join. My talk was "Recognizing the Other: Sameness and Difference in a Jewish Theology of Christianity." When invited to speak, I considered as the major question: How does a Jewish seminary fit into a consortium of nine Christian seminaries? and more generally, How can we appreciate both the similarities and the differences between the two faiths? My desire was to avoid a generic unifying pluralism and instead to focus on the past and present attempts to compare the specifics of the two faiths. My talk showed that a comparison is not as simple as a choice of "same" or "different," but the relationship is rather an overlap of different models of interconnection. I stated that interreligious comparisons remain "a field of tension between similarity and difference, between a sense of religious interconnection and recognition of the distinctiveness of the other tradition."[2] An edited version of my talk was published several months later.[3]

I was not expecting, however, to wake up one morning to find that the well-known sociologist of religion Peter Berger had read my talk and dedicated an online article to my thesis. I have long respected Berger's theological observations, feeling that he well understood the current trends of theological belief. I was delighted with his appraisal of my article: "Brill's own approach is nuanced, taking seriously both the differences and the commonalities between Judaism and Christianity." He goes on, "beyond the ideas of intellectuals who write books to the 'lived religion' of the many more people who have not read these books." Berger summarized my approach as, "He makes the important point that the differences between Judaism and Christianity are not greater than the differences present *within* each. He rejects abstract 'essentialism,' which looks at every tradition as an inert construct remaining unchanged from generation to generation." Finally, Berger concludes: "It is my impression that Brill is correct in his view on the growing openness on the Jewish side."[4]

My openness in this book has three interrelated goals. The first is to explain where the dividing lines are between the religions in an age of openness. During the polemical ages, any difference was magnified into a chasm, minor variances were treated as unbridgeable divides. My approach leaves differences in place but seeks to explain the differences. Second, to explain to Jews why Christian theology is not inscrutable and to Christians how Judaism is a very different theology. Third, to show the unacknowledged deep convergences in theology in the last half century. Our theologies converge from mutual exposure to modern life and thought, and by means of exposure to the thought of the other community. However, my goal is not to create a common covenant or blending of the distinct religions. There remain irreconcilable differences despite the recent convergences.

From Disputation to Dialogue

Let us briefly survey the timeliness of this growing openness. The historical attitude of Christianity toward Judaism has been one of hatred, persecution, and tragedy. The relations between two religions could not have been any more awful than those between Judaism and Christianity. For centuries Jews suffered discrimination and persecution in countries that defined themselves as Christian, culminating in the unspeakable horrors of the Holocaust built on a long history of church-supported antisemitism.

Starting with the early church, for example Chrysostom and Ambrose, there was outright hostility among church leaders toward Judaism. The early Church of Nicaea, as well as Athanasius, and Constantine held Judaism in very low regard as "an offensive, anti-Christian faith." This produced a two-millennium animosity. Christians considered Jews as damned and as working for the devil. Jews were accused in the ritual killing of Christians, desecration of the host, and poisoning of Christian wells. The history of Christian attacks against Jews including the killing and burning of Jews in blood libels and in auto-da-fé is etched in Jewish memory. The cross is a holy symbol of salvation for Christians but was, for premodern Jews, a demonic signal of terror and anti-Jewish violence. In Christian-Jewish dialogue today there are those who still wish to accentuate the historical burden of guilt and failure of the Christians and the church.

The Vatican II document Nostra Aetate in 1965 was a sea change in Jewish-Christian relations in which Christians switched from being enemies to friends. During the post–Vatican II era, there was a period of getting acquainted between the Jewish and Catholic leadership. On the Jewish side, books and articles appeared concerning Scripture, antisemitism, and the Holocaust, but little theology. The pioneers of dialogue, Marc Tanenbaum, Ben Zion Bokser, and even Abraham Joshua Heschel, did not engage seriously with Christian theology on topics such as the Trinity, the Incarnation, or original sin.[5]

Since the late 1990s, there has been a turn toward theology, but almost all Jewish thinkers who wrote at the time still considered Christian theology (Trinity, the Incarnation, salvation) as inscrutable. They claimed Jews cannot understand the Trinity or Christian theology. However, and despite differences, they said that we can acknowledge that both religions worship one God and follow a morality grounded in the divine. In a vein of ethical pluralism, some Jews involved in interfaith considered Trinity, the Incarnation, and salvation the same as the Jewish idea of upholding creation by making the world a better place and to work for a better future. For these pluralistic thinkers, both faiths say the same thing in different ways; Christianity just uses Christian signals and symbols and Jews use Jewish symbols.[6]

I entered the field of interfaith encounters decades after the great strides made in Nostra Aetate reversing a millennium of anti-Judaism. John Paul II went further by acknowledging Judaism as a living faith, recognizing the Holocaust, and making a historic official visit to the state of Israel. The original participants of the early 1960s were passing away, including my own teacher Rabbi Walter Wurzburger, who originally brought me into the interfaith discussions.

At this time, I was involved in a discussion at a forum where a proponent and an opponent argued about Judaism and Christianity commonalities, which turned entirely on the binary question of same and difference as well as the binary dichotomy of pluralist or exclusivist. Either Judaism and Christianity are the same or they are different. Either we accept a common Jewish-Christian covenant after decades of dialogue or we reaffirm that we have irreconcilable differences. I interjected that there are other positions aside from "same" and "different;" thus the writing of my series of books on the topic began. There is not just black and white, but also multiple shades of grey.

My Position

I do not believe a summary of the differences between the religions is as simple as a choice of "same" or "different" but rather an overlap of different models of interconnection. Recent scholarly work shows theological separation between Judaism and Christianity is not as contradictory as previously thought. We need to set up lines based on the new scholarship on the rabbinic and medieval periods as well as the interplay of modern thought. The two religions are of a converging and diverging history. Rather than irreconcilable noncomparable differences, we now can explore a variety of relationships, parallel, divergent, and convergent, and we can begin to understand each other, as well as be able to engage in comparative theology.

If I compare the specifics of Christian theology as presented in an introductory Christian theology volume to Jewish theology, we find that if the author sets out six points of a Christian theological idea such as original sin, Jews are likely to share three to five of them. Hence, both religions can be put in the other's terms. Theological points can be put onto a scale of similarity and difference. Not a yes/no or same/different dichotomy but a range of factors in common and those in difference. In many cases the similarities are due to scriptural, philosophic, and structural connections, so that even the differences show signs of interrelation.

My goal is not a quantification of similarity and difference, or an abstract checklist. Rather, my goal is to point out that our popular theological language usually fails to break issues down into component parts. Looking at component parts helps us move beyond binary thinking toward the difference between the faiths, from there we can enter the ever more important issues of liturgy and lived religion.

In comparing the two faiths, the first thing that I need to point out is that the Jewish narrative of the Exodus, Sinai, and the monarchy in Israel is quite different from the Christian narrative of the birth, life, passion, death, and resurrection of Christ. We have different fundamental narratives. Yet, we cannot remain just with the abyss of opposing narratives of Sinai or passion, Torah or Christ. On some topics, my results are closer to the way that we write books comparing Catholicism to the Reformed Church or Lutheranism. And on other topics, the comparisons are closer to the comparison of rejected early first-century Christian positions to those that became doctrinally accepted.

The different goals between Judaism and Christianity are not like the difference between two people travelling from Washington, DC, to either Boston or Honolulu but rather two people starting in Washington, DC, and then each going to a different city in Massachusetts. They both share many of the same roads and both must cross the George Washington Bridge. There is a common starting point, overlaps in routes, and then similar but different end points. We are from a common spiritual neighborhood in the first centuries, afterward we greatly diverged, we gained elements of commonality in medieval Aristotelianism, we greatly diverged again, and now in the contemporary era of modern thought we are converging again.

We need to realize that many of the differences between Judaism and Christianity are not greater than the differences within Judaism or Christianity itself. There may be a greater difference between the portrayal of God in Exodus, *Tanhuma*, Maimonides, *Zohar*, Hermann Cohen, or Rabbi Kook than between points of convergence between the faiths. Surprisingly, many Jewish theologians have also avoided discussing the complexity of the Jewish conceptions of God, whether rabbinic, medieval, or modern period, midrashic, kabbalistic, and Hasidic, looking only at the rationalism of the early twentieth century. A strict neo-Maimonidean rationalist, who excludes most midrash and kabbalah as not aligning with rationalism or with modern sensibilities, would not be comfortable with many of my comparisons. To do comparative work, one needs to work with a broad palette of prior ideas.

The differences between the religions are real and we should not get lost in undifferentiated pluralism, but Judaism and Christianity can be compared. We need openness to the otherness and to see difference between the faiths but not to see difference where there is no difference.

Finally, despite my focus on theological topics, there are similarities and differences that are not theological. Lived religion emphasizes the role of the cultural and historical forces and the living communities themselves. The process by which the descendants of Jewish and Christian immigrants are now meeting in the suburbs, a place where both are currently in similar habitats based on similar trajectories of integration into the United States, is just as crucial for the comparisons. Specific points of contact in Boston, San Antonio, or Paris yield different results. Location and context are important, in that, there are many forms of Judaism and Christianity, many different interpretive contexts and theologians. These chapters will be read differently in different contexts.

For interfaith work to be meaningful, even an academic book like this one, we need hospitality consisting of more than just the one-time meeting, rather the hospitality that creates openness to allow theology to come to be. We need to listen to the other faith without preconceived notions. We seek the hospitality of the other faith that allows us to go out of our comfort zones and be humbled or surprised. A hospitality with the other faith that invites further conversation, humility, listening, and mutual respect. Interfaith work should expose us to moods, sensibilities, attitudes, and inward passages that we would otherwise seldom have cause to understand in our current religious commitment.

When one crosses over into the religious life of another religious believer and learns the truths that animate what the other believes, the study also means coming back to your religion and asking new questions about its historical choices, and contemporary options. One must also learn about the other religion in its own terms. Jews are not waiting for a messiah in the Christian sense and Jews are not worried about hell; Christians, unlike Jews, see the Trinity as monotheism and Sin with a capital *S* as the human condition.

One of my firm principles is the need to get up out of the armchair and encounter the other religion. Do not essentialize the other religion from a textbook of world religions. Contemporary Jewish thought is not automatically the ideas of midrash or medieval Jewish philosophy, and Christian theology is not necessarily the same as patristic, medieval, or nineteenth-century Christian thought.

Some contemporary Jewish thinkers have yet to notice that the current Christian theological view is not the same as the view learned in a college medieval history class. Many Jews think Christians still understand their faith in medieval scholastic or Neoplatonic terms and are adamant about contemporary Christian beliefs based on something they read in their college textbook. They may still refer to Catholicism in its medieval or pre–Vatican II forms and still think of Protestantism as teaching sixteenth-century formulations. The Jewish side, including some active members of dialogue who seek commonality, still seems unaware of contemporary Christian theology such as Karl Barth,

Rahner, Moltmann, or Walter Kasper. Jews should acknowledge that Christians understand their faith in modern terms, just as modern Jews understand their Judaism in modern terms.

A pioneer who tried to acknowledge the closeness in contemporary thought was Pinchas Lapide (1922–1997), theologian and an Israeli ambassador in Milan. He had wonderful, productive dialogues with Jürgen Moltmann, Karl Rahner, and Hans Kung back in the 1970s and 1980s.[7] Lapide acknowledged that Judaism has many metaphysical and logos theories similar to Christianity, endeavoring to make a genuine effort to find some commonality between Christian Trinitarian language and Hebrew biblical imagery. Lapide related to Christianity as bringing, albeit encrusted, the monotheistic belief in the God of Abraham, Isaac, and Jacob to the gentile world, therefore he relegated Trinitarian language as a theoretical excretion formed around the monotheistic belief at the heart of Jesus's message.[8] The interfaith scholar Leonard Swidler writes in the foreword to the Lapide-Moltmann dialogue that this conversation yielded "exciting new insights into the meaning of reality that neither alone had more than an inkling of." Encouraging for future work, Swidler exhorts, "As a result . . . each is more profoundly a Jew and a Christian, respectively, but at the same time each is profoundly closer to each other."

This commitment to encountering the other religion in its contemporary form is especially important as a corrective to pluralists who may not be concerned or exposed to religious difference or lived religion. We do not know anything exhaustive about the other side but need to create openings for understanding. We need to put away the preconceptions of difference and work for commonality, but then discover the boundaries. We must give a charitable reading of the other faith and at the same time accept the insurmountable difference.

Concurrently, we need a commitment to a specific home orientation. We can be travelers and guests in the home of another. But then we needed to return to our own home. There is no home in general or religion in general. No primordial faith deeper than any one religion, but an engagement of one cultural religious system as understood by someone of a different system. One learns about the other side and uses one's imagination to enter the world of the other, then compares details. Encountering another religion allows the imagination to stretch beyond its established religious boundaries. It is through the imaginary insights and experiences of other religious traditions that one may come to a new awareness of distinct aspects of one's own religious tradition.

In the process of convergence ignoring the theological, symbolic, contextual, and liturgical differences is foolish, and seeing where the similarities lie is crucial. Yet, as a good guest or even as a tourist, we must pay exquisite attention to detail and aim to work on a thick description. Many aspects, especially the liturgical and ritual aspects remain foreign territory even after concepts are understood.

The goal is to avoid imposing one's home categories on a different religion. There was a need for me to distance myself from my home tradition and learn the questions, presuppositions, and outlooks of Christianity. But in my case, with a doctorate in Catholic theology and courses in Catholic thought under my professional belt, Christianity is a field for comparison that I have lived with for decades.

Surprisingly, my resolution to finally write this book came from an encounter with Hinduism. I had a fellowship to go to India and study Hinduism. In some respects, approaching Hinduism was easier than approaching Christianity because Jews did not have a prior negative relationship with Hinduism. Polymorphic Hinduism may seem theologically distant from Judaism. However, in the process of engaging with the diversity of Hindus and Hinduism, I saw the ability to open new vistas and to allow understanding of similarity and difference where previously the comparison was thought not possible. If I can do a theological comparison with Hinduism, a religion further from Judaism and one in which I have not been trained, then I certainly can compare Christian theology with Jewish thought. We should consider that Jews and Christians may be related in the same way that the various paths of the dharma—Hindus, Buddhists, Jains, and Sikhs—are related. They share common language but have different interpretations. Surprising to many, I can write a parallel book to this one about comparing Judaism with Islam, Buddhism, or Confucianism, as I have written such a book comparing Judaism and Hinduism.

Outline

The book is limited to six chapters, containing six major Christian theological doctrines. I was tempted to add five additional doctrines but limiting the discussion to six conveys a clear direction and method. I am not discussing the Holy Spirit, miracles, divine name, kingdom of God, and saintliness. I especially wish that I had included the Holy Spirit because many Jewish authors confuse the indwelling of the Holy Spirt in a saint with the Incarnation. They are both rooted in the broader ideas of incarnational thought, but the divine nature of the saint is technically only realized through the Holy Spirit. In addition, contemporary Christian thought has many thinkers who emphasis the role of the Holy Spirit in human life.

This book is an outgrowth of my course on comparative theology and much of the material in this book has been tested in the classroom. I focus on the Christian theologians that I know from graduate school and the Jewish theologians that are part of my education. I centered in my thinking on Rabbis Jonathan Sacks, Jospeh Dov Soloveitchik, and Abraham Isaac Kook. I focused on Rahner and Moltmann as two models of contemporary Christian thought, both of which show a convergence of contemporary thought, and from there branched out to Barth, Hans Urs von Balthasar, Emil Brunner, Kendall Soulen, or Kasper as needed. In addition, Barth, Balthasar, Kasper, Moltmann, and Soulen all explicitly acknowledge that we are living in a post-Holocaust world in which discussions of theology are now engaged in post-Holocaust reconciliation.

Chapter 1 deals with the Trinity, a seeming irreconcilable difference based on centuries of polemics. Yet on closer look, the differences can be explained by, and have more to do with, the narrower differences of monarchism compared to perichoresis (both terms to be defined in the chapter) and more importantly and paradigmatically, the contemporary

Trinitarian positions of Karl Rahner and Jürgen Moltmann inhabit a theological world understandable and translatable to Jewish thought.

Chapter 2 is on the Incarnation, the great Christian mystery of faith, asking whether it could be seen in Jewish terms through the rejected versions of Arianism and Docetism. And once again, the chapter shows that contemporary thinkers no longer use medieval language, rather a modern language shared with Jewish thinkers, leading both religions to reevaluate the biblical heritage of the idea.

Chapter 3 discusses the doctrine of sin as a root metaphor and original sin. The chapter shows that Judaism does have a fall of Adam, a sin of Adam, and inherited sin, but not a doctrine of Sin, with a capital *S*, that requires a salvation. In addition, the chapter shows how modern Christian thinkers are moving beyond Augustine's view of original sin.

Chapter 4 discusses salvation and atonement showing the role of both repentance and atonement in Judaism and Christianity. As well as the trend in contemporary Christian thinking toward understanding salvation as overcoming alienation, in addition, there is a strong universal inclination in current theology.

Chapter 5, on messianism, shows how the two religions traditionally define messianism differently, but originally had a common background. In addition, the chapter shows that contemporary Christian messianism offers this-worldly amelioration and premillennial dispensation, both understandable for Jews.

Chapter 6 is different from the other five chapters. Traditionally, Judaism was considered by Christianity as a broken covenant. In this chapter, we look at the recent trends to accept that Judaism has an ongoing covenant and Christian attempts to avoid supersessionism, the doctrine that Christianity replaces Judaism. This chapter shows the great strides of the last twenty years and serves as a vista of the current era of understanding and reconciliation.

Each chapter is approximately one third background in classical texts and two thirds twentieth century and contemporary thought. For the early centuries, I rely on the current scholarship about rabbinic and patristic texts to show the tension of same and difference from the early centuries. The contemporary texts are my specific focus in order to shift the center of discussion to the current lines of division. I am focused on theology and not intellectual history. And most importantly, I am not including the nonnormative minor voices, despite their theological innovation, such as Shabbatai Tzvi and Sabbatians, Joachimites, or Swedenborgians.

Early Judaism and early Christianity were from a common cultural world sharing ideas and attitudes. The intellectual and religious world of the first centuries was still a period where Jews, Christians, and those who were both, or neither, shared cultural ideas and tropes. Jews and Christians, to the extent that they were differentiated, shared Second Temple ideas from before the first centuries, shared Greco-Roman surroundings, and shared many ideas, texts, and practices in an era before the ways of the two religious parted. As the theologian Moltmann, along with Cardinals Ratzinger and Kasper, affirmed, we shared a common spiritual neighborhood. The neighborhood had many border crossings and joint activities.

The book chapters generally start by looking at rabbinic Judaism and patristics and does not deal with the Hebrew Bible directly. Therefore, it is important to note that the Hebrew Bible differs in organization, content, and translation from the Christian Old Testament. Jews and Christians share a Bible, but our Bibles are not the same. The books are arranged differently, the Jewish version ends with the book of Chronicles and a vision of a restored kingship and ideal life. The Christian version ends with Malachi and Elijah pointing to the coming of Jesus. The Jewish Bible is based only on the Hebrew text, the Christian one is also based on the Greek Septuagint. And the translations into English are different at many points.

We have different fundamental stories. Jews read the Bible as an Exodus from Egypt as the Jewish foundational story of the Jews becoming a people, Passover is about freedom from slavery and God creating the Jewish people, freeing them from Egypt, and then bringing them to Sinai and then to the land of Israel. Christians read the Bible as God's offer of grace and a story of salvation for original sin, needing redemption, needing Christ to come and save humanity. One side tells a story of God's special relationship with the Jewish people, taking them out slavery, and giving them the Torah at Sinai along with the inheritance of the land of Israel. In contrast, Christianity is about God offering an invitation to humanity via a covenant fulfilled in the coming of Christ and the removal of original sin along with salvation of humanity through the passion, crucifixion, and resurrection of Christ. Traditionally, Jews read the Bible through the Oral Law and its process of midrash, while Christians use the method of typology to see the story of Christ.

Many Christians, especially in countries without an active Jewish presence, still treat Judaism as a precursor to Christianity. To use a film metaphor, they see Judaism as a prequel instead of its own movie made by a different director, written by a different team, in a different original language, and for a different audience. Comparing the Hebrew Bible to the New Testament is not the same as a comparison of lived Judaism to lived Christianity.

Cardinal Kasper reminds us that the differences between Judaism and Christianity that are fundamental for both communities involve such key issues as the Christian confession of Jesus as the Christ, Messiah, and the Son of God, which are directly related to the Trinitarian understanding of the universal salvific significance of Jesus Christ.[9] Jews, in contrast, are concerned about Torah study, *mitzvot*, and the application of law. "Judaism and Christianity are not different versions of one religion but different faith with different agenda but using a common book and common early century materials."[10]

Both Judaism and Christianity have a great variety of thinkers, theologies, and positions on basic issues. I have no intention of essentializing either religion, even if at times I do not always qualify a statement about either. I recognize there are many Jewish positions different from my own. I also acknowledge that this book deals with complex doctrinal Jewish and Christian thinkers. An engagement with Eastern Orthodox Christians, Mennonites, free churches, and low doctrine Christians would have produced a different book.

Today when Jews read Jürgen Moltmann and Karl Rahner, and Christians read A. J. Heschel and Emmanuel Levinas we need to temper any essentialism. Currently, Jewish scholars teach and speak in Christian divinity schools, Christians teach and speak in Jewish graduate schools, and we both read each other's works. This book could not have occurred twenty-five years ago when the scholars on both sides still saw irreconcilable differences.

This book is not about truth claims or any updated form of the older style polemics and dogmatics. Therefore, I am not determining the truth of a theology, how Christianity relates to the Jewish concepts of foreign worship, or what the Jewish chosen people concept means. I am not asking which opinion is more valid or logical. I am certainly not looking to create a Jewish theology of Christianity, a common theology, a shared mission, a partnership, or an irenic convergence. I am not looking to create a universal idea or experience that we share. My goal is to act as a reader of texts and ideas in comparison, to basically show that contemporary Jewish and Christian theology are not the stereotype of diametrically opposed religions they are portrayed to be.

I am specifically leaving out from the discussion those Jewish and Christian thinkers who work to create a common covenant theology bridging between the two faiths, since that approach is not about comparison and contrast, rather a common covenantal call. I am not singling out the relationship of Judaism and Christianity because my method would also work with other religions.

Another way to see my project is from a personal perspective, the study of another religion can be a form of faith seeking understanding of the other religion, an act of seeking wisdom. A comparison focuses on the details of contrast and commonality for personal insight, helping the understanding of my own faith stretching the theological imagination. But the activity avoids the bigger questions of salvation, truth claims, common mission, or theology of religions. One simply accepts that the other religion exists and then asks, What can I learn from it? or How can I understand it from within my own commitments? This book is simply my trying to understand six Christian theological concepts from within Judaism.

If there is any one observation from writing this book, it is to note that Jewish thought's approach to theological ideas is more metaphorical, metonymic, and fluid, in contrast to Christianity's doctrinal definitions. But even here, one should not essentialize or overstate this dichotomy. Nevertheless, Jewish thinkers generally have the flexibility to choose specific ideas and exclude others. Some Jewish thinkers are scholastic and philosophical, or view God as transcendent, while others have a more narrative, immanent, or mystical approach. There are no clear lines of which passages of midrash and kabbalah are to be accepted, as well as no catechism of how to define topics in Jewish theology. My palette is broad in this book to be able to make comparisons, beyond any specific Jewish thinkers.

I wish to thank those who offered comments on various versions of talks and chapters, especially Nathaniel Berman, James E. Brenneman, Lawrence Frizzel, Abdulla Galadari, Adam Gregerman, Steven Kepnes, Matthew Levering, Jonathan L. Milevsky, Matthew Novenson, Anthony Sciglitano, Daniel Joslyn-Siemiatkoski, Rachel Slutsky, Matthew Tapie and my students for the last decade in my comparative theology classes. I thank the Catholic Theological Union (CTU) and Malka Simkovitch for inviting me to deliver a Shapiro lecture for CTU, my colleagues in comparative theology at the American Academy of Religion, and those who attended my Oesterreicher lecture. Finally, a special thank you to our administrative assistant Jay Wolferman.

On the Steps in Rome

I was in Rome in 2005 for a conference on the fortieth anniversary of Nostra Aetate. Among the many delegate speakers was a priest who was proud to tell me that he studied at Hebrew University. We had taken many of the same classes at different times and knew many of the same people. This reflected the transformation of our era in that Christians were studying Jewish texts in a Jewish institution in supportive way.

At one point over the course of the week, I was standing with my wife in front of the Il Gesu Church in Rome. This priest joyfully walked up to us and declaratively proclaimed, "Can't you feel the *shekhinah* here!" My wife and I looked to each other astonished about this Rabbinic Hebrew locution from the priest, which we found surprising. The priest sought a common bond between the two religions using the term *shekhinah* from the stock of common first-century ideas. His outburst probably did not create the anticipated spiritual commonality, since Jews and Christians use the term in different ways. For the priest, the term referred to the Holy Spirit, whose transformative presence enters people's lives. Jews use the term to refer to the presence of God in exile with the Jewish people or a sign that God is near to us in our synagogues or on the Sabbath, but certainly not about a church. We appreciated the Hebrew gesture; a single expression of joy can show openness and reconciliation, as well as commonality and difference.

CHAPTER ONE

Trinity

"I BAPTIZE YOU in the name of the Father, and of the Son, and of the Holy Spirit" is the liturgical formula used in Baptisms, affirming the Trinity as the core belief in God for Christianity. Trude Weiss-Rosmarin proclaims that this is the divide between Judaism and Christianity. For her, Jews have undifferentiated monotheism whereas the Christian Trinity is tritheism, a concession to polytheism.[1] In her estimation, the Christian Trinity is irreconcilable with Jewish monotheism, adding two unnecessary gods to biblical ideas. Can the positions be bridged? Can Jews get beyond treating the Trinity as tritheism?

Hebrew Bible and Rabbinic Views

In a Jewish understanding of the Hebrew Bible, God is a single being, a unique eternal Thou, the creator, judge, lawgiver, liberator, father, king, beloved, and shepherd. God is said to be, "merciful and gracious, slow to anger, and abounding in steadfast love" (Exod 34:6), but God is also a vengeful warrior. As an act of divine providence, God delivered the Israelite slaves from the Egyptians with, "a mighty hand and an outstretched arm" (Deut 26:8). In addition, the God of the Bible is accessible to humankind. God speaks through prophets and performs miracles for all to see.

Rabbinic literature portrays God in ways similar to the God of the Bible, specifically the continuity of describing God in multiple human terms. The rabbis stressed an intimacy in the relationship between God and man. God is the father to whom each individual could turn in direct prayer for his needs and at the same time the king ruling over all. The rabbis added new terms reflecting attributes, for example, *shekhinah*, as divine presence representing immanence; *gevurah*, the divine powers; and *makom*, place, representing all-encompassing transcendence. Each divine name captures but one dimension of the human experience of the divine, thereby providing a kaleidoscope of countless lenses and depth of vision of the experience of God. But in sum, all these terms point to a single oneness of God.

Trinity

Trinity, in Christian doctrine, is the unity of Father, Son, and Holy Spirit as three persons in one Godhead. The doctrine of the Trinity is a central Christian affirmation about God, rooted in the fact that God came to meet Christians in a threefold figure: (1) as Creator, Lord of the history of salvation, Father, and Judge, as revealed in the Old Testament; (2) as the Lord who, in the incarnated figure of Jesus Christ, lived among human beings and was present in their midst as the "Resurrected One"; and (3) as the Holy Spirit, whom they experienced as the helper or intercessor in the power of the new life.

Antecedents in the New Testament for the doctrinal Trinity include the verse in Matthew, "Go therefore and make disciples of all nations, baptizing them in the name of the Father and of the Son and of the Holy Spirit," (28:19); and the apostolic benediction: "The grace of the Lord Jesus Christ, the love of God, and the communion of the Holy Spirit be with you all" (2 Cor 13:13). This is not yet the concept of the Trinity, but triadic structure reflects the early, formalized ritual of baptism. The Gospel of John opens by designating Christ as the Logos ("word"), which, the Church Fathers claimed as proof that Christ was preexistent.

Justin Martyr (100—c. 160 CE) claimed that each time God appeared in the Hebrew Bible, this was in fact a form of the preexistent Christ. Therefore, Christians retained the oneness of God who emanated his word, the Logos, in Christ. Christianity was not new; their beliefs were based on the ancient traditions of the Jews. Tertullian (155–200 CE) was the first to use the Latin term Trinity, which he describes as a "divine economy" as in the household or monarchy of God. God the Father laid out the divine plan, God the Son carried out the will of the Father, and God the Spirit motivated the will of God in believers (*Adversus Praxean*, 27).

The doctrine of the Trinity developed gradually over several centuries, reaching definitive meanings through controversies and formal church councils.

Two early approaches understood the Trinity in opposite ways, either as subordination or as modalism. In the first, the divine in Christ as the Word, or Logos is subordinate to the Supreme Being, a hierarchy. Alternately, the divine as the Father, Son, and Holy Spirit is seen as three modes of the self-disclosure of the one God but not as distinct within the being of God itself, the three-fold nature is just an attribute of God. The first tendency recognizes the distinctness among the three persons but assumes their inequality creating subordinationism through lower emanations. The second approach affirms unity, but at the cost of the distinctness as persons creating a modalism, where the divine parts are only faces or aspects of an undifferentiated divine. Both of these approaches, as we shall see, could be understood in Jewish terms, in that both preserve a supreme undifferentiated divine who either has lower emanations or has many faces.[2]

Arius, in Alexandria taught that God created everything including Christ. Indeed, the very terms "the Father" and "the Son" indicated that Christ was subordinate to God, called subordinationism. The bishop of Alexandria excommunicated Arius, but other church leaders took his side. In 325 CE, Constantine called for an empire-wide council to resolve the matter of the Trinity, in which the fourth-century council, the council of Nicaea, and the subsequent council of Constantinople in 381, delineated the distinctness of the three persons and their unity as a single orthodox doctrine of one essence and three persons. The councils stated the crucial doctrinal formula in its confession that the Son is "of the same substance [*homoousios*] as the Father," and, by the end of the fourth century the doctrine of the Trinity substantially took the current form, maintained ever since. The phrase "three persons" derives from the Athanasian Creed that says: "And in this Trinity none is before, or after another; none is greater, or less than another. But the whole three Persons are coeternal, and coequal."[3] The debates on the Trinity were quite esoteric and included philosophical ideas of the universe. Was Christ a being like, but not identical with, the Father, or was he of the identical essence of the Father? The Council opted for the second choice in that God and Christ were identical in essence and that Christ was a manifestation of God Himself on earth. Having Christ identical to God the Father, confirmed the view that Christ was preexistent and helped to create the universe.

Bitheism, Theos, Monarchism, and Modalism

With the essential two positions of Rabbinic Judaism and Christian Trinitarianism in place, there is still a need to address the theological differences already present in late antiquity that are important for discussing contemporary issues. This book is not going to give an overview of the Rabbinic texts or the Church Fathers and church councils that formulated these positions, just the final decisions, relying on contemporary scholars of late antiquity for these points.

The important historical point for understanding this chapter is that, according to many current scholars, Rabbinic Judaism did not have a simple undifferentiated view of God. Historians accept that Judaism in antiquity had a variety of intra-divine structures, logos theories, angelic divine forms, divine manifestations, and bitheism. There were widespread ideas of complex structures of the divine in first-century Judaism, the crucible that formed both religions. These ideas continued in the later Tannaitic and Amoriac eras as well as into medieval esotericism and kabbalah, even if rejected by medieval rational philosophers. Many strands in Judaism did not relinquish the complex views of the Jewish God.

To consider one example that plays a large role for a Jewish understanding of early Christianity, bitheism or binitarianism, a position where God has two aspects, a transcendent God and a lower manifestation of God. Peter Schäfer and Larry Hurtado show the complexity and overlap between views of the divine in various first-century groups that later coalesce into the divergent religions of Judaism and Christianity.[4] Current historical research shows that during this period there was no pure Jewish monotheism contrasting with Christian Trinity, rather Judaism also had a more complex view of aspects of God. Daniel Boyarin calls on Jews to stop vilifying Christian ideas about God as simply a collection of "unJewish," perhaps pagan, ideas.[5]

Many of these first-century ideas continued in later Jewish thought and were not foreign to Jewish metaphysical conceptions of God. Many contemporary scholars each in their own way show a continuity of these ideas and later Jewish ideas. An earlier era of rabbinic scholars downplayed the hypostatic and mythological tendencies in rabbinic thought, treating them all as metaphor without acknowledgement of any hypostasis or manifestation of God in the rabbinic view of God.[6] Contemporary scholars, however, see these concepts such as the *shekhinah* as hypostasis and as having continuity in later Judaism.[7] Even ideas such as bitheism, a doctrine where there is a higher and lower aspect of the divine, are still shown in the *Targum*, Talmud, and later midrash, and from these sources the ideas reappear in medieval kabbalah.[8] Moshe Idel, the scholar of Kabbalah, has a six-hundred-page tome on Jewish concepts of Divine Sonship presenting Jewish thinking about God including Logos, intra-divine structures, and bitheism.[9] This book on comparative theology accepts the scholarship on rabbinic Judaism and kabbalah at face value, situating itself after the broad acceptance of border crossing between Judaism and Christianity in the early centuries and that kabbalah is strongly related to rabbinic texts. In addition, Moltmann, himself, cites later kabbalistic texts and modern Jewish thinkers influenced by those texts.

In a volume comparing religious views of the divine and ultimate reality, Anthony J. Saldarini uses this historical material to present Judaism as having a complex view of divinity, thereby displacing the pristine concept of Judaism as an "ethical monotheism" found in many authors in the early twentieth century, post-Kantian Jewish thinkers like Hermann Cohen, Leo Baeck, and Martin Buber.[10] Modern Jewish thought in Western Europe under the shadow of Protestant

Christianity, sought to differentiate Judaism from Christianity and at the same time work within the confines of Modern German thought. Immanuel Kant, especially, presented Judaism as an abstract monotheism, understood in prophetic ethical terms or rationalist terms. Little use was made of the traditional rabbinic texts. But the materials presented in the aforementioned works on rabbinic and kabbalistic thought support the view of a complex Jewish divinity. These Jewish ideas of a complex deity and bitheism that are parallel to early Christian ideas are likely not directly historically related to Christianity. Both are relying on scripture, common Second Temple sources, and common understandings in the early centuries of a multilevel monotheism in which God has a manifestation and has personified forms of divine presence.[11]

Early Judaism and Christianity come from the same spiritual neighborhood of multilevel monotheism, but the difference is that Judaism chose the approach of a spiritual hierarchy, not a Trinity. Judaism accepts what became known in Christian thought as the monarchist position or more specifically the form of monarchism called adoptionism (or dynamic Monarchianism). Monarchism, in its rigoristic form, was an early Christian heresy that considered the second and third parts of the Trinity as lower than God, the Father. In many ways this is the crux of the difference between the faiths. Judaism is monarchist; there is a hierarchy of divine parts, the *shekhinah* (or *gevurah* or *kavod*) is lower than the abstract God. The *shekhinah* and infinite divine are not indwelling together like the Trinity. The differences between the religions are not one God compared to three gods, rather Jews consider the intra-divine structures including the *shekhinah* as lower on a hierarchy. Christianity as expressed in the creed is explicitly antimonarchist, rather the creed is based on a concept called perichoresis in later centuries, the three persons of the Trinity indwell together and are mutually interrelated without hierarchy. Judaism's hierarchy is an emanation scheme. This is the Christian heresy of monarchism. Jewish bitheism, in which God is a monarchist Father who remains above his manifestations, is in contrast to a Christian logic of the Trinity, where the divine persons dwell together. Later, Jewish theories of *kavod* in philosophy and kabbalah, despite their acceptance of intra-divine structures, continued this same monarchism and hierarchy.[12]

In addition, much of later Jewish thought is a form of modalism, where the divine parts are just modes or attributes of one God without separate persons. Such is the view of most Jewish philosophers, who assume the one God who has the basic attributes of all knowing, all powerful, and benevolent. All other persona, hypostases, manifestations, or actions of God are either just a mode of the one single divine or a lower manifestation. For a concrete example, the third century Christian movement of Sabellianism, a specific form of modal monarchism, held the belief that the Father, Son and Holy Spirit are three different modes or aspects of God, not the same as the Jewish position but closer to it, as opposed to a Trinitarian view of three distinct persons or hypostases within the Godhead, defined as three distinct, coequal, coeternal persons whose distinction does not divide the one substance. Jewish thought, especially Jewish philosophers, treat all the variations in God language as just attributes, or modes. In contrast, creedal Christianity affirms that the Father, Son, and Holy Spirit are separate persons with eternal hypostatic reality as sperate persons.

Finally, during the second century, Jews and gentile Christians divided on the Jewish God. Some early Christian thinkers distinguished between the abstract high God and the God of the Bible. Christians considered the high god of the Jewish tradition as the high god of philosophers and not the active God of the Bible. These early gentile Christian theologians considered the philosophic high god as the Father of Christ. But they considered that the high god was not to be identified with the active deity of Jewish scriptures. Hence, there has to be a lower Son who proceeded from the Father who acts in the Bible. The God of the Bible is the Son who has change, passion, sorrow, love. Some such as Irenaeus and Tertullian may have still considered the God of the Bible as the high God, but over time the split became more common. As a corollary, for some gentile Christian theologians in the second century, God the Father lost his Jewish identity. God the Father was seen as the abstract *theos*, the high god of all. For our purposes in this paper, this point is useful for contrast to Jewish thought that always considers the abstract high god as the same as the personal and active God of the Bible without a need for a Father and Son.[13] Even though Judaism does not distinguish between a Father and Son, nevertheless, many of the ideas of bitheism do have elements of this logic.[14]

Medieval Encounters

One more consideration before approaching the modern material. Jews spent half a millennium under Islam where Jews studied Islamic kalam and falasifa, which emphasized the absolute oneness of God without any differentiation, a pure abstract monotheism. Medieval Jewish thinkers understood the Jewish intra-divine structures of the early rabbinic centuries solely as metaphor in order to preserve the pristine unity of God.

Saadiah Gaon (882–942), for example, would not accept bitheism or even monarchism, the terms for God are only metaphor and attributes. However, he did see the *kavod*, the divine glory as a lower created being used by God. Saadiah saw Jews, Christians, and Muslims, as sharing a belief in monotheism even if he saw the Christian formulation of the Trinity as incorrect and as defective from the position of true oneness.[15] Some medieval Jewish philosophers such as the thirteenth century thinker Isaac Albalag suggested that if Christians framed things as modalism, then they could agree. But medieval Christian creed did not affirm modalism.[16]

In the medieval polemics between Jews and Christians, Jews spoke of the divine as modalism and Christians presented an Augustinian position of divine personhood. For example, the thirteenth-century Rabbi Moshe ben Nachman, or Naḥmanides (1194–1270), in his account of the disputation in Barcelona with Pablo Christiani wrote:

> Fra Pablo asked me in Gerona whether I believed in the Trinity. I said to him, "What is the Trinity?"
>
> He said: "Wisdom, will, and power."

> Then I said: "Rather, He and His wisdom are one, He and His will are one, He and His power are one, and if so, wisdom, will and power are one. Even if God had accidental qualities, they would not be a Trinity, but they would be one substance with three accidental properties . . ."[17]

In short, Nahmanides gave a modalist answer. Yet, as a kabbalist, one who had a received tradition about the esoteric interdivine structures, called *sefirot*, Nahmanides considered the *shekhinah*, the presence of God, as a separate lower manifestation of God Himself. God has a lower discrete aspect called the *shekhinah*, thereby weakening his own answer.[18] However, the concept of *shekhinah* in the kabbalistic view of the divine is clearly hierarchical as the lowest element in divine manifestation and lacks independence, hence monarchism. Nahmanides in his presentations of the interdivine structures, the *sefirot*, explicitly went out of his way to defend divine unity working out the proper relationship of the lower entities to the divine unity. It is worth noting that Nahmanides's commentary on Exodus 3:13 distinguishes the divine as a triad, the unknown—"I Will be Who I will be," God as power of creation and miracles—the Tetragrammaton, and the God as the natural order—Shadai. A comparative discussion of divine names could start with this Jewish triad.[19]

In Christian terms, the kabbalah lacks eternal distinction in relation to the other parts of the divine, without perichoresis, defined above as the parts of the divine indwelling together and mutually interrelated without hierarchy.[20]

Modernity

The nineteenth century was a nadir of traditional Trinitarian thought, a lull that lasted for a century until the twentieth century theologians Karl Barth and Karl Rahner returned to doctrinal views of the Trinity. In fact, a significant number of Protestant groups were functionally Unitarian despite the liturgical Trinity. Friedrich Schleiermacher (1768–1834), the German Reformed theologian, was critical about the Nicene approach to the Trinity and more receptive to thinking that God is revealed through three personalities, in which the Godhead "is never revealed to us as it is itself." Therefore, the Trinity was not essential to the hidden Godhead, who reveals himself as God in creation by showing different faces.[21] Schleiermacher has been accused of Sabellianism and of not being a Trinitarian theologian. Unfortunately, despite his reformulation of the doctrinal Trinity, there was no theological rapprochement with Judaism because of his strong contempt for Judaism, shared by many in the nineteenth century.

Rahner on the Trinity

Karl Rahner (1904–1984) was a German Jesuit priest who is widely considered to have been one of the foremost Roman Catholic theologians of the twentieth century. He is best known for his integration of an existential philosophy of personalism with Kantianism and Thomism. He was an influential presence at Vatican II and was personally friendly with the important American Jewish theologian, Abraham Joshua Heschel.

In a very short dense volume, Rahner formulates his modern differences from classical formulations of the Trinity.[22] Most notably, Rahner, avoids the word "person" about the Trinity. Rahner writes that, in the modern era, "person" means consciousness and activity but originally the word only meant "concrete substance." The three parts of the divine are the very same thing as concrete substances in three modes or three distinct appearances of the same thing from different angles, although here such appearances are objective and lasting. The Trinity does not have three persons in the modern sense of the word, which would be tritheism, in that they do not have separate consciousnesses. The term he uses to describes the three parts, or instances, of the Trinity is "three existence ways" of one God; albeit relative, all is one essence in unity.

In addition, if the parts, or instances, are not separate then there is no classic procession of Father—unoriginated, to the Son—begotten, and both to the Spirit—procession. In Rahner's view all proceeds from the Father alone and the three subsistences of the Trinity are to be considered as distinct modes of a single God. They are differentiated but not separate. There is one divine essence and all proceeds from the Father, and the bond of the Father is relative to the other two. Rahner presents perichoresis, the coindwelling, as an act of self-communication of truth and love from God the Father to humanity.[23] Divine communication occurs in these three, and only these three, manners of subsisting, based on the two necessary moments of divine self-communication: knowledge and love. Rahner explains that the apparent differentiation of self-communication in truth as the Son and love as the Spirit must, in fact, first obtain in God's single self, prior to interaction with the world, in order for the differentiation in the world to be a real triune self-communication of the single God.

These positions refocus the common understanding of the internal process in the Trinity to emphasize his approach. Rahner writes: "For these modalities and their differentiation either are in God himself (although we first experience them from our point of view), or they exist only in us, they belong only to the realm of creatures as effects of the divine creative activity."[24]

Beyond the scope of this chapter is an extended discussion of Rahner's insistence that the "immanent Trinity"—the inner Being of God—is the same as the "economic Trinity"—the process of worldly salvation and grace. The three metaphysical existence-ways are the same as the three functions of the Trinity in human lives. Rahner rejects classic Catholic distinctions between the inner being or essence of God and God's relationship to and saving activity in the world. This is an essential point in modern Christology and deserves its own study. However, for our purposes, it is enough to note that for Rahner, this means that the understanding of the metaphysical persons of the divine is the same as triune divine persons offering salvation and grace. In many cases this leads to separation of the philosophic analysis of the Trinity from the purposes of incarnation and salvation.[25] From the perspective of the various modes of Jewish thought, Judaism generally does have an unfolding of the metaphysical divine but no temporal mission of the divine itself for salvation, neither a divine mission of salvation or of grace, and therefore, no parallel to an economic Trinity. Hence, we will focus on the immanent Trinity.[26]

Catholic theological discussions often repeat a standard set of evaluations of Rahner's view of the Trinity. These include, that Rahner is weak on the role of persons, social trinitarians think he does not have serious familial relationships of mutual love between parts of the Trinity, and that his position is close to a form of modalism. Modalism is a rejection of the doctrinal formulation of the Trinity, unacceptable for a Catholic theologian. However, it is important to note that these criticisms bring his view of the Trinity closer to a Jewish perspective, but the question is how close?

Since modalism, in which the three persons are not distinct, is a position that Judaism can theoretically accept, given its presence in Jewish philosophic and kabbalistic positions, it is important to reflect a bit longer on the question of Rahner's similarity to modalism. Marc Pugliese in an important article, concludes that Rahner is not a modalist. And the conclusion of his article may have put its finger on the Jewish-Christian divide.[27] For Pugliese, the question of modalism can be reduced to two chief concerns. First, the question of whether Rahner's theory can lead to denying necessary, eternal, distinctions within God which are fundamental to a Christian understanding of God's Being. Does God as have an abstract nature apart from the world and apart from God's external acts of self-communication that would ultimately be a unity without essential distinctions?[28] He answers that Rahner would answer in the negative. There is no abstract nature outside of the three persons of the Trinity. Here, again is a division between Jewish and Christian conceptions of God. The Trinity is not about a unity above any distinction, even when Christian theologians describe the first person of the Trinity that way. Jewish thought almost always affirms an abstract nature for God above the world and the numerical distinctions of the *sefirot* of the kabbalah are always seen as contingent on the infinite divine above the world.

Second, Rahner explicitly affirms there is only one Absolute Person, not a plurality of three subjectivities with individual consciousnesses.[29] Rahner understands the traditional tripersonal God as unipersonal with three manners of subsisting. While not willing to drop the word person due to longstanding tradition and for practical and liturgical purposes, Rahner seeks to explain what the church means by person as "a distinct manner of subsisting". The three existence ways are not masks for God to wear divorced from the content of the deity, but, rather, without them, the substantially real deity could not exist. This means that God is intrinsically tripersonal, a difference from Judaism that returns to the language of Absolute Person.

Pugliese is helpful in sorting out the complex issues involved in the discussion of the Trinity. He shows that the modalist thinking of the third century Sabellians which was rejected by the Church meant that God had different "masks" with the same individual being behind them. Those masks, however, themselves are not essential to, nor identical with, the one individual being behind them. Rahner too rejects this view that the persons of God are mere created masks and not essential to, nor identical with, the one individual God behind them. For Pugliese, the modalist error, which Rahner avoids, is not the lack of predicating modern "personality" to the divine persons, rather, he avoids treating the divine persons as mere masks or mere manifestations without real necessary distinctions in God from eternity.

But modalism is in fact, the Jewish position. As noted above, the rabbinic midrash and medieval kabbalah, in most cases, present the intra-divine structures as masks and ways of God's manifestation. The Jewish understanding of inter-divine structures generally do not have their own volition. Rather, they are emanations, which God uses as forces, mechanisms, or mediums to interact with the world.

I must mention another Christian theologian as part of my presentation of Rahner, Karl Barth, the Swiss Reformed thinker (1886–1968), a major voice in twentieth-century theology who wrote before Rahner, in his early writings, similar ideas to Rahner's but did not devote many paragraphs to the topic.[30] Similar to Rahner, Barth avoids the term "person" in regards to the Trinity in that the word originally meant something other than the modern meaning of personality. Barth directly proposed that the Trinitarian formula be updated to "ways of being," to replace the word "person."[31] Barth rejects "three persons" because the word persons communicates that there are three *personalities* or self-consciousnesses in God. In Barth's later presentations, however, he makes statements that place him clearly in the eternal subordination and eternal submission Trinitarian position, in which his divine unity "is both One who is obeyed and Another who obeys".[32]

Jürgen Moltmann

Jürgen Moltmann (1926–2024), professor of systematic theology at the University of Tübingen in Germany and one of the most widely read theologians of the second half of the twentieth century was actively engaged in dialogue with Jewish scholars. Moltmann explicitly wrote as a Christian post-Holocaust theologian writing after the process of Christian reconciliation with Judaism, and with a solid knowledge of modern Jewish thought.

Moltmann had a self-proclaimed distinctly Christian understanding of God that begins with the Triune Christian God, what is called a "social doctrine of the Trinity" where the persons of the divine plurality are engaged in a loving relationship and evidenced in the divine missions of each person of the Trinity. For Moltmann, God's essence is from eternity a love that is capable of suffering and ready to sacrifice and give itself up to suffering. The Christian primordial experience of God is of the suffering and self-abasement of God, a God who is freely affected and changed by the suffering world.[33] For Moltmann, "the cross of the Son stands from eternity in the center of the Trinity." Moltmann focuses not only on the suffering of God on the cross but also on the suffering within the Triune God. There was a "cross in the heart of God" before the cross was raised upon Golgotha. In the death of the Son the eternal heart of the Trinity was revealed.

Moltmann explains how he saw the carnage and tragedy of World War II and he therefore starts his thought from the sense of human suffering after World War II and the Holocaust. Moltmann asks as the basic of his Trinitarian scheme: Why did the divine permit Auschwitz? Moltmann writes that "it is not merely possible to see Golgotha and Auschwitz in a single perspective; it is actually necessary." In order to be true, a doctrine must offer a viable theodicy shedding light on the Holocaust and Auschwitz, must advance Jewish-Christian dialogue, and must remember that Jews were sufferers and Christians were perpetrators. In addition, a viable theology should have ecological concern, give a platform for Christian political activism, and both illuminate, and be illuminated by, the preoccupations of feminism. Above all, theological statements must be validated by experience.[34]

During his early period (1945–1948), Moltmann experienced God both as the power of hope and as a presence in suffering: the two themes that were to form the two complementary sides of his theology in the 1960s and early 1970s.

In his early work *The Trinity and the Kingdom*, where he freely engages with Jewish thought, he seeks to explain the social Trinity using the Jewish concepts of *shekhinah*, *tzimtzum*, and *tikkun olam* as understood by Elie Wiesel, A. J. Heschel, Franz Rosenzweig, and Gershom Scholem, as well as his readings of rabbinic thought. Moltmann starts his Trinitarian thought with Wiesel's description of his experience at Auschwitz as a shattering expression representative of what he calls the "rabbinic theology of God's humiliation of himself."[35]

Parenthetically, there was a debate almost fifty years ago about Moltmann's approach as a means of interfaith dialogue. Many Christian theologians of the Holocaust in the 1970s, such as A. Roy Eckardt, blamed the Holocaust directly on Christian teaching of contempt for Judaism as symbolized by the Trinity, without distinguishing between the anti-Judaic teaching of contempt and the teaching of the Trinity. For these theologians engaged in the early decades of Jewish-Christian dialogue, any mention of the Trinity, even if done sympathetically, was automatically implicated in perpetuating antisemitism.[36]

Moltmann's First Movement of the Trinity
Shekhinah

Moltmann divides the coming to be of the divine movement to the world into three movements: indwelling, suffering and kenosis, and glorification, which he correlates with the Jewish ideas of the *shekhinah*, *tzimtzum*, and *tikkun olam*.

The first movement of the Trinity is God's self-distinction, and immanent indwelling in the world. Moltmann explores the meaning of this indwelling and activity of the second person of Trinity, from a variety of perspectives, including Eastern Orthodox, Catholic, Lutheran, and Jewish. In his chapter on Jewish antecedents of the second person of the Trinity. Moltmann makes an important declaration that the very Christian ideas of the incarnation of the divine Logos and the indwelling of the Holy Spirit developed in the same "spiritual neighborhood" as the Jewish ideas of exilic of the divine and *shekhinah* theology.[37] He compares the opening prologue to John's gospel as analogous to the *shekhinah* that descends and indwells in the desert tabernacle, we read about the divine Logos that descends and indwells (*lit.* tabernacles) among God's people as Jesus of Nazareth, the Word become flesh. He argues in his book that the doctrine of the Trinity can be traced back to its Second Temple origins and developed in harmony with Jewish experiences of God.[38]

Moltmann wrote that Tertullian's formulation of the Trinity uses the Greek philosophic terminology of Neoplatonism. However, Moltmann continues, "as the New Testament shows, in actual fact the concept of a lower aspect of God goes back to the Israelite theology of the *Shekinah*." The rabbinic doctrine of the *shekhinah* is one of the primary theological frameworks that Moltmann uses to interpret his own, as well as the world's, experience of suffering.[39]

According to Moltmann, the God who lives in heaven and among the wretched of his people reveals a double presence, that he finds developed by Abraham Heschel in his interpretation of the prophets, and which Heschel calls, "a bipolar concept of God."[40] Heschel's writings on divine pathos, in which he argues against a passionless God by showing a divine willing to engage in self-humiliation, and come down to humans in forms of the *shekhinah*, serves Moltmann's concept of God is a God who is freely affected and changed by the suffering world. In Heschel's bipolar concept of God, God is at once wholly free in God's self and at the same time committed to the people of God in covenant and affected by their history.[41] Picking up on this concept Moltmann asserts:

> Heschel has shown that the Jewish experience of God cannot be a simple monotheism, because on the basis of the experience of the divine pathos it must come to an awareness of this *self-distinction* of God. Every self-communication presumes a self-distinction. Whoever speaks of the communicability of God presumes a relationship in which God can step over against God.[42]

Rather than the dichotomy described above where Jews are portrayed as having an abstract high God, necessitating early Christians to have a second person of God who engages with humanity, Moltmann finds bitheism in Heschel's Judaism, where the infinite Jewish God makes himself known as the most moved mover, a form of dipolar theism.[43] Thus historically Jews and Christians shared first century concepts of intra-divine structure and bitheism. Moltmann, however, reads the rabbinic *shekhinah* as a synonym for God's presence as the second person of the Trinity. As noted, according to Moltmann, the Christian tradition expanded on the Jewish *shekhinah* tradition and began to perceive a series of mutual indwellings, which the Church Fathers later describe in terms of *perichoresis*. But Moltmann acknowledges that whereas the Jewish *shekhinah* tradition perceived the transcendent God and the immanent *shekhinah* as different from each other. Christian tradition perceived a series of indwellings, Even so, Moltmann reiterates for emphasis "nowhere is there any talk of three gods."[44]

I must point out that, despite Moltmann's reading of a similarity, the biggest difference between Judaism and Christianity is that Jewish thinkers read the *shekhinah* as a lower element in a divine hierarchy created by God. For Jews, the *shekhinah* and the *kavod* accompanying Israel in the desert are a created lower level, or a created apparition, similar to Arius's fourth-century subordinationalism, which was rejected by the council of Nicaea. The Trinity as the crucified God is based on the need to understand the passion of Christ, but Heschel's presentation of pathos is based on the prophets of the Hebrew Bible such as Amos.

In addition to Heschel, Moltmann uses Franz Rosenzweig's presentation on the *shekhinah* in *The Star of Redemption*, which also includes the notion that God suffers with the Jews in exile.[45] Rosenzweig treats the *shekhinah* as the persona of God without any kabbalistic hierarchy. Rosenzweig's unique locution probably betrays Christian theological influence, and in turn, is, for Moltmann, a useful text for a theological bridge between Judaism and Christianity. For Moltmann, following Rosenzweig, the people suffer exile and persecution, and the *shekhinah* suffers with them. The *shekhinah* suffers exile and ignominy, and "the people suffer with the *Shekinah*."[46]

Yet, Moltmann does not conflate Christianity and Judaism, he notes that for Franz Rosenzweig, unlike Christianity, this deliverance is ostensibly in the "hands of human beings." Human action is what counts in Judaism, not divine action. In another place, he states that a Jew does *mitzvot* for the divine rather than the divine needing to act for the sake of humans. The economic Trinity in Israel is Torah in the flesh—in the hands of the people Israel. The Jew, according to Moltmann's reading of Rosenzweig, fulfills the endless precepts "for the sake of uniting the holy God and his Shekhina." For instance, every time a Jew confesses the Shema Yisrael they "confess God's unity," which is "nothing less than the process of redemption."[47]

Moltmann surprisingly uses a rabbinic text, the Mishnah of Sanhedrin VI:5, to exemplify his approach to the second person of the Trinity.

> When a human being suffers what does the Shechinah say? My head is too heavy for Me; My arm is too heavy for Me. And if God is so grieved over the blood of the wicked that is shed, how much more so over the blood of the righteous.

We have a Christian reading of the Mishnah about the *shekhinah* suffering as affirming the second person of the Trinity. Once again

Moltmann emphasizes the common spiritual neighborhood rather than an attempt to Christianize the rabbis.

The Second Movement
Tzimtzum

Moltmann's second movement of his Trinitarian unfolding is about God's self-humiliation, co-suffering, and estrangement. The movement to incarnation was to suffer with humanity as a kenosis of his infinite divinity. Moltmann explains this movement as a move from omnipotent theism to incarnation and again uses the kabbalistic concept of the *shekhinah*. But in order to explain the self-limiting of God, Moltmann turns to the sixteenth century Jewish mystic Isaac Luria's doctrine of *tzimtzum*, as presented by Gershom Scholem.[48]

According to Gershom Scholem, as read by Moltmann, *tzimtzum* means concentration or contraction, which in kabbalistic thought signifies a withdrawal of God from the world. Moltmann compares the way the first movement of the Trinity naturally leads into the second movement as an act of *tzimtzum*. As Moltmann understands it, "God has released a certain sector of His being, from which He has withdrawn—'a kind of primal, mystical space'; and into this, accordingly, He can issue from himself in his creation and his revelation."[49] This means that creation begins with a self-humiliation on God's part when he determines to be self-limited. This withdrawal—this "exile"—into God's own self that allows for the nihilo in which creation by God can occur. Transposing this into a Trinitarian key, Moltmann writes that the "relationship of the Father, the Son and the Holy Spirit is so wide that the whole creation can find space, time, and freedom in it."[50]

Moltmann presupposes a self-humiliation inward, a *tzimtzum*, a contraction, that is the culmination of a history of divine self-humiliations, the goal of which is the very redemption of creation and the reconciliation of all things to God. This Trinitarian event, as Moltmann understands it, is deepened by the *shekhinah* tradition because the Son in the triune God, like the *shekhinah*, participates in humankind's destiny, making the sufferings of his people his own.

The *shekhinah* accompanies Israel into the humiliation of exile and there co-suffers in solidarity awaiting redemption and return. Christ experiences the humiliation of the cross, the "exile" of death, and there co-suffers in solidarity awaiting resurrection and return.[51]

Tzimtzum for Moltmann means incarnation and kenosis, which he identifies with both the *shekhinah* and *tzimtzum*, as terms for contraction and kenosis. According to Moltmann, God's self-humiliation, his *tzimtzum*, is ultimately realized and is nowhere greater than on the cross. Moltmann argues that on the cross the Father and the Son are so deeply separated that their relationship is cut off. While the Son suffers death, the Father suffers the death of the Son. This Christology that has no equivalent in Judaism.

But to evaluate this from a Jewish perspective, *tzimtzum* does not mean *shekhinah*. There is a kabbalistic emanation hierarchy in which Lurianic *tzimtzum* exists in the emanation or as an unfolding of God, which becomes reread as Moltmann's first movement of the Trinity, that of emanation and indwelling. Furthermore, in Lurianic *tzimtzum*, the contraction is a cosmic catastrophe creating a hollow, a gap, an aporia, the opposite of a redemptive conscious kenosis. Beyond that, in Scholem's reading, the contraction expressed deep alienation from the divine. *Tzimtzum* leaves an empty space that is then filled with divine light; the contraction itself is not a description of a part of the divine, for Jews contraction is cosmology. Moltmann conflates rabbinic thought with sixteenth-century kabbalah, stating that Luria, taking up a midrashic teaching of the *shekhinah*, that refers to God "concentrating" his *shekhinah*, becomes transformed into teaching God's concentrated form.[52]

For Moltmann, in contrast to the Jewish perspective of divine contraction as presented by Scholem, Christ preexists and solves the problem of the void through incarnation as the contraction, the *tzimtzum*. Christ is the contraction of kenosis providing a salvific divinity to the world. In contrast, for Jewish thought the void is a kabbalistic cosmology of distance from a primordial divine, a structure of limitations of reality, and a chain of hierarchical emanations. *Tzimtzum* remains a hierarchical emanation indicative of our distance from the divine. The repair of the contraction in Lurianic thought needs a new emanation of light into new reconstructed vessels to bear the light. The repair requires searching for the sparks of divine light scattered like shattered glass into the void of this world; and the repair requires the human performance of *mitzvot*, especially done with kabbalistic intention.

The Third Movement
Tikkun Olam

The third movement of his Trinitarian theology is God's redemption, restoration, and eschatological union. For Moltmann, glorification is the end goal of every Christian's life journey and an aspect of Christian soteriology and Christian eschatology. The process first involves the believer's sanctification, where they are made, and are being made, holy as a continual process where the Holy Spirit works to mold believers into the image of Christ.

According to the Lukan Pentecost narrative, the Spirit, like the divine *Logos*, also descends and immanently indwells among God's people. Only this condescension, unlike the Incarnation, is an indwelling in human hearts (Rom 5:5). Moltmann adds, "What once happened in Solomon's temple, when God's Shekinah entered it, resting, and dwelling there, now happens in the bodies of believers. The living, physical community becomes the temple of the divine, life-giving Spirit."[53]

Moltmann concedes that whereas the Jewish understanding of the *Shekhinah* tradition perceived a kind of "double presence"—God and *Shekhinah*—the Christian experience perceived a kind of triple presence, which includes the pnuematological indwelling of the Holy Spirit in redeemed humanity and the ecclesial community as a whole.

In his book on ecclesiology *The Church in the Power of the Spirit*, Moltmann asks whether the Christian act of belief, which unites believers with God through the Holy Spirit, is similar to the Jewish activity of *mitzvot* or *tikkun olam* (ethical responsibility). While Moltmann understands this eschatological union to be entrusted to the work of the third person, the Spirit, he nevertheless makes room for the Church's own participatory acts of what Moltmann calls *tikkun olam*, which he defines as the uniting of human beings with one another, in the union of "society with nature and in the uniting of creation with God through the church."[54]

Therefore, according to Moltmann, Jews achieve restoration through the performance of *mitzvot*. This is a kind of Pelagian self-perfection process to repair the world. And Moltmann himself sees this as an important difference from Christianity, which needs the third person of the Trinity for Christ's redemption of humanity. As mentioned previously, in Moltmann's reading of Rosenzweig, the eventual redemption for Jews is effected by Israel's unifying of God and in their acts of *tikkun olam*, their religious practice and their ethical acts.

Given his extensive use of Jewish theological notions to creatively construct a new understanding of the Trinity we may want to join the scholar Geiko Muller Fahrenhaz who asks: Does Moltmann's use of Judaism work? Is there an actual compatibility here between Jewish and Christian theological thinking or is it just typological similarities? As to whether Moltman's theology could have any relevance to Jewish theology, Muller Fahrenhaz says, "I have my doubts whether Jewish theologians could regard Moltmann's argument, which all too quickly moves from questions through a supposition, as a compelling exegesis."[55]

In places, Moltmann seems himself to answer the questions with uncertainty. Moltmann questions his own use of Jewish categories but then uses them anyway. Moltmann himself expresses reservations in the way in which he makes use of the Jewish tradition. He admits that the Jewish tradition "does not permit the full and real presence of God in his Shekinah and his Spirit to be thought."[56] Yet, Moltmann himself tries to close the gap between Judaism and Christianity in his own thought, so that the analogy can be closer to compatibility.

Comparison

What are the insights gained from comparing Rahner and Moltmann on the Trinity to Jewish thought? First, to reiterate my opening discussion of the differences. Jewish thought situates itself as modalist, not Trinitarian, Jewish thought is monarchist not Trinitarian, Jewish thought is often docetic, only describing how the divine makes itself appear, only a semblance of divine reality, not Trinitarian.

In addition, an observation true for this entire book: Jewish thought leaves the terms for intra-divine structures as fluid, free-floating signifiers of Jewish texts rather than fixed creedal statements. Thus, Jews in general avoid the doctrinal controversies so endemic to Christianity, such as the Filioque controversy. In late antiquity and in the age of Christian polemics the dividing lines between the faiths are already set. The debates are about modalism, monarchism, Docetism, Arianism, as fixed ideas. Jews and Christians made different decisions in the third and fourth centuries that undergird today's differences, as well as those in our post-polemical age. In many cases, Jewish thought is similar to the positions rejected as heresy in the early Christian councils. This has led to recognitions of differences as well as newly found convergences. However, as historical scrutiny clearly shows, the two faiths grew out of the same sources, and both have conceptions of the divine with intra-divine structures.

Recognition of these similarities is already very significant. Pinhas Lapide who did recognize these similarities, found Rahner's modal Trinity closer to Judaism's vision of the divine than Moltmann's dynamic Trinity. In addition, Lapide already pointed out that for Christians, the Trinity is a fixed theological view of God affirmed in the creed and liturgy. The need for three divine elements working together is basic to Christian theology. In contrast, Lapide shows that the whole rainbow of Jewish expressions of God includes a gallery of verbal images, which neither are now nor ever have become hardened in creeds or "stone-hard concepts on which one could build a putative knowledge of God." He continues, "rather what we have in all these images are metaphors toward the unutterable," forms of poetry and personal formulation.[57]

No Jewish thinker or believer has to affirm *shekhinah*, *kavod*, and *tzimtzum* of God as anything but metaphors in a sea of rabbinic metaphors. Judaism has no fixed divine configuration, so its theology varies from a philosophic negative theology without hypostasis to kabbalistic structures of the divine. On one extreme, some Jewish philosophers accept a negative theology and treat all language of the divine in rabbinic texts as mere simile or metaphor, but many kabbalists who take the God language seriously still seek to preserve the unity of an Absolute God by means of treating God language as attributes, and still other Jewish thinkers have grand imaginary metaphysical schemes with thousands of divine parts. Judaism varies from philosophic simile to parabolic knowledge to infinite literary complexity.

For example, the Jewish rationalist Hermann Cohen saw God as an ideal, an archetype of morality. An ethical monotheism of one unique God unlike anything else, worshiped through living ethically. Many modern, liberal Jewish thinkers followed in similar paths. On the other hand, some kabbalists such as Rabbi Isaac Luria (1532–1572), describe a complex map of intra-divine structure arranged into a baroque hierarchy with thousands of divine levels. But these different philosophic views are regarded as interpretations subject to debate within Judaism. By contrast, the doctrine of the Trinity as defined precisely in the creed is at the very heart of Christianity.

Jewish thinkers also define intra-divine parts of God differently. Most notably, regarding our discussion of Moltmann, the Jewish *shekhinah* is not the Son of Man or Logos. The *shekhinah* in midrashic and kabbalaistic Judaism is often feminine, bridal, and an image of fecundity and mothering.[58] In contrast, the *shekhinah* in Moltmann's Christian thought is the second person of the Trinity, an incarnate male Son, known through the mystery of faith. The same range of differences are found in discussions concerning the Father in both religions, or a comparison of incarnation or revelation.[59]

Rahner's near modalism without familiar relationships between divine parts allows Jews to say that his view is similar, for all ostensive purposes, to the Jewish view. The difference is the implication of the economic Trinity and perichoresis. Rahner assumes that God's perichoresis, the co-indwelling, is needed as an act of self-communication. Judaism, in contrast, can envision God as an abstract nature apart from the world without essential distinctions. And as noted above, the numerical distinctions of the kabbalistic hierarchy are always seen as contingent on the infinite divine above the world. For Jewish thought, God language when about real entities is about created masks or veils and not essential to, nor identical with, the one individual God behind them.

Moltmann's dynamic movements in the divine would make some sense to a kabbalistic reading of Judaism as well as those modern Jewish thinkers who use forms of kabbalistic thought such as Rosenzweig, Heschel, or Abraham Isaac Kook, even if they would ultimately reject Moltmann's formulation. Yet, to these thinkers, Moltmann's view of the dynamic movements would be an alternative schema of the divine but not a different conception of God.

Here again, similar to Rahner, the difference in the conception of God would be the implication of the economic Trinity, not the immanent Trinity. For Moltmann, God's essence is from eternity a love which is capable of redemptive suffering. When the Son suffers death, the Father suffers the death of the Son. In contrast, Jews achieve restoration through the performance of *mitzvot.* To use the idea of a root metaphor, the core difference is a root metaphor of mitvah performance or a root metaphor of divine salvation. But the difference is not the conception of God. The difference is also that Christians live in a world that is "already here" in which God redeems humanity even if kenosis is needed, while Jews consider the world as firmly "not yet" especially after the contraction of God and the breaking of the vessels, and after the Holocaust.

Moltmann made an important declaration that the very Christian ideas of the incarnation of the divine *Logos* and the indwelling of the Holy Spirit developed in the same "spiritual neighborhood" as the Jewish ideas of exilic of the divine and *shekhinah* theology. But then both religions developed in very different directions even if they are returning for some convergence at the end of the twentieth century. This is especially shown in how Moltmann used modern Jewish thought to define the Trinity. This is the point that makes the topic of this book an important perspective. Despite, divergences from the early common roots, there are currently signs of convergence again.

A Trinitarian position such as Rahner's influenced by modern thought converges with Judaism leaving most of the difference over self-communication and attributes. But this comparison is not a clear black and white dichotomy between the religions.

The Jewish difference from Moltmann's position, is seemingly greater and more substantive than from Rahner's position because Moltmann's formulation of the Trinity consists of three persons. However, Moltmann's use of midrash, kabbalah, and modern Jewish thought shows that the specific differences are about details in the formulations.

This chapter dealt with two creedal high Christology thinkers, however if we had looked to non-Trinitarian thinkers such as Oneness Protestants or some Anabaptists, we would have had even more to reframe the discussion. A place for further discussion is Eastern Orthodox theology, which rejects the filioque, rather affirming the theological concept that the Son proceeds from the Father, meaning that there is a clear conceptual hierarchy, a monarchia or primary, within the divine. For Eastern Orthodoxy there can only be one cause of the Godhead—God the Father. The Father is the source of the Son and Spirit with an "eternal submission of the Son to the Father."[60] This clearly hierarchical structure deserves comparison with Jewish positions.

Miroslav Volf, the Yale Divinity School theologian, may have placed his finger on the difference between the two religions in seeing the Christian divine as having a mutually interior being and perichoresis, implying that for others, such as Judaism, the intra-divine structures are only numerical, or external. "The unity of the triune God is grounded neither in the numerically identical substance nor in the accidental intentions of the persons, but rather in their mutually interior being . . ."[61]

Conclusions

Cardinal Kasper in his book on the Trinity reminds us that the Trinity is a unique Christian understanding of God that is unlike the unique Jewish understanding of God, even if both are based in the Hebrew

Bible and the common thought of early centuries.[62] I do not want to elide that difference, or make the Jewish and Christian readings the same. I do not want to confuse or conflate the two religions. But I do want to move beyond the widespread view that Jewish thought has a pristine monotheism and Christianity has tritheism.

At this point, we already have undone the assumptions of Trude Weiss-Rosmarin who made Judaism a pure abstract monotheism in diametrical opposition to Christianity. The two religions are not different in a zero-sum way, either historically or conceptually. Rather, some elements are the same and some elements are different. And now they have mutual influence on each other. In the end, the two religions remain as two distinct religions, or two different constructions of religion with different theological views of God. These different views create quite different positions when viewed liturgically, homiletically, and spiritually.

Nevertheless, this book seeks conceptual understanding and mutual edification. Many Jewish theologians have avoided discussing the complexity of the Jewish conception of God or they have foreclosed discussions of theological similarities with Christianity before discussions have even begun. Rather than irreconcilable, noncomparable differences, we now can explore a variety of relationships, parallels, divergences, and convergences, and we can begin to understand each other, as well as be able to engage in comparative theology.

CHAPTER TWO

Incarnation

IN THE POPULAR song *Mary Did You Know?* the verse goes, "Mary did you know that your baby boy would save our sons and daughters?" The Incarnation of the Son of God as a baby through the Virgin Mary as a miraculous conception and then as the teacher Jesus, and finally as a unique crucified savior was all part of a divine design to redeem the world from sin.[1]

Jewish thinkers have always found the Incarnation as incomprehensible and never understood why God needed to become human. Trude Weiss Rosmarin declares:

> Judaism is an ethical monotheism not predicated on a person . . . Judaism, therefore, has no need for the kind of religious assurances and consolations that Christianity finds in the doctrine of the incarnation of God in Jesus. On the contrary, this doctrine seems to the Jew an infringement upon and a diminution of the incomparable Uniqueness and Unity of God.[2]

Since Jews do not see a need for a redeemer from sin, they do not see a need for a divine human incarnation. Most of the time, Jews have seen incarnation as ridiculous and pagan, distinguishing between the Jewish personal God and the Christian personified God. Anything that needs to be done can be done by God alone and in addition in Judaism the divine and the human are two realms with a vast theological chasm between them. Judaism cannot accept the Incarnation of the Son of

God because Judaism does not hear this story, and because Jewish faith does not testify to the story.

This chapter looks at the classic definition of the Incarnation and potentially similar ideas in Judaism, then turning to the contemporary convergence.

Incarnation as defined by the Church

The term *incarnation*, from the Latin *carnis* (flesh), literally means "enfleshment" and reflects the Christological doctrine that Jesus was fully human and fully divine, the Son of God in the flesh. The Gospel of John starts with, "In the beginning was the Word" implying that Jesus was the divine logos. Later in the same chapter, "and the Word became flesh and lived among us" (John 1:14) implies that the divine logos was incarnate as flesh.[3] Paul writes of the Son becoming flesh: "God sending his own Son, in the likeness of sinful flesh and of sin" (Rom 8:3). Paul identifies Jesus with God and sees God indwelling in the corporal Jesus: "In Him dwells all the fullness of the Godhead bodily" (Col 2:9). The concept of God as incarnate was traditionally retrograded into Isaiah by the gospel writers themselves "His name shall be called Immanuel (meaning 'God with and among us')" (Isa 7:14, Matt 1:22–23).

In patristic interpretation of the New Testament, Jesus was considered as the eternal Logos made manifest as the divine Son. The shared divine nature of the Father and Son is shown as "the Father is in me and I in the Father." (John 10:36,38) According to the Gospel of John, Jesus says: "He who has seen me has seen the Father" (John 16:9). St. Athanasius links this to "I and the Father are one" (John 10:30); and thereby establishes the consubstantiality of the Father and the Son. The effect of the Incarnation on the human will of Christ was to leave the will free in all things human save only sin, in that, it was impossible that any stain of sin should soil the soul of Christ.

At the start of the second century, many thought that Jesus was already considered divine. Pliny the Younger, governor of Bithynia in Asia Minor, learned that "on an appointed day," Christians habitually met before daybreak and recited "a hymn to Christ, as to a god" albeit he may have been understood as subordinate to the Father. These hymns, which go back to the earliest days of Christianity, sharply contradict the popular notion that the concept of the Incarnation is only a product of fourth-century theologians: Athanasius simply argued theologically what the church had been singing for two centuries.[4]

Some scholars take a maximalist position about the concept of God in early Christianity, maintaining that early Christians simultaneously considered themselves monotheistic, yet considered Jesus not as a simple messenger of God, but worshiped him as the Son of God. They maintain that the early Jewish Christians worshipped Jesus at a very early date, no more than two decades after the Christ event and most likely during the first decade. In contrast, scholars taking a minimalist position have insisted that Jesus was not worshipped until the late first century CE or the early second century. Some claim that Christians did not believe Jesus was God until the latter part of the first century. Some claim that the many held a position of subordination to preserve monotheism or that they only prayed through Christ and not to Christ. The early Christians honored Jesus as God's Son in the sense that he was God's agent par excellence, having an unprecedented relationship with God, but not as being himself God.[5] However, as noted above, the Councils of Nicaea and Chalcedon determined that Jesus was both fully human and fully divine.[6]

The Chalcedon Council concluded in 451 that the Incarnation implies three facts: (1) the divine person of Jesus Christ, (2) the human nature of Jesus Christ, and (3) the hypostatic union of the human with the divine nature in the divine person of Jesus. The doctrine of the Incarnation as accepted by church council recognized Jesus to be "truly God and truly man . . . in two natures, without confusion, without change, without division, without separation." The Incarnation is the mystery and the dogma of the Word made Flesh.

However, there were contrasting interpretations of the Incarnation that were not accepted by the council. This chapter cannot convey the diversity and complexity of the many positions of the early Church, but in broad terms, the rejected positions can be summarized into the following three different approaches. One opinion strongly emphasized that the divine nature and the human side were only as appearance, Jesus was purely God and merely appeared as a human form (a position called Docetism). Another stressed the human side and Jesus the man was able to become divine (a position called adoptionism), already rejected at Nicaea. A third position stated that the divine Word indwells in the human Jesus as two separate sides. God indwells in the human who is just. The indwelling of the Word in Jesus is, however, more excellent than the indwelling of God in the just man by grace, for that reason the indwelling of the Word purposes the Redemption of all mankind as a consequence. In this approach, Mary is the Mother of Christ (Christotokos), not the Mother of God (Theotokos).

Interestingly, these rejected positions could be more readily accommodated into Judaism, God appears in the image of a man in a docetic manner, or a holy man could have the divine rest upon him as a form of adoptionism. Both have Second Temple era Jewish antecedents, and both continue within Jewish thought (see below on God appearance as a body in the book *Shiur Komah* and the ascension of Enoch and Elijah). But these positions are different from the Western Catholic doctrine of Chalcedon.

Cardinal Walter Kasper notes that these positions show that the divine and the human do not form a natural symbiosis. In his Christology, Cardinal Kasper emphasizes that Chalcedon unambiguously held on to the statement "that God and man do not form a natural symbiosis. In the Incarnation, God does not become a principle within the world; he is neither made into a spatial reality nor into one of time. God's transcendence is upheld as much as is the human person's independence and freedom."[7] The Church Father Irenaeus defended the concept of the Incarnation, yet called the concept of God becoming flesh the scandal of the Incarnation. Irenaeus identified the Incarnation thus, as a note that by worldly and rational standards, the Incarnation of Jesus—God assuming flesh—is truly scandalous.

This is the unbridgeable dividing line between the two religions as they are now, Jews do not worship Jesus, through Jesus, or any another being besides God and consider these traits as foreign worship. The scandal of the Incarnation is indeed a scandal for Jewish thought. If we are comparing the doctrinal incarnation to Jewish views, then this scandalous unnatural combination is the division, not the rejected views. The Jewish reaction to this doctrine as formulated in the fourth century, when there was a clear divide between the post-council church and the Rabbis of the Talmud was an absolute rejection of incarnation in which God does not have a son and humans do not become divine or offered a share in the divine nature. Rabbi Abbahu (d. ~320, Casearia), Talmudic amora offers a polemical response to his perception of the Christian position. Abbahu comments on the phrase "beside me there is no God" (Isa 44:6) to mean God's explicit denial of a father or a brother or a son (Ex. Rab. 29.4). In addition, he said: "if a man tells you 'I am God' he is lying" (J.T., Ta'an. 2.1, 65b).[8]

In addition, the divide lies in the fact that the incarnation is tied to salvation, the redeemer must be a divine person to redeem humanity. According to the Augustinian perspective, after the fall, human will is unable to fully turn to God. No human could restore the human will. Humanity is not to worship and serve anything other than God. Therefore, the one who redeems humanity must be God. Anslem, in contrast to much contemporary Christian thought, states that only Jesus Christ as the divine-human mediator as a human can render to God the positive honor He is due, and also bear the negative consequences of humanity's failure to honor God.[9]

Divine Immanence

One of the recent ways of reconciling Jewish and Christian thought is to look at the topic of divine immanence in the Hebrew Bible, thereby considering the incarnation as only an intensification of divine presence of God immanent in the tabernacle and temple. This is the approach of Jürgen Moltmann, Cardinal Walter Kasper, Elizabeth Johnson, and the Biblical scholar Gary Anderson,[10] as well as the approach of the Jewish theologians Pinchas Lapide and Michael Wyschogrod, thereby opening vistas for discussion beyond this chapter.

Michael Wyschogrod thinks that the doctrine of God's incarnation could be understood as a kind of intensification of God's covenant with Israel. Wyschogrod argues that the covenant between God and Israel results not just in a closeness and intimacy between them but includes an indwelling of God in the people of Israel whose status as a holy people may be said to derive from this indwelling. Although the incarnation is not foreseeable based on the Hebrew Bible, once the fact of the incarnation is assumed, as it is by Christians, then incarnation can be regarded as an extension of the Bible's basic thrust. Wyschogrod identifies the incarnation with the holiness of the Jewish people, the entire nation of Israel; however, most other theologians and scholars think the better analogy is the tabernacle.

For Wyschogrod, a Biblical approach would see no reasons "within the essence of the Jewish idea of God," which exclude a priori God's "appearance in human form." According to this position, the idea of the Incarnation in general is not antithetical to Judaism. To reject the Incarnation on a priori grounds would be to impose external constraints on God's freedom, a notion fundamentally foreign to Judaism. According to this view, when Christians say, "We believe in the Incarnation, that the Son of God became man in Jesus Christ." Christians consider this intimacy between God and his creature as an event in the long-term history of God coming down to the world starting with the tabernacle.

Looking back on the differences between the rabbinic and Christian positions at this point, Jews had God immanent in the world in the tabernacle, while Christianity extended the immanence to God as incarnate in the world. The verse in John, "The Word became flesh and made his dwelling among us" (1:14) actually uses the word "tabernacled" (*eskēnōsen*) to describe the incarnation.[11]

In the Hebrew Bible this divine immanence is described as God's dwelling in or among the people of Israel: "Then have them make a sanctuary for me, and I will dwell among them" (Exod 25: 8). Also, "I will dwell among the people of Israel, and will be their God" (Exod 29: 43, 45). God is dwelling among the people of Israel after the Exodus out from Egypt, so he can be their God.

The immanence continues in the Jerusalem Temple. When Solomon began building the Temple, the house of God, in Jerusalem, God said: "Concerning this house you are building, if you will walk in my statutes and obey my ordinances and keep all my commandments and walk in them, then I will establish my word with you. And I will dwell among the children of Israel" (1 Kgs 6:12–13.) God has thus two dwelling places for his intimate presence: the Temple and the people of Israel.

Jumping ahead to the rabbinic period, by the first century, the term *shekhinah* (God's indwelling) took on a greater role within Judaism as a name for this divine presence. The term originates in the Hebrew Bible with God's glory "dwelling" over the tabernacle (Exod 40:35) and indicates both divine presence and continuity. *Shekhinah*, as used in the rabbinic concept of divine immanence, conveys divine presence on earth and is used as a synonym for the divine glory. "When [Israel] went into Egypt, the *shekhinah* went with them; in Babylon the shekhinah was with them" (Talmud, *Megillah 29a*). However as noted in the chapter on the Trinity, the *shekhinah* is a hierarchical manifestation of the divine, monarchistic and hypostatic. In contrast, the prologue to John's Gospel and the early Church Fathers developed divine immanence as the Logos becoming flesh who lives as a human. This leaves a gap between a manifestation of divine presence but not actually God in the Jewish religion and an actual incarnation in a person in the Christian religion.

Anthropomorphism and Embodiment in Jewish Texts

Moving from biblical to rabbinic texts, Jacob Neusner examines the notion of anthropomorphism in rabbinic literature claiming that the Rabbis have an incarnational theology. He defines incarnational as anthropomorphism, "the representation of God in the flesh, as corporeal, consubstantial in emotion and virtue with human beings, and sharing in the modes and means of action carried out by mortals." God's attributes are represented as identical to those of a human being. That is why the character of the divinity may accurately be represented as incarnational: God represented as a person consubstantial in indicative physical traits with the human being.[12] God having a body, God having representation, and God having emotions are all incarnational. Neusner does not present a substantive union of the divine and human, rather a divine in the image of the human. He argues that some earlier rabbis held to a doctrine of incarnation; he is fully aware of the theological connections this has for Christianity because he sees that the biblical evidence of the Old Testament leads to the incarnation, a God with a body and emotions that can be represented.[13] However, this identification of anthropomorphism with incarnation is not what Christians mean by incarnation and at best would be a heretical docetic approach. Yet, Neusner is important for clearing space to discuss the topic in that many scholars were fundamentally hostile to acknowledging anthropomorphism in rabbinic thought.[14]

Christoph Markschies shows that Jews did have personified images of God's body as shown in synagogue mosaics, in the biblical books of Ezekiel and Daniel, and the apocryphal books of Enoch, Apocalypse of Abraham, and the Apocalypse of Zephaniah, as well as in later Merkavah ("throne-chariot") mysticism with its work *Shiur Komah* (the measure of the mystical body [of God]), which contains "speculations as to the gigantic scale of divine bodies" (167).[15] These texts offer images of an embodied God. Yet, Markschies concludes that in Judaism, "Nothing approaching an incarnation, 'a rendering in flesh' of such privileged divine intermediary figures within a concrete earthly body (as indeed of the Nazarene Jesus), may be found in any of these Jewish texts of highly varied provenance."[16]

Moshe Idel, the scholar of Jewish mysticism, in his groundbreaking work *Ben: Sonship and Jewish Mysticism* looks at forms of descent from God and divine embodiment in Jewish thought showing that these ideas of divine embodiment are ancient themes in Mesopotamian literature and continuing into Second Temple Jewish literature such as Enoch traditions, which assume that Elijah, Enoch, and the patriarch Jacob become divine, or part of the divine throne.[17] He specifically frames the discussion as one of being a Son of God. The relationship between the divine realm and the human realm may take several familial forms, including the relation of a divine father, a divine or higher son, and human who may be considered lower sons. This relationship goes both ways creating a continuous link between the human and divine realms. But most importantly, he separates sharply these ancient Jewish themes of Sonship from Christian conceptions of incarnation, because the latter version created a singular and ultimate version that only occurs with the concurrent ideas of virgin birth, a unique son, incarnation as flesh, sinfulness, atonement for Sin, incarnation as revelation, and the sinless perfection of Jesus.

For Idel, Christianity combined two extremes of becoming divine, both found in Judaism without the symbiosis of Chalcedon. The first is Elijah becoming divine and the second, divine becoming manifestation in lower form like Metatron or the Shiur Komah, in contrast, Christianity simultaneously raised a human to the Godhead and had the divine incarnate into a human.[18] Elijah became divine but not God, and the angel Metatron never became manifest in the flesh. The Talmud even cautions that Metatron should not be worshiped because he was an angel and not a deity (TB Sanhedrin 38b).

The incarnation, according to Idel, however, is not an intensification of prior Second Temple trends, rather about the moment of a specific person, Jesus Christ, seen as divine at a specific moment offering a new Torah. Decisively, Christians limited this specific moment to a small window of time, a specific person—Jesus, specific goal of salvation as the Christ, and added an eschatological element for the redemption of the entire world.

In contrast, Judaism, according to Idel, has ideas of divine descent as the embodiment of the divine Torah, in which Torah takes on a garment or a spiritual body thereby allowing God's embodiment in sacred texts, for example, the imagery of the enclothed garmented Torah in the *Zohar*. Or the divine is manifest as a body in various forms, for example, the book *Shiur Komah* (the measure of the mystical body), which presents God's partial manifestation in a human form. An audacious image of divine embodiment in Judaism is the Talmudic passage envisioning that God wears a pair of Tefillin, on which is written his expression of love for the Jewish people:

> "Who is like Your people Israel, a unique nation upon the earth" (2 Sam 7:23). R. Abin son of R. Ada in the name of R. Isaac said: How do you know that the Holy One, blessed be He, puts on tefillin? For it is said: "The Lord has sworn by His right hand, and by the arm of His strength." (Isa 62:8) "By His right hand": this is the Torah; for it is said: "At His right hand was a fiery law unto them." (Deut 33:2). "And by the arm of his strength:" this is the tefillin; as it is said: "The Lord will give strength unto His people" (Ps 29:11). (TB Berakhot 6a)

God is portrayed as living a life of embodied keeping of the commandments in tandem with the Jewish people. It is important to note that these forms of embodiment are not dependent on whether God has a body.

Nonetheless, can God have a body in Rabbinic Judaism? The Church Fathers thought God is immaterial based on their Greek philosophy training. Conversely, they assumed that Jews conceptualized God as corporeal. According to Justin Martyr, the Rabbis conceived of God as having hands, feet, and fingers. Origen declares that the Jews imagine God as being similar to a human being.[19] There is a manifestation or hypothesis of God with anthropomorphic form, as noted by many scholars. From a historical perspective, Rabbinic Judaism would appear to hold that (1) God has a manifest body, (2) this body can be seen but not by everyone, therefore not an ordinary body, and (3) it is forbidden to represent God visually, unless the representation is indirect. However, rabbinic thought permits representing God embodied in verbal, oral, or written form. Daniel Boyarin encapsulates how rabbinic Judaism and early Christianity disagree on the question of the divine body. Rabbinic Judaism starts from the idea that God is immediately corporeal but not incarnated, while Christians assumed God is incorporeal but incarnate.[20]

In sum, ancient Jews most likely accepted God had an unseen body and Christians did not, for Christians God had an incarnation. Christianity's dualist perspective envisioned God as first invisible and immaterial before being incarnated, making himself visible. The Christian concept of the body emphasizes the duality of the soul and body and the tension that exists between them. Jesus is God made visible as a body and as a name.[21] In the end, the differences resolve around immanence in a person compared to divine immanence in a tabernacle, and the incarnation of the spiritual into a physical body compared to the somatic whole of an unseen body of God. Jewish thought has an unseen body of God indwelling in the tabernacle and Temple, while Christians have an incarnation of the God into a physical human body.

Medieval Era

Medieval Jewry in Muslim lands followed Islamic philosophic conceptions and saw God as a simple incorporeal unity. Maimonides explained God as a divine being, first cause, who is indivisible and non-corporeal. He relegates the Christian ideas of the Incarnation and Trinity to a defective conception of religion, which he considered a form of foreign worship unacceptable to monotheism. In addition, the medieval Jewish rational tradition, including Maimonides, relegated all references in rabbinic literature to God's body or God's manifestation as mere metaphor alone since God is strictly incorporeal in all senses.

In Christian lands, Jews treated the Christian worship of Jesus as a representation of the divine encapsulating it with a rabbinic legal concept that Christians are associating a non-divine being with God thereby lessening the monotheistic status of Christianity. The term used was association (*shituf*); a human Jesus was associated with God during worship thereby substantiating from a Jewish conception that incarnation is impossible. In any event, for medieval Jews, Christians were seen as having the Creator of the world in mind even though when Christians mention God's name, they needlessly also have in mind another thing—Jesus. Jews paid little attention to specific theories of the Trinity, Incarnation, or Jesus.[22]

In the polemical context of a debate with Pablo Christiani, Nahmanides, the thirteenth-century Barcelonan Jewish commentator approached the discussion from the perspective of needing to win the argument to prevent forced conversions. Nahmanides demonstrated, from numerous biblical and Talmudic sources, that the Christian concept of incarnation ran counter to rabbinic Jewish belief showing that the biblical prophets regarded the future messiah as a human, a person of flesh and blood, without ascribing to him divinity.

Beyond this, Nahmanides reduces the idea to an absurdity in which the concept of incarnation "seems most strange" for "the Creator of Heaven and Earth to resort to the womb of a certain Jewish lady, grew there for nine months and was born as an infant, and afterwards grew up and was betrayed into the hands of his enemies who sentenced him to death and executed him." For him, "The mind of a Jew, or any other person, simply cannot tolerate these assertions." Nahmanides sees too much drama, too much materiality, too much messy birth and infancy, and too much of an outrageous particularist story. There is no logical overlap according to Nahmanides, between incarnation as a material person and Judaism.[23]

Modern Era

In the modern era, incarnation remains a tenet of Christian faith, but many modern Christian thinkers view the incarnation with a greater focus on the blueprint of creation rather than as solely a means of absolving humanity from sin. For example, Friedrich Schleiermacher considered the incarnate appearance of Christ as the aspirational ideal of humankind, the necessary completion of creation, not an addition to creation that responds to the appearance of sin.

In modern Christian thought, this distinction becomes the debate between infralapsarian and supralapsarian understandings of the incarnation. The infralapsarian position thinks the Incarnation was part of the plan of creation itself, while the supralarsarian position thinks the incarnation was contingent upon sin. Incarnation can either logically precede or follow sin. The majority report throughout Western

Christian history is the supralarsarian position, God would not have become incarnate had humanity not fallen into sin. Modern thought generally holds the infralapsarian position focusing on God's incarnation as the plan of creation, Judaism is closer to these infralapsarian positions.

Karl Barth holds the traditional position; Karl Rahner sees the incarnation as a mystical bond of humanity and God; Jürgen Moltmann sees the incarnation as God bearing human suffering; and Elizabeth Johnson thinks the incarnation means God identifies with the entire created world.

Karl Barth

The first of the four moderns is the Swiss Reformed theologian Karl Barth (1886–1968) who places incarnation front and center as the revelation of God. "In the incarnation, the humanity of Christ becomes the sole means of revelation of the eternal Word."[24] Barth believed that God is unknowable by the finite human, and he rejects all forms of natural theology. Revelation comes to humanity only through Jesus Christ as God's choice as both the means of revelation and the object of revelation. On the other hand, Barth asserts that Christ would not be a revelation if he were not human because Jesus Christ is both revelation to humanity and of humanity. God may have become flesh and human but, Barth denies that human nature possesses a capacity for becoming the human nature of Jesus Christ.[25]

Barth contends that the human Jesus Christ reveals "that man is the man of sin, and what sin is, and what it means for man."[26] In Christ we see the fleshy human nature "in its perversion and corruption."[27] Thus, the human Jesus Christ becomes a mirror in which every human being can see himself as this man and as a sinner, revealing the nature of sin and the sinfulness of the human race.[28]

The sinlessness of Christ was a pure obedience, "which no other human can render" and he substitutes obedience in the place where "otherwise sin necessarily and irresistibly takes place."[29] Christ bore the sinful nature innocently since the sin was not his own from disobedience. He lived life in the form of a human on the basis of Adam's human act, but he did nothing that Adam did.[30] God's freedom, for Barth, for the Word to became flesh is grounded in the divine covenant and election of humanity. God did not have to will to become human but did indeed will to be God for us and not God without us.

Barth's approach with its emphasis on sinfulness, incarnation as revelation, and the sinless perfection of Christ, builds directly on the Christian theological scheme and has little in common with rabbinic or Jewish thought.

Karl Rahner

Recent trends in Christian theology have generally rejected Augustine's and Anselm's formulations of Incarnation, rather they consider the Incarnation as an intended part of creation, part of a prelapsarian goal of Christ becoming close to creation.

"The statement of God's *Incarnation*—of his becoming *material*—is the most basic statement of Christology," observes Karl Rahner, the moment in which the divine Word emptied itself and became flesh, emptying the Word into human nature.[31] The doctrine of the soul after incarnation expresses our partnership with the God who took human nature as the vessel of divinity. Rahner rejects the erroneous idea that Jesus's human nature was no more than a disguise, a suit of clothes that could be shrugged off because "the climax of salvation history is not the detachment from earth of the human being as spirit in order to come to God, but . . . the coming of the divine Logos in the flesh, the taking on of matter so that it itself becomes a permanent reality of God."[32]

Rahner asks, What does it mean for God to be human? Rahner argues that only by means of incarnation can humanity perceive the truth of human nature, because it's only in Jesus that we witness a person fully given over to God. Human nature's meaning is to be given up to God, abandoned; humanity is fulfilled and finds itself by giving oneself up to God: The Incarnation shows us that being human means having the potential to be completely inhabited by the Word of God. All theology, says Rahner, is therefore anthropology, and all anthropology is Christology. To know what it is to be human is to know Christ, and to know Christ is to know God. Human freedom is not about sin and depravity or the remedial need to redeem humanity from the covenant of works. Rather, through incarnation, humanity is reconciled with Christ's ultimate divine offer and the ultimate acceptance of the divine. Incarnation as the real symbol of that offer of God, an intensifier like a hug of a relationship.

Jesus of Nazareth is the true symbol in whom God can self-manifest in the human condition, and that through Jesus we can become true humans. In this sense, Jesus Christ is the real symbol of God and of human beings in whom we can know both God and the human person. "The principle that God's salvific action on man, from its first foundation onto its completion, always takes place in such a way that God himself is the reality of salvation, given to man and grasped by him in the symbol, which does not represent an absent and merely promised reality but exhibits this reality as something present, by means of the symbol formed by it." Rahner claims that the doctrine of the Incarnation should be the main chapter of a theology of symbolic realities, and this chapter would consist of an exegesis of Jesus's saying: "Whoever has seen me has seen the Father" (John 14:9).[33]

According to Rahner, the ancient Hebrews believed in a transcendent God, who reveals himself freely to humanity, and human beings can only grasp the divine presence of the revelation through mediated realities.[34] God is not a concept or a static being. God truly wants to talk to human beings face-to-face, as a presence, in which God's presence is mediated through symbols. We can call God's self-communication in the Hebrew Bible as God's manifestations or theophanies since many Fathers of the Church understood theophanies in the Old Testament as a sign of the pre-incarnate Logos. Theophanies are always mediated. For instance, when God speaks to Abraham, the Bible presents an angel speaking in the first person as God. For Rahner, such divine self-communication takes place ontologically in Jesus Christ in whom God speaks to human beings face-to-face. All human history is a movement toward the Incarnation, which illumines the future of humankind. (Covenant theology does not play a role in his thinking.)

In Jesus, God is not just present as in the Hebrew Bible, but God becomes human. Rahner points out that we must avoid mythological misconceptions in which the human side of the Godman is portrayed as a passive puppet or as a "mask through which God makes himself known." The Incarnate Logos became direct reference to the Wisdom; the angel of the Lord is understood as reference to the existence of the pre-incarnate Son as the second person of the Trinity.[35]

In the Incarnation God breaks any clear barrier between the divine and the secular world because now we no longer say simply that God is in Jesus, but that Jesus is God. Jesus of Nazareth is God's Word in history. God did not simply self-communicate through Jesus of Nazareth, but in him God became man. God did not just speak through a human being, but as a human being.

Rahner notes that Christians tend to reflect only on the historical mediation of the Incarnate Word during his earthly life. But for Rahner, the humanity of Jesus plays a fundamental role not only in the past, but also in the present and for all eternity "as the permanent openness of our finite being to the living God of infinite, eternal life"[36] Rahner claims that the ecumenical councils developed a philosophical language may not express appropriate meaning nowadays.

Rahner acknowledges that we are dealing with absolute divine mystery, which limits human approach.[37] The theology of the Incarnation is a fundamental divine mystery, fundamental for Christian spirituality in terms of following Jesus not only because we do not know the divine in itself but also because our understanding of the human being is not self-evident.[38] We cannot understand God-self if we do not understand our own human nature and existential condition in the world. In that sense, Rahner asserts that we cannot say anything about God without also saying something about human beings, and vice versa. For Rahner, an experience of God is not something extraordinary, rather God-self speaks to the human person throughout their everyday life. Every human person receives the divine grace to be open to hear God's word as a personal and interior experience of God.

The New Testament and the church's tradition have related to Jesus Christ as the Incarnate Word of God while keeping their monotheist faith in the immutable and transcendent God.[39] Karl Rahner takes seriously the church's teaching on the hypostatic union of the human and divine natures; in that he considers the human created nature of Jesus as already assumed by the Logos of God. For Rahner, originally we could not speak of the second person of the Holy Trinity without mentioning the Incarnation because the Son was always with the Father and with the Holy Spirit. However, after the Incarnation of the Logos of God we no longer can refer to Jesus Christ without implying his humanity as incarnate Son.

There are those who think that Rahner is emphasizing the two extremes of the Incarnation at the same time. For Rahner, Jesus was a real human Israelite who expressed Jewish values and at the same time was the Eternal Logos before incarnation so that the incarnation is almost docetic. Therefore, Colin Gunton calls Rahner a degree Christology, in which Jesus is greater than humans by degree and not by kind, then Rahner turns around and affirms that the Logos is eternal. For Rahner, Jesus was a divinized human. Being human means being open to the mystery we call God and giving oneself to it; incarnation is highest form of giving of oneself. We have potency for hypostatic union and mystical connection. At the same time, incarnation is God speaking out in an immanent word within the sinful world.[40]

Rahner's simultaneous degree Christology of a divinized man who is the pinnacle of human divination along with incarnation as symbol of the eternal Logos is in many ways combining certain aspects of both, and simultaneously held, Docetic and Arian approaches, the Son is an eternal Logos beyond the incarnation and also Jesus who becomes divine. There are other possible ways to understand Rahner, and many would disagree with this characterization of his thought as combining divination with eternal Logos, but this approach allows the Jewish theologian to place the incarnation against the Jewish positions.

Jewish thought can follow many a Rahnerian paragraph argument but then Judaism loses him by his Chalcedon conclusion. Jesus as a Jewish human person who does not become fully God or as a divine figure who does not become human, are both possible in first-century Jewish thinking but rejected due to the Chalcedon conclusion. In the twentieth century, Martin Buber could accept the notion that Jesus was a great teacher, a mere human being, teaching Jewish doctrines, but without any sense of a divination or incarnation.[41] To the extent that a follower of Rahner presents Christ as Jesus who is universal in the human soul, and not as the specific product of the second person of the Trinity and a miraculous birth, then Judaism and Rahner can find common language about religious anthropology.[42]

Nevertheless, fundamentally, Judaism, even without a concern for salvation, does not think an incarnation is needed to give oneself over to God. Humanity was designed to know God, love God, and commune with God. Judaism is certainly uncomfortable with the idea that the God of the Hebrew Bible is only a transcendent God who needs the compliment of a loving immanent God and uncomfortable with the idea that Christ is the singular higher manifestation of God's love. Jews find that idea supersessionalist and even anti-Jewish, in that in Exodus, God takes care of the Israelites as if on eagles' wings and Deuteronomy is concerned with loving God, cleaving to God, and God taking care of us. Neither Exodus or Deuteronomy are considered in Jewish thought as a pre-incarnate Christ, even if understood in some early Jewish texts as due to God's Logos.

Jürgen Moltmann

Jürgen Moltmann finds that the rationale of the incarnation is not in sin, but in creation. Incarnation is the perfected self-communication of the triune God to his world, as well as a step taken "for the sake of perfecting creation."[43] We are told that human being are made in the image of God (Gen 1:26–27), which Moltmann takes as a promise: In Christ "we have the fulfilment of the promise made to man that he will be 'the image of the invisible God.'" Consequently, according to Moltmann, that Christ is the true man and "it is therefore in union with him that believers discover the truth of human existence." In other words, even if humankind had never fallen, Christ would still have become incarnate in order that humanity should have a clear idea of what was meant by being in the image of God.[44]

The second idea in Moltmann's Christology is the divine suffering involved in the life of Christ and particularly in his cross.[45] Moltmann wished to change the discussion from what he considered as the traditional preoccupation with what the cross meant for Jesus to a different focus on what he saw as a revolutionary preoccupation with what the cross means for God.

Moltmann espouses the dialectical (as opposed to the analogical) principle in his approach to the knowledge of God, in which being is revealed not in its like but in its opposite. Love, for example, is revealed only in hatred and unity only in conflict. Similarly, God is revealed only in his opposite. The *god-ness* of God appears only in the paradox of divine abandonment on Calvary. Our personal natural sense of the divine does not expect divine *kenosis*, a divine self-emptying or divine capability to suffer. That is why such an idea is a *scandalon*.

Moltmann stresses this dialectic as fundamental to the concept of the incarnation. "Out of God's passion there arises the divine sympathy. Through the incarnation God shares and understands our finitude. Through the cross, God enters our godforsaken." Thereby, God unexpectedly becomes contracted, in the language of the Jewish kabbalah as a divine contraction (*tzimtzum*), through kenosis to connect to humanity, as explained in the Trinity chapter. "He humbles himself and takes upon himself the eternal death of the godless and the godforsaken so that all the godless and the godforsaken can experience communion with him." Hence "the godforsaken and rejected man can accept himself when he comes to know the crucified God who is with him and has already accepted him."

Jürgen Moltmann in *The Trinity and the Kingdom of God* writes: "The incarnation of the Son is more than merely a means to an end. Christology is more than the presupposition for soteriology." The incarnation was an end in itself, its own goal of reconciling God with the world. "Once the incarnate Son of God has achieved the reconciliation of the world with God, he himself becomes superfluous." For Moltmann, "the justification of the sinner is more than merely the forgiveness of sins," rather a reconciliation which perfects nature and creation. So, "the Son of God would have become man even if the human race had remained without sin." The Incarnation is specifically the Son becoming man so that we learn what is the nature of the true man, in the image of God, as promised in Genesis.[46]

Moltmann differentiated between what he called a "fortuitous" and a "necessary" incarnation. If the incarnation is necessary, then it is as a soteriological need for the Son of God to became a man in order that he could save humanity from our Sin. If incarnation is fortuitous, then the incarnation displays a fulfilment of the love of God and of his desire to be living amid humanity, to "walk in the garden" (Gen 3:8) with us. Moltmann favors "fortuitous" incarnation primarily because he feels that to speak of an incarnation of "necessity" is to do an injustice to the life of Christ.[47]

Against Barth's tendency to speak of the second coming of Christ (*parousia*) as merely a revelation of what Christ already is, Moltmann insists that the eventual return brings in something new, in that, Christ does not merely unveil the salvific meaning of Christ's death, rather he brings the fulfilment of the whole history and promise of Christ.[48] Moltmann finds that the rationale of the incarnation is not in sin, but in the very purpose of creation to create a kingdom of God, simultaneously the perfected self-communication of the triune God to his world, as well as, a step taken for the sake of perfecting creation. The cross is an affirmation of God's solidarity with the pain of humanity rather than a divine act of atonement for sin. In fact, Christ would have come even if Adam had never sinned. As a result, Moltmann is totally dismissive of the Anselmic view of the incarnation as what he calls "an emergency measure . . . the functional presupposition for the atoning sacrifice on the cross."[49]

The Jewish position does not require the incarnation to attain God's closeness with humanity because God is available to all (see chapter 6 on covenant) or for God to bear human suffering (see chapter 3 on Original Sin).

Elizabeth Johnson

Elizabeth Johnson (b. 1941), professor emerita at Fordham University, developed a Christology that directly rejects the Anselm approach to theology: God was incarnated to shower good and blessing on creation, and that means not just on humans or Christians but all of God's creation.

Similar to a Jewish reading of the Hebrew Bible, Johnson sees the presence of God's incarnate blessings in the blessings of Genesis, Exodus from Egypt, and community of Second Isaiah about to return from exile. The God of Israel is a saving and redeeming God of Exodus long before the Incarnation—this redemption comes through a deep knowledge and solidarity with the people and the promise for action to deliver. "It is the Creator God who is called Redeemer and Savior. These and other texts sing out an unequivocal assurance that the God who created the people is now acting as Redeemer, claiming back from another's authority, overcoming every obstacle to restore them to their own life in God's covenanted family."[50]

Continuing themes we saw in Moltmann of a redemptive quality to incarnation, Johnson holds that incarnation frees humans from both sins before the divine as well as political and economic oppression. "This redeeming work clearly has a political dimension; people robbed, plundered, and taken into captivity are being released to return to their native land. At the same time, given that the exile was interpreted as punishment for the nation's misdeeds, this moment of redemption also entails the forgiveness of sins, for the individual but also for the whole community."[51] The redemptive covenanted life was the very plan of God's creation in which both the individual and community are restored before God.

This vision of a return to the divine in an individual, political, social, economic, and religious sense can also be found in the thought of the Jewish thinker Rabbi Abraham Isaac Kook whose vision of return to God combined repentance from sin with full restoration of human potential and freedom from oppression and lack. "The power of renewal adds holiness to all creatures. The concealed inner force of our souls is also revealed, and it perfects the soul in thought and deed."[52] For Kook, Judaism was a "divine idea" that encompasses the universe in its totality and seeks to overcome divisions of secular and religious, material and spiritual. But for Rav Kook the divine idea is immanent in the people of Israel and its activities, not the working of the Trinity in Christ.

The Trinity, for Johnson, exists eternally in a *perichoresis* of mutual relations: "God is love" (John 4:16).[53] In such a relational theology of God, the transcendent Holy One does not enter the world for the first time in the historical person of Jesus Christ. Rather, the Triune God is pervasively present as self-communicating love throughout the cosmos from the beginning of time to the end. This infinite immanence is alluded to in the Bible by the figures of Spirit, Word, and Wisdom, among others. Johnson's work is the closest to a Jewish position in its focus on the forms of divine immanence in the Hebrew Bible along with the redemptive qualities of this immanence. The dividing line between Jewish and Christian forms is the Trinity and Jesus.

Elizabeth A. Johnson advocates a Hebrew Bible creation theology affirming God's presence with and love for all creation. The rabbinic tradition proclaims, "that there is no place devoid of divine presence" (*leit atar panui minah*), hence God is found in everything and every being.[54] So too, Johnson extends the notion of God's solidarity and presence to the entire creation through the incarnation. Using the lens of a Wisdom Christology, Johnson argues that the resurrection "pledges a future for all the dead, not only the dead of the human species but of all species."[55]

Conclusions

In the contemporary era, Christian and Jewish thought converge in looking toward the divine presence in the tabernacle and the Second

Temple era mediator figures as a common ground. No longer is the incarnation only the scandalous mixture of irreconcilable divine and human of the Chalcedon creed, rather it is another example of coming from a common spiritual neighborhood.

Yet, Jews with an embodied Torah have no overlap with Anselm's view of the incarnation as needed to overcome original sin. Jewish thought rejects the idea of worshiping Jesus or considering him or any other human as God. Discussions of God's body or docetic appearance in midrash and kabbalah do not close the gap because Incarnation was traditionally connected to redemption from sin and integrally tied to the concurrent ideas of virgin birth, atonement, a unique divine Son, and incarnation as flesh.

More basic is that Judaism, even without a concern for salvation, does not think an incarnation is needed as a revelation or to give oneself over to God. Humanity was designed to know God and love God. Jews find that any suggestion that Jesus as Christ is needed to reach God as a negation of a Jewish understanding of the Bible or even anti-Jewish. Jewish thought as creation theology saw the creation of the world as good without the need for a change to nature or history. In addition, much of Christian thinking traditionally reads the Incarnation as a mystery and a *scandalon*, hence beyond ordinary categories. As noted above, the Jewish position does not require the incarnation to attain God's closeness with humanity or for God to bear human suffering.

The formulation of Elizabeth Johnson which focuses on original blessing in creation, however, does begin to close the gap between the two religions. She advocates a Hebrew Bible creation theology affirming God's presence with, and love for, all creation before the incarnation of Christ, but there is still the need for the incarnation in Christ. According to Johnson, God is found in all creation and God's wisdom in all things is a form of the Incarnation. Judaism can agree with this. Finally, her considering the incarnation as divine immanence, divine providence, and concern for his people as shown in Genesis and Exodus culminates in Jesus, yet the function of incarnation is closer to Jewish theism and Jewish views of immanence in Genesis and Exodus.

Bigger Conclusions

The author and theologian Dorothy L. Sayers stated that "the dogma of the Incarnation is the most dramatic thing about Christianity, and indeed, the most dramatic thing that ever entered the mind of man; but if you tell people so, they stare at you in bewilderment. The event of the Incarnation of the Son of God—Jesus Christ, brought about change, not only in history, but to history itself." The belief that God, the creator of everything in heaven and on earth, descended through the Son and that his Son and Word became flesh and man, is very foreign to the Jewish understanding of God.[56]

From the Jewish perspective, Martin Buber spoke of the absence of God's Incarnation as being something specifically Jewish: "the non-incarnation of God who reveals himself to the "flesh" and is present to it in a mutual relationship . . . constitutes the ultimate division between Judaism and Christianity . . . We 'unify' God when living and dying we profess his unity; we do not unite ourselves to him." For Buber, the anthropology of Judaism is about our lives of meeting and fulfillment, not Christian incarnation.[57]

In contrast, some recent Jewish thinkers have thought differently and sought to overcome the impasse. For example, Pinchas Lapide reflectively and empathetically notes:

> If I contemplate the Incarnation in this way, it is basically neither idolatry nor deification of the creature and not at all an attempt to seize hold of God, as some Jews maintain, but in the final analysis only a further development or the taking it to the logical conclusion of that Hebrew doctrine of salvation that understands the loving bestowal of God in his humanity as the basic dynamic of all world history.[58]

Yet he emphasizes, that he is unable to believe in the incarnation.[59] Similarly, the Jewish theologian Andre Neher wrote about the incarnation that: "The Christianity whose theology is able to frighten only hypersensitive Jews appears" to be a biblical view "taken to its final conclusion."[60]

I must point out that the theological concept of Divine incarnation is not the same as the various forms of human theosis, deification, divination, and incarnational anthropology, which do have Jewish parallels, but which deserve their own discussion under the rubric of the Holy Spirit.[61]

In a charitable reading of Christianity, as noted above, twentieth-century theologian Michael Wyschogrod suggests, controversially, that the divinity of Jesus is not radically different from the holiness of the Jewish people.[62] If God loved Israel, then he could have miraculously become incarnate if he wanted to. The God of Israel is "a God who enters into the human world and who, by so doing, does not shy away from the parameters of human existence, including spatiality." God remains the transcendent God, "But this transcendence remains in dialectic tension with the God who lives with Israel in its impurity (Lev 16:16), who is the Jew's intimate companion, whether in the Temple of Solomon or in the thousands of small prayer rooms"

Yet, and with emphasis, Wyschogrod walks back his suggestion: "There is a good reason for the severity of the Jewish rejection of the incarnation." In that, "No matter how close God comes to humankind in the Hebrew Bible," God remains the eternal judge of all things human and cannot become the frail and temporal human being.[63] Wyschogrod concludes that for Jews, the doctrine of Jesus Christ as Son of God or as "the incarnate Word of God" exceeds the limits of Judaism, even though Jews can acknowledge that the contemporary view of incarnation develops central Jewish themes.[64] The concept of incarnation is generally viewed as one of the main dividing lines between Judaism and Christianity when understood as the doctrinal scandalous symbiosis of the infinite divine and fleshy human to offer salvation.[65]

To which a Christian might note that the free decision of the sovereign God of Israel to take up his dwelling in the one Son of the Jewish people, Jesus of Nazareth, makes it impossible for Christians to speak of God without including his relationship to this Son. Nor can Christians speak of God without the historic trajectory from an eternal Christ to a specific incarnation in a specific time and a specific place. That is to say, the incarnation in a Jewish body makes the connection of the

Christian understanding of God tightly connected to Judaism and the Jewish people as the location of his incarnation.

In light of this Christian retort, Michael Wyschogrod, despite rejecting incarnation, "linked Christian understanding of Incarnation with the demand that Jesus not be separated from the Jewish people along with a sense of connection to the Jewish people."[66] The Son of God, God's Word, became a human being in Jesus of Nazareth; he did not become a human being *in abstracto*, in general or in a neutral way. Rather, for Wyschogrod, "Jesus became Jewish flesh, a Jew, the son of a Jewish mother, and as such he became a concrete human being."[67]

This approach was exemplified by Pope John Paul II in a 1997 address to the Pontifical Biblical Commission who spoke of the New Testament's inseparable link with the Old Testament and Jesus's human identity. By emphasizing that Jesus became a Jew, the Incarnation of the Son of God becomes a connection with the Jewish people: "Jesus' human identity is determined on the basis of his bond with the people of Israel, with the dynasty of David and his descent from Abraham. And this does not mean only a physical belonging." Jesus of the Gospels took part in the synagogue and the reading of Jewish scripture. Thereby, "Jesus also came humanly to know these texts; he nourished his mind and heart with them . . . Thus, he became an authentic son of Israel, deeply rooted in his own people's long history."[68] For Pope John Paul II, God becomes a human to identify with the Torah, Jews, and their suffering. This is not a Jewish perspective, but certainly, as Michal Wyschogrod notes, it is a biblical one.

CHAPTER THREE

Original Sin

THE POET JOHN Donne in a hymn wrote: "Wilt thou forgive that sin where I begun, / Which was my sin, though it were done before?"[1] These two lines encapsulated the concept of inherited original sin, staining each and every person at birth. The weight of sin and its formulation as original sin is one of the main theological pillars of Western Christianity.

Trude Weiss Rosmarin declared, "Judaism has no room for anything resembling the Christian doctrine of Original Sin".[2] Indeed, since St. Augustine first formulated the concept, Jewish and Christian scholars have seemingly stood diametrically opposed on the issue of original sin. In the nineteenth and twentieth centuries, many Jewish thinkers voiced a sharp dichotomy between Judaism and Christianity on the topic of original sin. For a clear example, Rabbi Samson Raphael Hirsch (1808–1888), the champion of German Neo-Orthodoxy, declared that "every human child comes from the hand of God as pure as Adam did, still today every child is born to mankind pure as an angel." For Hirsch, in no manner whatsoever is mankind placed under a ban for his first disobedience.[3] Since Judaism is about fulfillment of duty using one's God given free will and self-control, being Jewish is in itself an "emphatic protest" against original sin.[4] Following Hirsch's logic, modern Jewish thought has since largely publicly rejected original sin as a doctrine.

This chapter contests this sharp binary division between the Western Christian position on sin as contrasting to rabbinic conceptions. The concept of sin is more than a zero-sum issue, in which Judaism either lacks a concern with sin and original sin or veers to the opposite extreme to affirm that Jews have historically had a doctrine of original sin. Both religions have shared roots in the same cultural world of the biblical fall of Adam. Judaism possesses several of the components of the theory of original sin, such as Adam's fall and inherited sin, but ultimately lacks the Augustinian concepts of a damaged nature, inherited by future generations, with infinite guilt that must be removed in salvific redemption in Christ. And now, modern Christian theologians such as Brunner, Rahner, and Moltmann conceptualize sin closer to Jewish understandings of sin, while Jewish theologians such Soloveitchik exhibit understandings of sin closer to Christian conceptions.

The Christian Idea of Original Sin

Early Christian thought coupled the human condition of evil and suffering together with the action of redemption by Jesus Christ. There is evil because Adam committed a primordial sin in Eden, he fell, dooming future generations of humanity in the process, and Christ redeems mankind through his sacrifice on the cross.[5]

Paul's concept of salvation offered by Christ understands Genesis as the primordial sin of Adam bringing sin to the world. This frames the Christian discussion through the lens that we live in evil and sin, in which sins need to be forgiven or redeemed by Christ "who gave himself for our sins to deliver us from the present evil age, according to the will of our God and Father" (Gal 1:4). Similarly, "so Christ was offered once to bear the sins of many. To those who eagerly wait for Him, He will appear a second time, apart from sin, for salvation" (Heb 9:28). Taken together, these passages assert the idea that humans are essentially prisoners who sit in darkness and blindly wait for someone to save them. Furthermore, Paul creates a typology of death in Adam, life in Christ: "we also rejoice in God through our Lord Jesus Christ, through whom we have now received reconciliation. Therefore, just as sin entered the world through one man, and death through sin, so also death was passed on to all men, because all sinned" (Rom 5:11–12). For Christians, Jesus Christ offers reconciliation for the sin of Adam, which brought death to the world. This correlation of death in Adam with a needed birth in Christ expressed in Galatians, Hebrews, or Romans are obviously unknown to Jewish scriptures.

In the early centuries, there was still much Christian debate on the role of human agency and human will in relation to sin. Justin Martyr (second century) thought the fault of sin lies at the hands of the individual who committed it, unlike later formulations of original sin. According to Justin Martyr, "each man committing evil by his own fault" (ch. 86), each person, "like Adam and Eve, brought death upon themselves" (ch. 124). Origen quoted Romans 5:12–21, rejecting the existence of a sinful state inherited from Adam, rather Adam's sin sets an example that all humanity partakes in, but is not inherently born into. Greek Father's, in general, emphasized the cosmic dimension of the fall, namely that since Adam, human beings are born into a fallen world, but held fast to belief that man, though fallen, is free. Cyril of Jerusalem (313–386) taught that humans were born free of sin, but he also believed that, as adults, humanity was naturally biased towards sinning.[6] A position found in both Jewish and Christian sources. The early Greek Fathers held fast to the belief that man, though fallen, is free and that the fault of sin lies at the hands of the individual who committed it, similar to the rabbinic view.

Tertullian, however, taught a hereditary transmission of sin transmitted through the sin of lust from sexual reproduction. Cyprian develops this idea, writing that the infant "born has not sinned at all, except that carnally born according to Adam, he has contracted the contagion of the first death from the first nativity." The origin of death, however, as told by the fall in Genesis, is not the same as an original sin.[7]

In the fourth century, Augustine developed the verses by Paul into a full rich theology of the fall and original sin, thereby overshadowing much of the earlier debate on sin and human agency. For Augustine, Adam's sin represented the permanent fall of mankind's intellect and will. Originally, Adam had a divine ability to choose good and thereby avoid sin, but those gifts were lost after the original sin. The first sin was a turning away from God through pride and subsequently future generations were born into sinful conditions. Augustine assumed everyone needs redemption due to the severity of the original sin of turning away from God, teaching that the punishment of the first parents—Adam and Eve—for their sin included the inability to produce offspring that would not resemble themselves in sinfulness. When Adam sinned, so did all men of his posterity, the entire human race ruined because he transmitted his guilt to all humanity by means of original sin. Even newborn babies are tainted with sin through the desire to reproduction leading back to Adam and Eve. Baptism removes original sin, but the consequences of original sin, such as tendency toward evil, remain.[8]

In the sixteenth century, Martin Luther (1483–1546) asserted that humans inherit Adamic guilt with a state of sin from the moment of conception. He explicitly rejects any sense or way that "natural man is made righteous by his own powers, thus disparaging the sufferings and merit of Christ." John Calvin (1509–1564) took Augustine's doctrinal framework much further, declaring that humans are totally depraved with a complete corruption of nature with nothing humans can do to rectify the situation. His theory of total depravity holds that people have an inherently sinful nature, a complete alienation from God, and a total inability to achieve reconciliation with God based on their own abilities. Christ is the only answer. Calvin taught that people are unable to impose their will upon God, that God is the only entity capable of making moral decisions due to the reality of divine predestination. Calvin asserted that our state of total depravity pervades all areas of human existence, including heart, emotions, will, mind, and body.[9] Just as a bad tree brings forth bad fruit, this corrupted nature brings forth individual sins and depraved humanity.

There is much to discuss concerning the council of Trent, Arminianism, various catechisms, and different formulations of will and grace, but they are beyond the scope of this book. Nevertheless, in all formulations, the Christian needs salvation through the Triune God, the Incarnation, justification, and a messiah to be free of original sin. All humans owe an infinite debt to God due to sin which they cannot pay, but in his infinite goodness can pay as an act of salvation.

The Early Jewish Theological Neighborhood

The concept of sin and the fall of Adam developed in many different directions in the Second Temple period and first century.[10] The non-canonical books such as 2 Baruch, 4 Ezra, and Apocalypse of Moses show that Second Temple Judaism(s) had a variety of approaches to sin. Rabbinic Judaism and Christianity religions share many of the Second Temple narratives of Adam's sin of a fall from Eden that present inherited sin, a corruption of original goodness for all humanity, and of a post fall propensity to sin.[11] But in the early centuries the two religions predominately veer in different directions. For rabbinic Judaism, Genesis 3 does not mention or even imply anything like original sin, only a fall of humanity and a corruption of original goodness, yet, generally Judaism assumes that humanity has free choice to sin or do good. Christians retain a stronger view of sin through the Pauline, and then Augustinian, lens of the doctrine of original sin.

The dominant approach of rabbinic literature is that the Bible exemplifies a succession of human failure—Adam and Eve, Cain (Gen 4), Nephilim (Gen 6), the tower of Babel (Gen 11), the complainers and grumblers (Num 11), the rebel Korach (Num 16), and so forth.[12] Rabbinic texts believe sin generally requires constant vigilance to choose the correct path, to choose life. While there are Jewish texts on the corruption of human will and intellect at the original sin, the rabbinic texts hold that the succession of human failure is not an inherent given condemning mankind. There is no one fall corrupting all humanity, but rather over the course of life many decisions are needed to choose the good and then repent if sin or the wrong path was chosen. During the lifelong struggle measured in the prosaic continuous choice to fight the evil inclinations within us, rabbinic Judaism, generally assumes a need to be on guard against the evil inclination that causes foolish moral choice. Humanity sins, fails, and makes mistakes, but God in his love and loyalty always forgives.[13] The Christian position of Justin Martyr could be easily compared to the rabbinic Jewish position. As a counter statement, there are some rabbinic statements that say there is no death without sin, "The soul that sins, it shall die." This statement in turn generates a rabbinic discussion of those who never sinned but still died because of the sin of Adam.[14]

In what may have been anti-Christian formulations, some rabbinic text are seemingly directed against the notion of a corrupting original sin. The Talmud states, "Adam was created from the dust of the place where the sanctuary was to rise for the atonement of all human sin," meaning that sin should never be a permanent or inherent part of man's nature.[15] Even Adam, who sinned in the garden only nine hours after creation, received God's pardon that day, and God continues to pardon now.[16]

Perhaps the best way to understand the rabbinic Jewish position is to note its similarity to the beliefs held by Christian heretic Pelagius (c. 355 AD to c. 420 AD), who taught that sin did not taint human nature and that humans have the free will to achieve human perfection without direct divine intervention, in which the coming of Christ made perfection achievable. In the Pelagian view, sin was not an inevitable result of a fallen human nature or a taint from birth, but instead came about by free choice and bad habits. Jesus is an exemplar of a life without sin, but some Hebrew prophets also serve as exemplars of a sinless life. By teaching the absence of sin as an insurmountable problem along with the idea that humans can choose between good and evil, Pelagianism advocated a position closer to that of rabbinic Judaism. Pelagius considered the coming of Christ as allowing perfection through self-volition, rabbinic texts assumed the same about the ability to attain perfection through Torah.

Notably, rabbinic texts present humans as created with two inclinations: the good inclination (*yetzer ha-tov)* and the evil inclination (*yetzer ha-ra*). Contrary to mainstream Christianity, rabbinic thought assumes that there is some positive value in having seemingly negative character drives if the drives are channeled properly, subduing but not doing away with one's evil impulses. Lust and desire are positive when channeled into positive purposes functioning as leavening in the dough. A famous rabbinic statement credits the lust, desire, and greed of the evil inclination with a positive purpose for motivation to build a house, find a spouse, and have a family. Humans have certain passions that can be used for good or for bad, but they only become evil with improper use in individual choices.[17]

Turning now to Adam's fall, which has a broader range of interpretations within Second Temple and rabbinic Judaism, we see a divergence from early Christian concerns. For example, in one Jewish text, Adam was originally a gigantic luminous being whose body spanned the earth with a stride that crossed continents with a few steps. The fall would transform a giant-sized Adam, reducing him to our current human size. The fall was an end of an original antediluvian era before the current state of ordinary humans. In a similar change from an original state, the fall permanently altered fruit trees from their original design of having their wood as eatable, making human nourishment easy, to only having eatable fruit.

In addition, rabbinic texts developed a parallel between Adam and the people of Israel, noting that God exiled Adam just as he later exiled Israel from their land. Just like Eden was the paradise lost, the land of Israel is the lost paradise of the Jewish people. For Judaism, the exile from the garden of Eden was the start of a world order of exile, historical trauma, and eventual return for the Jewish people. The continuous nature of this fall from the garden into history has since come to define Jewish history. The focus is national, and cosmic, not individual.[18]

Nevertheless, the rabbinic corpus does indeed contain several statements that possess many, but not all, elements of a theology of original sin, in which Adam and Eve sinned, and became stained with hereditary concupiscence. This Talmudic passage has many similarities with the theory of original sin: "Rabbi Yohanan said: When the serpent came upon Eve, he infected her with filth. When Israel stood at Mount Sinai their filth ceased, but gentiles, who did not stand at Mount Sinai, their filth never ceased" leaving the rest of humanity to bear the guilt and taint of the filth of sexual sin. Yet, according to this passage, the Torah has transformative qualities that alter human nature. This midrashic line of thought later finds a home in subsequent Lurianic kabbalah-inspired texts, specifically exclusivist views.[19]

Finally on the role of women in the sin of the garden, Second Temple period literature, specifically the Wisdom of Sirach (25:14), condemns women as the source of sin and bringers of death into the world, which reveals a very negative view of women (Sir 25:13–26:18).[20] This theme is carried over into rabbinic literature in midrash and Talmud, finding multiple articulations such as her copulating with the serpent.[21] Eve brought ten curses to women, albeit some of them are also atonements, including menstruation, childbirth, rapid aging, the need to stay at home to be modest, head covering, and bringing death to the world. This cluster of rabbinic ideas of the sin of Eve is often surprising for most modern Jews who have never heard of these passages and does not carry over into any modern denomination or theology of Judaism. Christianity generally did not retain these early positions on women.[22]

Medieval

Maimonides and Naḥmanides

The philosopher Moses Maimonides (d. 1204), in his *Guide of the Perplexed*, described the sin of Adam as an allegory of the universal human condition of rejecting knowledge, truth, and morality preferring a disordered realm of a desire-driven world of falsehood. For Maimonides, the intellectual study of the *Guide* along with training oneself toward philosophic religion naturally brings one back to a prelapsarian garden of morality and intellect.[23]

In contrast, Thomas Aquinas (d. 1274) sees original sin as causing three losses: "stain, corruption of natural good, and debt of punishment."[24] The stain is the loss of grace through sin, thereby the natural good is corrupted. Humanity is disordered by human will not being subject to God's will, thereby humans remain entirely sinful, disordered, and with a lack of virtue. The debt of punishment is that sinning warrants eternal damnation. For Thomas, since the fall of Adam, human society has lived in a state of spiritual disorderliness of excessive greed, pride, and sexual passion. Man could do nothing of his own free will to rectify the condition into which his original sin led him, "none of these three can be restored except by God" because Adam, even before the fall, needed grace, as the infused virtues of faith, hope and love. For Aquinas, reason and will are natural and only tainted by the fall, however, faith, hope, and love are supernatural and need divine grace. According to Maimonides's approach, in contrast, Judaism does not have two of the three losses at all, the stain of sin or debt of punishment, only the corruption of natural good. However, the natural good according to Maimonides can be corrected naturally through the natural virtues. Maimonides lacks supernatural virtues beyond the natural and no divine gift is needed for the operation of the natural virtues. Even Torah in this context is natural.

The difference between the religions lies in how the fall gets corrected, naturally or through supernatural grace. Aquinas distinguished the supernatural gifts of Adam before the fall from what was merely natural, considering the former as lost, privileges that enabled man to keep his inferior powers in submission to reason and directed to his supernatural end. Even after the fall, however, man kept his natural abilities of reason, will, and passions. To the extent we speak of natural virtues, Judaism can share a common framework with Christianity, but not of stain and corruption or a redeeming grace.

Another traditional medieval Jewish position was expressed by the thirteenth-century thinker Nahmanides (d. 1270), a rabbi engaged in Jewish-Christian polemics who clearly stated in his Barcelona disputation, with clear knowledge that he is rejecting Christian positions, that individual souls are created pure and sinless with no sin passed down between them. In addition, Nahmanides stated that there is no need for an infinite atonement of the offering of Christ because sin is not infinite nor is there fear of eternal damnation. Judaism has the concept of repentance, of our own turn to the good, which is all that is needed.[25]

Publicly disputing the claim that Adam's sin was nullified by Jesus, Nahmanides asserts that the Christians have created a convenient theory. Nahmanides points out that the explicit punishments of Adam and Eve for their sin are detailed in Genesis (3:16–19), such as having to work by the sweat of one's brow, which is still in effect; therefore, the sin of Genesis was not atoned by Jesus. Furthermore, Nahmanides states that the Hebrew Bible lacks the Christian concept of the eternal punishment of the souls in hell. Finally, Nahmanides declares that this claim of original sin is not subject to empirical verification; no one can disprove it. He suggests that the Christians send someone to give eyewitness verification from the afterlife before they ask people to believe.[26]

Paradoxically, Nahmanides in his non-polemical writings proceeds in a different direction, as one of the first mentions in Jewish literature of an original sin (*het kadmon*). For him, the legal imperatives of the Torah are binding only after the fall due to sin. Only after the fall, do human beings have free will and a desire to do evil. For Nahmanides, "Originally Adam lacked autonomy and his own will." When Adam gained free will, he required the discipline of the *mitzvot* because he was no longer predetermined to follow God's will. The fall does not mean corrupted by sin, or a moral taint, rather a fall from doing God's will in a fixed manner to human free will requiring discipline. Nahmanides does think death is natural since man is a composite being, but if Adam had not sinned, he would not have died since his soul would have naturally cleaved to the divine will. But after the sin, man as a mortal has volition and choice, but no inherited sin. Adam's postlapsarian freedom and lack of guilt is thusly almost a 180-degree opposite of the Augustinian Christian approach.

According to some interpretations of Nahmanides, he interpreted the fall as a fortunate fall, a positive divine ordained fall, Adam could not have fallen from his elevated, prelapsarian, spiritual state unless God wanted him to disobey by showing his own volition. God did not want worship only from spiritual automatons, but from people with free will, who must struggle to serve God. Thus, there was no fall in the garden, rather a raised status, without moral guilt or need for salvation, rather a necessary decent for the sake of growth by means of the *mitzvot*, the original sin was not a curse, but rather an opportunity.[27]

Nineteenth and Twentieth Century Moderns

The Enlightenment taught the idea of mankind as good and blameless, rejecting the idea of original sin. The coinciding eighteenth-century

Evangelicalism backlashed against the Enlightenment thinkers' total rejection of original sin. Consequently, in 1757, English theologian and cleric John Wesley stated that since the reality of original sin cannot be provable under the Enlightenment's terms of natural religion, divine revelation was absolutely needed to teach about original sin.

Nineteenth-century liberal Protestant thinkers introduced a major shift in thinking about original sin, understanding the concept as a natural part of our consciousness, even without revelation. For example, Fredrich Schleiermacher considered original sin as only the incapacity and corruption induced by the natural human fall from Godly consciousness. Schleiermacher presented the doctrine of original sin without reliance on the myth of Adam, thereby separating original sin from a fall. Similarly, Søren Kierkegaard considered original sin as the human affliction with despair and anxiety to be overcome by a leap of faith. Kierkegaard's concept of anxiety as fundamental to human existence was later developed by many Jewish thinkers in the twentieth century, who, in their Jewish philosophic works, inadvertently separated the concept of anxiety from any initial connection to original sin.

The twentieth century, in the aftermath of the two world wars and the creation of the atomic bomb, fostered a post-war sense of human frailty. This newfound appreciation for the fragility of the human condition impacted Christian views on original sin. Protestant theologian Reinhold Niebuhr considered original sin a verified empirical fact, holding sin and evil as part of our fallen world characterized by man's self-centeredness, materialism, and egoism. Original sin is thusly a powerful symbol of the tensions of the human heart and the sinfulness of humanity. By removing the Augustinian understanding of the fall from considerations of original sin, Niebuhr's position on the human condition begins to converge with Jewish positions.[28]

From Niebuhr onward, existential theologians, such as Paul Tillich considered original sin as another way of talking about the fundamental questions of ultimate meaning, in which human suffering and confronting human mortality define our existence. Twentieth-century Christian theological thought continued to push aside many aspects of Augustine's doctrine to create more positive views of humanity, including an acceptance of free will.

Karl Rahner

Jesuit theologian Karl Rahner developed his view of original sin as the human condition, not because Adam and Eve fell in the garden, rather because of our own autonomous choices made in our human freedom. For Rahner, the theological concepts of original sin and original guilt refer to existential states of the soul like despair and egoism, in which sin is both our human condition and the result of personal decisions. He posits that we each make our own personal decisions for good or for sin, each person unique in her personal choices. But, nevertheless, we each fall. Rahner explicitly acknowledges that as moderns, we have lost the Augustinian view of sin.[29] Personal guilt from an original act of freedom, such as Adam's, cannot be transmitted to future generations because sin is the existential choice of "no" of personal transcendence toward God or against him. "By its very nature this free act cannot be transmitted, since it is entirely a free act. This freedom is precisely the point where a person is unique, and no one can take his place . . . and in this way escape responsibility for himself." Therefore, "original sin" in no way means a guilt or innate sin determined or imputed by God or biological heredity.[30]

Similar to Niebuhr, Rahner posits that everyone acknowledges that the world, in some manner, exists in a state of disrepair. "The pessimism of Christianity" is that we all are touched by sin and all our virtuous acts are tainted by guilt. Rahner affirms that Christianity, which possesses a "radical realism" concerning the fundamental state of humanity as touched by sin, promotes "the best service" for creating better people and societies. Rahner points out that Christianity, unlike the pessimistic state of atheistic existentialism, acknowledges that humankind is capable of salvation.[31] However, he precludes a real possibility of ever overcoming the guilt through optimism or natural amelioration in any sort; rather, we must rely on God's offer of salvation to save us from sin and guilt.[32]

Rahner notes that God's self-communication in the Trinity was "prior to [Adam's] free and good decision" thereby making the first sin a far more serious matter than it would otherwise have been without any communication from God. By rejecting God's self-communication and not simply a command of God, man suffers on an ontological, rather than merely experiential, level. "Original Sin, therefore, expresses nothing else but the historical origin of the present, universal and ineradicable situation of our freedom as co-determined by guilt." Original sin is rooted in "a rejection of God's absolute offer of himself in an absolute self-communication of his divine life." Because we ourselves have an apprehension of our own guilt, and because we can reasonably infer that all those around us are also guilty, we are forced to the view that there was an original instance of freedom awry, for otherwise the current environment of universal guilt is inexplicable.[33] The Christian faith, according to Rahner, affirms that sin in its essence is a free and definitive "no" to God, a rejection of God's gracious offer of self-communication. Human freedom is so radical and comprehensive, as to make even the acceptance of God an object of choice.

Rahner developed the concept that God has freely chosen to be ever present to each human being in intimate closeness as an offer of self-communication as a supernatural existential to offer salvation. The Grace of God is a "Self-communication of the absolutely holy God" designating "a quality sanctifying man prior to his free and good decision." The loss of such a sanctifying self-communication assumes the character of something which should not be, and is not merely a diminishing of the possibilities of freedom.[34] God also offers God's very person as an object of choice, and so makes possible a free "yes" or "no" to the true God. The horizon of God, which makes freedom of choice possible, becomes itself the object of decision. The decision to love or hate the neighbor, is simultaneously to render a "yes" or "no" to God, the creator of the human essence. Here we have a line of thought with resonance to the thoughts of Martin Buber, Emmanuel Levinas, and other Jewish thinkers.

For a Jewish perspective on Rahner, many Jewish texts affirm a natural state of disrepair that needs the Torah as the cure, so too many texts note that humans use their freedom to reject the path of Torah. However, for Judaism, the world is not determined by this fundamental theological guilt, disrepair, and sin. The guilt and disrepair do not require special intervention. In Judaism, the fall of the world still leaves space for humans to be partners in creation. Humanity may need a cure, but not as an intervention of Trinitarian self-communication, or incarnation. Hence, as Nahmanides wrote, there is no need for humanity to concern itself with the God-man Jesus Christ. A Jewish reading of Genesis is that everything God created was good, which he pronounced as *tov me᾽od*, meaning "very good."[35] Jews generally do not have a fundamental theological guilt or sense that the world went awry through sin. Jewish thought leaves room for humans in their freedom to repair the world, to be partners with God, and to strive to messianically redeem the world in action.[36]

Moltmann

Jürgen Moltmann connects original sin to his theme of the suffering borne by the Triune God, offering hope in overcoming the immense suffering in the world.

The concept of original sin and sin in general, for Moltmann, is the rebellion against God: "The first definition of sin is well-known: *man's rebellion against God* as depicted in the story of the serpent in Paradise and the sinful fall of Adam and Eve." There was a rejection of God's promise of creating man in his own image. The second moment of sin was in the voice of the serpent, who corrupted knowledge of good and evil. Adam and Eve ate this fruit and their eyes were opened. They felt ashamed of their nakedness, and they hid themselves from each other and from God." Moltmann explains that "the sin of man is obviously that he followed the voice of another being, specifically, he allowed the serpent to define his destiny."[37]

Rejecting many aspects of Augustine, Moltmann's approach focuses on the human fall from that original state of being in the image of God

(*Imago Dei*), existing in the "likeness of God." Moltmann explains original sin as both humanity's failure to be "like God" as well as humanity's desire to "not be like God." But Adam's sin "against God can also be seen in the fact that he no longer wanted to be "like God" and the image of God."[38] When humanity no longer lives according to the *Imago Dei*, humanity ceases to be human: "Humanity without acknowledgement of the divine is bestiality."

Moltmann explains that humanity's presumption and resignation is identical to the deadly sign of sloth, a state of melancholy sadness that decays a humanity that no longer desires to be like God. Moltmann describes sloth as "hopelessness, inertia, melancholy" as "apathy," and "the seed of sweet decay." Noting the prominence of sloth in human nature, Moltmann comments, "Temptation then consists not so much in the titanic desire to be like God, but in weakness, timidity, weariness, and in not wanting to be like God or to be what God requires of us. God has exalted man and given him the prospect of a life that is open and free, but man hangs back and lets himself down."[39]

To sum up, Moltmann's definition of original sin is: (1) *hubris* and *presumption* to be as God, and (2) *resignation* and *laziness* not to be like God's image on earth. Presumption and resignation are the roots of all actual sins: *presumption* not to acknowledge the Lordship of God and *resignation* to refuse the freedom God has given us. As a prime example of hubris, "Prometheus, who has stolen the divine fire, is the prototype of the rebellious sinner." While resignation, is the Sisyphus model of boredom and *ennui* of a life without meaning. Simply put, in the two sinful states we either rebel, or we give up hope and meaning.[40]

Moltmann frames the motivation for sin in an existential manner, claiming the awareness of sin is "the awareness of death which first creates fear for life, the fear of not getting one's fair share. This leads to a craving for life, and greed." In this statement Moltmann suggests that because humans are mortals who have not faced their finitude we are led into sin. Humankind can find hope in the redemptive work of Jesus Christ who restores the image of humanity. For Moltmann, Christian hope is life based on reality of the resurrection of Christ. Christian hope is "realistic" since it takes seriously the possibilities of sin with which life is fraught: "This new reality is the Kingdom of God come to us from the future, and making claims upon us now."[41]

Judaism differs from Moltmann in that rebellion from God's command is just an allegory for our foolishness, frailty, and freedom of volition. Sometimes, in Judaism the rebellion would be phrased as going after idolatry.[42] However, the rebellion is not reified as a fundamental state of humanity, an original sin. Human frailty, for Judaism is to know that humans have good and bad traits, often giving into the latter, but without an arc of sin and redemption. The hubris and sloth may be a cause of sin therefore fragile humans should turn to God in repentance. The Jewish theological axis is human frailty smallness and divine grandeur, not original sin and necessary redemption. Finally, in rabbinic thought remembrance of the day of one's death and human finitude leads to prevent one from sinning, while for Moltmann human finitude leads to sin, requiring divine hope, redemptive hope, to overcome sin.

Emil Brunner

In his classic work *Divine Imperative*, early twentieth-century Swiss Reformed theologian Emil Brunner offers a different view of the original state of humanity and the fall. He describes how man was created in the image of God and with the express purpose of being in community with God. Man is not just another animal; rather, man is to live a life of dignity and majesty living in the image of God: "The distinctive character of man, in contrast to the rest of creation, is based upon the fact that he is designed for freedom-in-God, for a personal existence which is distinct from God, and yet dependent upon Him." Humanity was meant to live in family, in community, and in culture: "God has not created us as angels, but as human beings of flesh and blood, human beings who can only manage to live their life in a human way by means of marriage and the family, civilization and culture, by means of the State and the system of law." Brunner sees natural man as endowed with responsibility as an independent moral agent and as having ultimate obligations to God. In so far as man is addressed as a moral agent, he is called to account prior to the proclamation of grace.[43]

Original Sin forced humanity out of this community, thereby removing the very basis of divine mandated human existence. Originally, man was created to be in communion with God, but through sin, man lost the ability to be in communion with God. Nevertheless, human nature to be in communion with God has not changed. Our soul choses God, but our sin makes us choose an idol. Sin has become a burden for all of mankind, perpetuated daily when we create a false God in our lives instead of worshiping Him.

Brunner thinks original sin pits man against God, where "God is only an alien Power, which forces him from the outside." What was originally holy is now unholy and oppositional to God. The Bible, for Brunner, speaks of the ungodly power that we all know only too well from our own experience, which is opposed to God. As surely as God is love, is my own lovelessness ungodly, diabolical, resistance against God's action.[44]

In order to overcome man's separation from the divine, God has given himself in Christ Jesus to this deranged world. God transmits his will to us in the darkness of this world, through the gospel of forgiveness and salvation. Brunner stressed the limitations of general revelation, the knowledge of God that does not include God's saving grace, as unable to lead human beings into a saving relationship with God, as imparting little if any information about a loving God, and plainly provided nothing for dealing with the problem of human sin.[45] Note that Brunner rejects a literal interpretation of Genesis and a causal explanation of sin. Rather, he emphasizes responsibility and commanded-ness. He reverses Kierkegaard's formula for the relation between individuals and humanity, stressing community and divine responsibility in the community itself.

The basic contours of Brunner's formulation of human responsibility—the choice to serve God or to sin, man's fleeing to sin, and then repentance, love, and the restoration of the relationship with God—can easily be affirmed in Judaism. The difference at this point is only that Jews consider the restoration as occurring by means of Torah, including the Torah's teaching on divine love and repentance, while Brunner states that the restoration is a redemptive grace of Christ.

Rabbi Soloveitchik on Original Sin

We see an interesting convergence on the topic of original sin between Emil Brunner and the Orthodox Jewish theologian Rabbi Joseph Dov Soloveitchik (1904–1993), whose thought was deeply influenced by Brunner's dialectic theology. My goal is not to survey modern Jewish thought or discuss liberal Jewish positions that lack any overlap with modern Christian theologian. Rather, to just give one example that can be used to create a horizon of convergence.

Both Brunner and Soloveitchik see man as playing a critical role in God's created world and proclaim that we have a divine imperative to live a life of dignity and majesty, rather than follow our bestial sin potential. Similarly to Brunner, Soloveitchik wrote that, if not for sin, then experience of God would be without disappointment. Instead, life after Adam's sin and the subsequent fall is one of defeat, resignation, and struggle. For Soloveitchik, the original sin presents an alternate view of God, a demonic God, as in Brunner. Before the serpent, Adam and Eve perceived God correctly as the cosmic Creator and worked alongside him in the garden of Eden with his direction and guidance. The serpent to the story casts doubts upon God's actions and motives, making God appear demonic and unholy. Rabbi Soloveitchik writes of this mistaken view, "The experience of God, according to the serpent, is demonic, uncanny, weird. Man should not fear God but should shudder or feel horror before Him . . . God is not the friend but the fiend . . . if man wants to gain freedom, he must rebel against Him and throw off His yoke." This mistaken view is an unforgivably primitive view of God, which denies the divine attributes and makes God less than the creator of the universe.[46]

Soloveitchik asks: What was wrong with the choice to eat from the tree that was referred to as good? He suggests that the concept of "good" can mean two very different qualities: good as an ethical quality and good in the esthetic sense. In the fall, "[t]he ethical motif collided with the orgiastic aesthetic one and was defeated." In other words, to be fully human is to be able to choose between the aesthetic and the ethical and the wrong choice, with sensuality "unhallowed by ethical appraisal" and thusly constituting "sin."

While Christianity suggests that man is tainted by this sin, Soloveitchik sees the sin as the beginnings of man's split personality. Man's ethical side is his "prosecutor-judge" that seeks to correct his aesthetic side.[47] For Soloveitchik, this sin did not corrupt man; rather, sin divided him into two aspects to his personality, one connected to God and one alienated from God. Therefore, Judaism is not in the business of saving man from sin so much as correcting the gap between these personalities.

Soloveitchik acknowledges the difference of approach to sin between Christianity and Judaism. Hereditary sin "as developed by Christian thinkers, is a metaphysical, objective quality, inherent in human natural existence" unlike the Jewish idea of sin that does not corrupt human nature. The Jewish idea is that the Jewish people or any other community of people can bear a sin, but not an individual. For Soloveitchik, the ethical man is one who strives to co-participate with God in the divine imperative. Original sin did derail this mandate and create a duality in mankind, but there are still mechanisms in place to return man to God, namely the covenant made through Abraham and Moses who established his precepts of Torah with a people to provides the ethical norms of God's plan of creation. Brunner's Christian approach has a much stronger enslavement due to sin, in which, man needs a special grace offered through the life, death, and resurrection of Christ.

Evaluation

If Original sin is defined in Augustinian or Calvinist terms, then Judaism does not converge with Christian ideas of original sin. Judaism differs in its Pelagianism, that assumes humans have the resources for our own betterment, and that sin can have a positive role. If we speak of a fall of Adam or a sin of Adam that needs to be repaired, then we may have many commonalities.

Looking at the topic of original sin afresh after the modern theological thought—Rahner, Moltmann, and Brunner—we can now evaluate the relationship of current approaches to Judaism. The most basic change for all of them is the rejection of the Augustinian dualistic approach to original sin. Most Jewish thought can readily acknowledge the fallen state of humanity and the need of a repair. Both religions agree that the choice to sin was made in freedom and teach a positive anthropology of humanity.

Rahner starts with a universal prelapsarian offer of God to humanity and then states that most people freely decline that offer in sin; therefore, compared to an Enlightenment view, Christianity is pessimistic about the human condition. Only Christ's self-communication to humanity sanctifies man to give a "yes" to God, thereby offering an optimism rooted in the removal of guilt. In contrast, Judaism generally treats individual sin as readily, morally, and naturally repairable and is more concerned about national exile and the fate of the Jewish people.

Moltmann also rejects Augustinian original sin with its guilt passed down through procreation, instead considering the human faults of hubris and sloth as the sins that make humans fall from their original creation in the image of God. Moltmann worries about the fall of the person from the image of God to animality, arrogance, and depression. Moltmann claims the awareness of human mortality causes sin. Judaism is more about the fall from an ideal state of serving God through our desires, volition, rebellion, or folly.

The Jewish difference from Brunner's theology can be simplified as a difference of corruption of humanity requiring Christ as opposed to the Jewish dual aspects to human personalities, in which the Mosaic covenant of *mitzvot* helps Jews choose the correct side.

The modern theologians we looked at offered images of humanity in the image of God, or being called by God, bringing their understanding of the human condition close to Judaism. However, at its core, the contemporary thinkers still had to explain that sin necessitates a redemption, a salvation through Christ. Further direction for comparison includes that the Eastern Orthodox Church never subscribed to Augustine's notions of original sin and hereditary guilt, instead focusing on the image of God undistorted within each person, thereby offering many more opening for comparison with Judaism.[48]

Symbolism of Sin

Paul Ricœur wrote his classic philosophic studies of the concept of original sin in *Fallible Man* and *The Symbolism of Evil*, where he treats original sin as a part of a cross-cultural need to address sin and evil in the world, beyond the specific Christian ideas about guilt and divine salvation. For Ricœur, Buddhists seek to overcome suffering through meditation, Zoroastrians see the evil as part of a dualistic world, Christians have a concept of original sin and redemption to explain reality, and Greco-Roman myths seek to restore a primordial order.[49]

Ricœur famously popularized that there is no concept of sin in the Hebrew Bible in the sense of a distorting stain upon the soul that requires a kind of supernatural atonement or cleansing process. The Hebrew Bible, according to Ricœur, speaks of three distinct categories of wrongs. There is *chet*, the misstep, literally meaning "missing the mark," as if one were shooting an arrow and hitting the outer rims of the target and missing the shooter's goal, its center. The second, *pesha* is a conscious rebellious act such as taking revenge, stealing, or murder. The third, *avon*, is an error, an unintentional act that nevertheless has harmful consequences. His goal was to create a sharp distinction of the Hebraic Bible and the Christian perspectives, not completely accepted by historical scholars. Rabbinic Judaism certainly, does have many concepts of sin that overlap with Christian positions, as shown in this chapter, which were not discussed by Ricœur.

Christians, according to Ricœur, see the world as needing a redemption from original sin as essential for their religious or theological grammar. The stain of guilt on the individual is the very reason for needing salvation. When a Christian says original sin, the emphasis is already on Christ's redemptive powers of man from his sinful condition more than Genesis.

Judaism does have some similar themes of sin and fall of Adam that grew out of the same spiritual neighborhood of the late Second Temple and first century. However, Jewish texts do not have this grammar. In addition, Jewish thinkers did not have a doctrinal need to decide between the many rabbinic texts on the issue because the fall of humanity and original sin was not a major Jewish theological framework. Judaism just acknowledges that we are no longer in the garden and sin happens. At the end of the day, for Jews, sin in its rabbinic understanding can be repaired by human action, repentance, and following the guidance of the Torah.

My point here, as elsewhere in the book, is that we should not present a zero-sum issue in which Judaism either shares all details of a concept with Christianity or she does not. We can separate the Western Christian doctrine of sin into sperate components and elements to evaluate properly.[50] Some of the elements include:

1. God's creation is perfect, and humans were created as good. But humans are not perfect in that they have imperfections, become flawed, and readily sin.
2. After the sin by Adam, human nature fell from an original perfection becoming flawed.
3. Adam sinned and left a taint of sin for all humanity as original sin.
4. All humans possess a bruised and damaged nature, perverted and distorted.
5. All humans have guilt that must be removed by a divine act such as Christ's atonement, baptism, or the experience of justification, depending on the tradition.

In general, traditional Jewish thought accepted the first three statements and modern Jewish thought limited the overlap to just the first two. Rabbi Solovetichik makes a point of accepting the first three and also the fourth, recognizing a covenantal method of removing the sin though Torah. The fifth premise is where the crucial difference lies. In sum, when Anselm is asked why God cannot forgive and atone without a redeemer, he states that to restore the fallen universe the honor that is due to God must be repaid. But humans cannot do it, because God is infinite and we humans are only finite. The Modern Christian thinkers we looked at do not share Anselm's premise. For Jews, there is no needed payback, finite or infinite. God can forgive and atone. The closest Judaism gets to the fifth premise is the aforementioned midrash, where Mount Sinai removes our lustful fallen nature, which is a rare rabbinic opinion in the sea of rabbinic literature.

To give a full picture on this topic, we can also list many forms of original sin that are primarily only in the Jewish texts and not the Christian ones:

6. Ten Punishments of Eve and her pollution of the world as a special fall for women.

The sixth element was presented above as Eve's sin in Second Temple era and rabbinic sources.

7. Sin as a positive force in that humans grow as religious individuals from the process of sin and return. Many Jewish mystical thinkers have formulated this approach as a fortunate fall.

The seventh element was presented in the above discussion of Nahmanides where Adam had to be expelled from the garden of Eden, as a fortunate fall, in order to be able to follow the commandments of the Torah with his own free will.[51]

8. Jews often metaphorically ascribe their sense of sin, alienation, and fallenness to the submission to life in the exile (*galut*), in which Adam's exile from the garden parallels the exile of the Jewish people after the destruction of the Temple in 70 CE.

In the Jewish idea of exile (*galut*), Jews feel a condition that limits the human ability to be in contact with God. A return from exile means "the longing for final redemption and for return to the Edenic state of harmony between human and human, between humans and the world, and between humans and God." Exile is a very different metaphor than sin, that opens to discussions of elegy, destruction, and degradation as a minority religion, as well as alienation.[52]

9. A rupture of the cosmos in creation, emanation gone awry.

This nineth element is a specific Jewish theosophic idea, often cited as an example of Jewish original sin in a colloquial sense, In the theosophic metaphysical scheme of Rabbi Isaac Luria (d. 1572), during creation there was a shattering of the original plan of creation through the sin of a cosmic demiurge of a primordial hypostatic Adam. In the shattering, the vessels holding the divine energy of creation fragmented like glass and became disbursed. All human souls were in primordial Adam's soul, so when he fell, the entire human race fell with him with disastrous consequences for the whole of creation and the divine being.

This shattering is clearly the fall of Adam and a primordial sin, the world is now fragmented, the divine is limited, and the sin needs to be undone. However, shattering is a cosmic flaw produced by the shattering of the world, not a moral sin producing guilt. The individual generally does not bear moral responsibility for the cosmic flaw. The process of redemption involves gathering the fallen sparks of divinity by performance of Torah and *mitzvot*, the actions of Jewish practice have restorative properties. The entire process of history is a struggle to restore the fallen world to its original perfection, a victory of order over chaos.[53] When Jewish ritual practice succeeds in restoring Adam's fall, then the messiah comes. The messiah does not redeem, rather his arrival is a sign of the completion of human action of resting the cosmos.[54] In Ricœur's categories, this rupture is a cosmic fall rupturing an original order and not a Christian conception of guilt and redemption.[55] The Lurianic fall of breaking vessels unleashes a cosmic significance to human action to repair the damage, unlike a Christian vision of needing a redeemer.

However, to come full circle with contemporary comparisons, Jürgen Moltmann read in depth about Luria's theology of scattered sparks of divine, which he considered as a useful description of Christ, the cosmic Adam, who engaged in kenosis to reach the God forsakenness of this world. For Moltmann, human action is needed to overcome the fallenness of the world to usher in the messianic age. (On his use of Luria's thought, see chapter 1 on Trinity.) In the new century, many of the differences are now similarities and convergences, even in their particular Jewish and Christian forms.[56]

CHAPTER FOUR

Salvation and Atonement

THE TRADITIONAL ENGLISH Christmas carol *God Rest You Merry, Gentlemen* joyfully exclaims ". . . Christ our Savior / Was born on Christmas Day/ To save us all from Satan's pow'r . . . / To free all those who trust in Him." Christianity is about salvation from sin and from Satan's continuous power of causing sin. The incarnated birth of Christ offers salvation to Christians if they accept him as Savior.

According to the binaries of Trude Weiss-Rosmarin, Judaism lacks any form of vicarious atonement. "The idea of 'vicarious atonement,' that is to say, the payment of the penalty not by the sinner but by a substitute, is irreconcilable with Jewish ethics. Judaism exalts justice as one of the foundations of the universe. It is unjust, and inconsistent as well, to sacrifice a perfectly innocent 'Savior' for the transgressions of the sinners . . . for justice requires that the sinner bear the consequences of his actions." She contrasts Jewish moral responsibility and repentance with Christianity's need for divine forgiveness. To attain forgiveness "in accepting Jesus Christ" goes against Jewish emphasis on human responsibility.[1]

This chapter breaks the discussion down into three smaller questions with some surprising answers. First, Judaism clearly is not a salvation religion, while Christianity is a salvation religion. Second, contrary to Weiss-Rosmarin's opinion, Judaism is certainly an atonement religion, in which saintly rabbis, biblical figures, death, suffering, punishment, and God each are said to offer atonement. Third, Rahner and Moltmann redirect the Christian concept of salvation to universal salvation of humanity through human freedom and rectifying this world, thereby narrowing the gap between the two religions. Many of the small building blocks of repentance, atonement, grace, and salvation are shared by both religions even when contextualized in different narratives.

Salvation in Judaism

Salvation in Judaism has been primarily conceived in terms of the collective destiny of Israel as the elect people of God. The prime case of salvation for Judaism is the narrative of the Exodus from Egypt bringing freedom from slavery, the guidance in the wilderness, the giving of the Torah, and then being brought to the Holy land. The Exodus serves as the model for all future salvations and its memory being impressively perpetuated each year by the ritual of the Passover Seder. The restoration of the Holy nation was generally linked with its Holy Land and the return of the Temple. The Hebrew word for salvation (*yeshuah*) concerns Jewish national destiny in general as any salvation from persecution or oppression. Salvation is also used metaphorically with a general meaning of liberation from straitened circumstances or from any other evils to a state of freedom and security (1 Sam 11:13; 14:45; 2 Sam 23:10; 2 Kgs 13:17). Jews also use the word salvation to pray for atonement from sin in the High Holy Days prayers, which start with special penitential prayers (*selichot*) before the Holy Day. Here too, salvation is collective for the people Israel.[2]

Salvation from the Perspective of the Early Church Fathers

The Hebrew word for salvation (*yeshuah*) was translated as *soteria* in New Testament Greek pointing to the end of days and afterlife, shifting the emphasis from national salvation to personal soteriology. Christianity's primary premise is that the incarnation and sacrificial death of Jesus Christ formed the climax of a divine plan for humanity's salvation consequent on the fall of Adam into sin, with a divine plan completed at the last judgment, when the second coming of Christ. This soteriological evaluation of history finds expression in the Christian division of time into two periods: before Christ (BC) and anno Domini

(AD)—i.e., the years of the Lord. For Augustinian Christianity, there must be an atonement for sin to avoid damnation, and to offer spiritual strength aiding man in his struggle against darkness, sin, and concupiscence.[3]

The gospels connect the bread and wine of the Last Supper as the redemptive blood of the new covenant. "This is my blood of the covenant, which is poured out for many for the forgiveness of sins" (Matt 26:28). Paul connects atonement to the blood of Christ "as a sacrifice of atonement by his blood, effective through faith" (Rom 3:25). "We have been justified by his blood, will we be saved through him from the wrath of God" (Rom 5:9). And the epistle to the Hebrews declares that "without the shedding of blood there is no forgiveness of sins" (9:22). These verses bind the concept of any atonement to the Eucharist and the blood of Christ.[4]

The earliest Christian document about salvation outside the New Testament writings is from Clement of Rome (96 CE). "We . . . are not justified of ourselves or by our wisdom or insight or religious devotion or the holy deeds we have done from the heart, but by that faith by which almighty God has justified all men from the very beginning."[5] A Christian needs faith and an inner conversion to inherit God's promises. Clement also expected a Christian to engage in acts of holiness, obedience, and hospitality.

Augustine become the predominate traditional theological language for Christian salvation, even though his formulation is not the only accepted opinion, Augustine understands the condition of sinfulness to issue from the corrupted human will, damaged by the fall, (as discussed in chapter 3). Augustine's view of salvation emerges logically from his understanding of the fallen human will: because the will cannot incline toward God of its own accord, God must initiate salvation. Augustine's view is that people cannot contribute anything to this process. Upon conversion to faith, God restores human free will and forgives sins. Christ played several roles in the process of salvation. First, the sacrifice of Christ paid humanity's debt of sin: the "debt has been paid by Christ." As "both Priest and Sacrifice." Christ offered himself for the atonement of human sin. Second, Christ took the death sentence for sin upon himself that "he might make null the death of the wicked whom he justified." Third, the sacrifice of Christ brought reconciliation: through the forgiveness of the cross, which thereby Christ "dissolved the enmity" that had existed between people and God. Fourth, Christ defeated the powers of evil on the cross, in that, in Christ "we have triumphed over the enemy." Fifth, Christ offered a living example of humility and good works.[6] Augustine's conception of atonement made the death of one individual, Jesus, the central act of atonement, necessity for all.

Pelagius, however, argued that Augustine radically underestimates the goodness and power of human nature even among the gentiles who do not worship God. Human nature does not appear to be as damaged and sinful as Augustine suggests. And if all people are equally sinful and unable to help themselves, it would be unjust for God to save some and condemn others. Judaism would agree with these comments by Pelagius on the goodness of human nature, on the lack of an original sin corrupting all humanity, the lack of a need for a savior, and that salvation does not come by means of faith. One of the most important distinctions between Christianity and Judaism is that the former conventionally teaches justification by faith, while the latter teaches that man has the choice to follow divine law. By teaching the absence of original sin and the idea that humans can choose between good and evil, Pelagius's position was close to the Jewish thought of the era. Pelagius wrote positively of Jews and Judaism, recommending the study of Jewish biblical law. Augustine himself accused Pelagius of Judaizing, Even more so, Pelagius held that Christianity is not about faith and belief, rather one's actions and virtue. Jesus was an exemplar of the virtuous life to be emulated, thereby accepting only Augustine's fifth purpose of Christ's salvation. There is no corrupted will needing a saving grace, Judaism, as Pelagius, would also place greater emphasis on action over belief. The same way Jewish thought is different from Nicaean Christian thought on the issue of monarchism compared to perichoresis, here Judaism is different from Nicaean views of atonement by having a position similar to Pelagius.[7]

The locus for Christ's atonement has many interpretations. Augustine (and Anselm) saw the crucifixion and death as a substitution in the paying of a debt caused by humanity's sinful nature offending God's honor. Origen, taught that Jesus's death is the ransom paid to the devil (or evil powers) to free humans from the bondage of sin. At the resurrection, the devil was tricked into trying to capture Christ, but he did not have any control over Christ, or in modern parlance the devil is a symbol of the evil miasma of society. A third opinion, popularized by Irenaeus, is that of Christus Victor. Jesus's life is a victorious struggle against evil, placing the locus at the Incarnation of the eternal God existing before time as part of the Trinity. The atonement is either located in the crucifixion as a sacrificial death, in the tricking of the devil at resurrection, or the very power of the divine incarnation.

In the Middle Ages the need for salvation becomes identified with being Catholic. All other people on earth, all other religions and peoples are condemned. In 1302, Pope Boniface VIII supported this conviction when he declared in his bull *Unam Sanctam* "that outside of this church there is neither salvation nor the remission of sins." Until the mid-twentieth century Catholics generally denied the possibility that non-Catholics can be saved.[8]

Jewish Views of Repentance

In the Hebrew Bible repentance, called *teshuvah* a Hebrew word translated as "returning," is interpreted as a turning back to something you have looked away from, principally a return to God. "Come, let us return to the Lord," the prophet Hosea (14:2) tells the people of Israel to return to God. In Judaism, everybody sins and makes mistakes, and everyone can return and reorient themselves, but there is no human condition called sin. The Hebrew word for sin (*chet)* references an arrow that has "missed the target." There is nothing inherently corrupt about that miss. Rather, a mistake was made—due to a lack of focus or skill.[9]

In rabbinic thought, humans possess free will making them culpable for his evil deeds (see M Avot 3:15–16), nonetheless there is not a righteous person on earth who does only good and sins not (see Eccl 7:20). Divine recompence is given to actions based on one's deeds, in which divine justice is perceived by the rabbis as functioning in tension with the divine attribute of mercy. The latter provides from the very outset the means to ensure salvation for all in the form of repentance.[10] In some cases, rabbinic texts use a marketplace model of spiritual merits and demerits, there is a proportionality of righteousness and sin. Repentance adds to one's merits to undo the demerits.[11] George Moore, the historian of early Judaism, points out that repentance "may properly be called the Jewish doctrine of salvation." However, repentance is not a process by which one makes initial entry into the grace of God and enjoys the benefits of his mercy, but rather a means by which one is restored to that proximity. According to Moore, "There is no failing in man, whether collectively or as an individual, which requires special divine intervention and which cannot be remedied, with the guidance of the Torah, by man himself." He continues, "To use other language, one is already 'saved'; what is needed is the maintenance of a right attitude toward God, even though without it, the mercy of God is of no avail."[12] Rabbinic Judaism has an affinity to aspects of the ancient Stoic ideal of virtue and the need for self-mastery and commitment to return to proper action after veering due to human frailty.

The difference between rabbinic Jewish thought and Augustinian Christianity bears similarities to the difference between Augustine and Pelagius, but an even closer connection is that some of the Greek fathers still have positions near to rabbinic modes of thought in which divine forgiveness is universal and conditional on the offender's repentance. For example, Origen ascribes crucial importance to human free will and requires the repentance of the offender in order to obtain forgiveness and hence salvation. Acts of contrition show repentance and conversion, (*metanoia*). Origen also notes thar God listens to the weeping of those who repent. Tears have always been a Jewish requirement for the Day of Atonement, albeit the practice has been neglected in modern practice.[13]

According to the Mishnah, only sins against God can be atoned for through repentance. Sins against other people can be atoned for only once the wrong has been made right, for example, restitution has been paid for a financial crime, and forgiveness received from the victim. "For sins between man and God, Yom Kippur atones. But for sins between a man and his fellow, Yom Kippur does not atone until he appeases his fellow" (Yoma 8:9). If one harms another person, God cannot absolve you of the wrongdoing, only the person whom you harmed. One must face the harm head on by committing to learn from mistakes, and then addressing the needs of those who have been harmed.[14]

Medieval Concepts

Maimonides (1138–1204) explains the process of repentance as three stages: confession privately before God, regret, and a vow not to repeat the misdeed. "Recognition of one's sins as sins" as a confession before God is an intellectual and moral conscience. Repentance involves knowing that certain actions are sinful and overcoming one's motives for sin as deeply as one can. The true penitent who finds herself with the opportunity to commit the same sin again, declines to do so. In a modern formulation of Maimonides repentance involves several steps: naming and owning the harm, starting to change, restitution and accepting consequences, and finally, making different choices as evidence of transformation, thereby accepting that actions have consequences.[15]

Catalan rabbi Jonah of Gerondi (d. 1264) argues that repentance only works through divine kindness (*hesed*). He quotes Jeremiah: "Turn back, O rebellious children, I will heal your afflictions!" (3:22). Repentance consists of divine healing of past sins that otherwise would require punishment.[16] For Nahmanides (1194–1270) every individual act of repentance from sin is less personal atonement than homecoming out of exile to the spiritual land of Israel, a return to a pristine original state of harmony with God on an individual and collective level. Repentance is part of a return from exile with its alienation, persecution, and distance from the ideal biblical vision back to the envisioned idyllic state.[17]

Atonement

The Hebrew word *kippurim*, sometimes translated into English as "atonement," conveys a sense of reconciliation with God. The Jewish daily liturgy proclaims: "forgive us father, for we have sinned . . . for you are a forgiver . . . gracious one who greatly forgives." But in Judaism, this is often understood as a collective atonement for the entire Jewish people, "Please forgive the wrongdoing of this people out of the extravagance of your loyal love just as all along, from the time they left Egypt, you have been forgiving this people" (Num 14:18–19) is the verse that is used in the liturgy for the Jewish Yom Kippur service, where appeal for forgiveness from personal sin is intertwined with collective forgiveness of the Jewish people as a whole. The language of the liturgy uses "we," not just "I." What matters is that Jews take responsibility for the entire Jewish people—past, present, and future—in relation to their fellow humans, and in relation to the God of Israel. As the Talmud puts it, "All Israel are mutually responsible for each other" (*Shevuot* 39a).

In rabbinic texts of atonement, there is a convergence of the same spiritual neighborhood with Christianity. Among the most notable example of vicarious atonement, are the various statements that the death of the righteous is an atonement for those still living. "Just as the Day of Atonement atones, so does the death of the righteous atone." (TB Moad Katan 28a). Nevertheless, it should be noted that the medieval Jewish rationalist tradition, saw this idea as problematic and devoted themselves to answering why the righteous suffer and shrinking this idea.

Biblical patriarchs are divine intercessors for atonement, and the pain of death and suffering are personal atonements. Even though there were divergent approaches already in the early centuries, nevertheless Judaism still has various forms of vicarious atonement or the need for suffering.[18] Medieval Rationalists were deeply bothered by any form of vicarious atonement and modern thinkers read these texts against the simple reading.[19]

Other forms of atonement in Judaism include suffering,[20] poverty,[21] the pain and travails of living in exile and the pain of living after the destruction of the Temple,[22] and above all, death atones for sin.[23] Positive actions that offer atonement include sharing one's table with the poor,[24] prayer, and the study of the Torah.[25] In addition, the Merit of the Patriarchs, the accumulated merit of Abraham, Isaac, and Jacob, can extend atonement to their descendants, the Jewish people, as a form of merit not grace. Similar forms of merit for atonement can be bequeathed by one's direct righteous ancestors, great righteous people, and even having pious posterity in one's own children. Finally, some Orthodox authors consider the sufferings of the Jewish people and Jews killed by non-Jews as offering atonement for sins.[26]

Sometimes a righteous biblical figure offers vicarious atonement for a whole generation.[27] An example useful for comparison with Christianity is the idea of Moses's offering himself up for the atonement of the Israelites after the sin of the golden calf as a fulfillment of Isaiah's "he bore the sins of many" (Isa 53).[28] This becomes a broader principle that "the righteous are seized by death for the iniquities of the generation."[29] The Zohar, a foundational medieval book of Jewish esotericism, formulates an explicit relationship between the suffering servant of Isaiah 53 and vicarious atonement. "When the Holy One desires to give healing to the world, He smites one just man amongst them, and in his merit heals the rest . . . As it says 'He was wounded for our transgressions, bruised for our iniquities' (Isa 53:5)."

However, greater than this array of vicarious atonement, the Mishnah (circa 200 CE) declares, that Israel is directly purified, without the need for vicarious atonement, by their Father in Heaven.[30] "Rabbi Akiva said: How fortunate are you, Israel; before Whom are you purified, and Who purifies you? It is your Father in Heaven, as it is stated: 'I will sprinkle purifying water upon you, and you shall be purified' (Ezekiel 36:25). And it stated: 'The ritual bath of Israel is God' (Jeremiah 17:13)" (Yoma 8:9). God offers atonement the way one immerses in a ritual pool. In a similar manner, one needs to repent (*teshuvah)*, by acknowledging sins, to commit to not repeating them in the future, and to ask God for forgiveness. Nothing else is required: not a Temple, not a priest, not a sacrifice, and not the merit of an atoning virtuous human. God himself purifies.

Surprising for many modern Jews, rabbinic thought contains the concept of Gehinnom (Gehenna, or purgatory) offering atonement and purification for the wicked, who when purified from sin ascend to the garden of Eden, the eternal paradise (see *Eduyyot* 10:2; *Yalqut Isaiah* 26; Numbers Rabbah 81). Gehinnom, whose depiction is based on the idolatrous fire of the biblical Valley of Hinnom, serves as a symbol of God's retributive powers. The Talmud divides people into those with more merits than sins, and those with more demerits, and places everyone else on a sliding scale. Rabbi Akiva's statement, "God punishes the wicked in Gehinnom of twelve months" (*M. Edeyot* 10.2) implies that everyone else spends less time purifying.[31] The Rabbis never develop this punishment into metaphysics or create a dualism of saved and damned. In line with this, the rabbis taught that all of Israel are allocated a portion in the world to come as well as the righteous of all nations (M *Sanhedrin* 10:1).

The language of having a savior offering atonement is not mainstream Jewish thought yet has been kept alive with the Hasidic movement. Rebbe Nachman of Breslov (d. 1810), an early Hasidic leader who died in Uman, Ukraine, testified, "Whoever comes to my grave, recites the Ten Chapters of Psalms (16, 32, 41, 42, 59, 77, 90, 105, 137, 150), and gives something to alms, no matter how great the sins, I will extend myself the length and breadth of Creation for him; by his sidelocks, I will pull him out of Gehinnom!" In 2024, over sixty thousand pilgrims annually descend on the Ukrainian city of Uman each Rosh Hashanah, to pray on his grave fully expecting Rabbi Nachman to lift them out of punishment for their sins.[32]

Salvation and Justification

For early Lutherans, "faith alone justifies." For them, St. Paul emphasizes the fact that grace is purely gratuitous; that no natural good works can merit grace nor the observance of the Jewish Law. Catholics may insist on the necessity of works of Christian charity and sacraments. Lutherans, however, hold that faith alone suffices for justification, and the observance of the moral law is not necessary either as a prerequisite or for obtaining justification. According to Luther, the faith that justifies is not, as the Catholic Church teaches, a firm belief in God's revealed truths and promises, but is the infallible conviction that God for the sake of Christ will no longer impute to us our sins, rather considering us, as if we were really just and holy, although in our inner selves we remain the same sinners as before.

In contrast, in Calvin's theology, only those predestined infallibly to eternal salvation obtain justification; those not predestined by God produce a mere appearance of faith and righteousness, and this to punish them the more severely in hell. This approach was the original position of denominations that have Dutch Reformed roots, but this predestined righteousness has no parallel with Judaism.

Moses Mendelsohn (d. 1786) responded to both the Lutheran and Catholic approaches. He emphasized that Judaism has no dogma in the Catholic sense of required beliefs for salvation, in addition, religion is not just faith. Rather, Judaism is revealed legislation, the system of *mitzvot*—laws, rituals, and ordinances, for the conveyance of the universal truths by means of symbolic language. Judaism has beliefs and doctrines, but one does not have to believe anything or assent to anything to be saved. Jews usually present this as an oversimplified divide of deed versus creed, but a more sophisticated version presents Judaism as system of life and Lutherans as faith in a one-time event of Christ to offer saving atonement.[33] Finally, as a universalist, Mendelsohn affirms that one does not need to belong to an established religion. The truths of religion are available to all people as part of universal reason.

Before looking at the twentieth century, an eighteenth-century convergence offers a distinct resemblance to Jewish phraseology. John Wesley (1703–1791), founder of Methodism, wrote that we need to be saved from our inclination to "miss the mark"—to fall short of the high standard for love and justice that God desires for and from us. Sin is a distortion of our relationships with God and one another. God's grace works to reset our compasses and lead us in the direction of restored, loving relationships. For him, the opposite of being "saved" is not "un-saved," rather being lost. What afflicts human beings so often is not knowing our true and intended place in the world. The God we experience is a God of mercy, who forgives the ways we miss the mark and relentlessly invites us to grow and be transformed for our own personal salvation and that of all of creation. He says repentance and good works "are necessary to full salvation." A process not an event. Sin is disease and grace heals the disease of sin, referencing Christ as the Great Physician.[34] This position, has a convergence with Jewish ideas and has Jewish parallels, for example, Maharal of Prague (Yehudah Lowe, d. 1609) thinks that sin is an entropy away from being centered in God, and those that sin are really just lost and dissipating. God's atoning restores the sinner to the correct path.[35]

Carl Henry

The influential American Evangelical thinker Carl F. H. Henry (1913–2003) offers a Christian position that does not show signs of convergence or commonality with Judaism. The gospel of salvation through Christ, for Henry, represents the Bible's fundamental message. Scripture promises man the only hope of his future, the "offer of redemption" grounded "in the death and resurrection and ascension" of Jesus Christ.[36]

Henry viewed Christianity as superior over other religions by possessing valid propositional information of God based on biblical revelation. God's major message in revelation is despite man's moral revolt against God, nevertheless God as Jesus Christ shows his love in the offer of a saving redemption. The natural human iniquities deserve and call forth unmitigated judgment, which God mercifully spares us on condition of faith in the righteous Redeemer, Jesus Christ. Henry's doctrine of the atonement is that of penal substitution in which Jesus mitigates the judgement upon humans. The death of Christ absorbs the full force of this judgment. He sees this theology in the Old Testament itself. Starting with the curse after the fall (Gen 3:15) and Abraham's near-sacrifice of Isaac (Gen 22), the day of atonement (Lev 16), and the suffering servant passage (Isa 5), concluding with the capstone summary of penal substitution in Romans 3–5.

In Henry's view, the central problem the atonement dealt with was sin. The Father sent Christ as a substitute, one who would not only suffer for sin but die to pay the full penalty for it. In paying this penalty, Christ defeated sin, allowing the sinful to go free and experience transformation. Christ's "holy life and substitutionary death" makes it possible for God to be reconciled to man; man, to be reconciled to God. Without the sacrifice of Christ on man's behalf, man must meet the dreaded wrath of God in its full force. Salvation provides for the victory over the temptations of sin in the here and now allowing the establishment of the kingdom of God.

Karl Rahner

Karl Rahner affirms that humans are by nature orientated to God, in that, human nature has an inner moment of grace or an unfolding of the divine within it. To be human, means that one is a recipient of God's offer of self as grace. Hence, all humans, even non-Christians have this grace from Christ, and can be considered what Rahner calls "anonymous Christians." Humans in their essence are oriented by God toward Christ and thus, the nature of humanity is to be self-transcendent seeking human self-realization of our divine natures. God created the world in grace that can only be known through human freedom to fulfill the divine potential of the self.[37] Human nature is never pure nature; rather human nature contains a supernatural order of this grace, even as sinner and unbeliever. This has done away with the dichotomy of saved and unsaved, believer and unbeliever, and needing a specific doctrine to be saved. This basic premise brings Rahner's position close to human initiative of repentance within Judaism.

In Rahner's theology, this grace that leads to human salvation, must be the grace of Christ. "For there is one God. There is also one mediator between God and the human race, Christ Jesus, himself human, who gave himself as ransom for all" (1 Tim 2:5). Rahner sees the church as the tangible presence of this grace in the world, and hence Christianity, as the inclusive religion for all. Yet at the same time, Rahner believes that Jesus Christ is the salvation for all people and hence that his presence can be found in all people and all religions. From a Jewish perspective, this emphasis on Christ seems more particularist than universal.

According to Rahner, Jesus Christ is present always and everywhere as an offer to all humans as the universal salvific will of God. And grace is always and everywhere present, always existent in an elevated offer of grace. This conviction follows from his agreement with the traditional Thomistic line of thought that grace presupposes nature and natural souls, grace assumes the creation of universal humanity. For Rahner, this means that natural creation and salvation are to be understood as interrelated moments of the life of grace.[38]

Salvation requires a response of faith to this divine offer of grace in one's life, according to Rahner. According to Rahner, a positive response to the divine self-communication occurs when one, "freely accepts his own unlimited transcendence." In other words, a human accepts God when she accepts herself as a being directed ultimately to God through knowledge, freedom, and goodness. Given this understanding, Rahner argues that a free person is not necessarily one who has a multitude of choices but rather is a person who surrenders herself to the mystery of God within life, precisely because our fulfillment is found ultimately in God who has given humans the capacity for a response through grace transforming the recipient's consciousness. Rahner's transformation of self directly opposes any penal version of atonement.[39]

Rahner argues that the demand of moral conscience necessitates humans to transcend selfishness through acts of faith, hope, and charity, and ultimately through acts of love of neighbor. The basic act in which man morally transcends himself is this love of the neighbor. Rahner equates giving ourselves to the neighbor in love with surrendering to God. Action is the way grace is shown, rather than through abstract doctrinal knowledge or in faith. Hence, a person who follows her conscience, or fulfils the absolute demand of love or endures darkness and suffering in hope, has achieved salvation by responding to God. Anyone who does not close herself off from God's offer finds his salvation.[40] At this point, a Jewish thinker can be relatively comfortable with Rahner's conception of salvation in its universality, naturalness, and call to moral action.

Rahner refers to grace as the "ontological self communication of God" reminding his reader that in the economy of salvation, God has revealed himself as three-fold, Father, Son, and Spirit. He argues that if this is to be a real self-communication of Godself then there must be an identity between the economic Trinity and the immanent Trinity. Therefore, Rahner argues that if grace really is the self-communication of God, then grace must bear this threefold, trinitarian character, sharing in the intimate life of the Trinity. Here the Trinitarian conception of God, differentiates the understanding of salvation between Judaism and Christianity. For Rahner, Trinitarian at his theological core, God's sharing of the divine requires a differentiated aspect of God, the Son, separate than the divine Father, and needing to be maintained in the Spirit.[41]

In Rahner's words, "We are saved because this man, who is one of us, has been saved by God, and God has thereby made his salvific will present in the world historically, really, and irrevocably."[42] According to Rahner, the human person would know herself to be incapable of absolute fulfilment by anything less than God on the one hand and yet incapable of attaining to God on the other. This dilemma is resolved by God's self-communication: "The goal which man cannot reach can become the real point of departure for man's fulfilment and self-realization." In short, God's self-communication is the "highest summit" of human life. For Rahner, the natural human person cannot find fulfillment without a special self-sharing of the Trinity to overcome human limits, albeit that all humans already have this special self-sharing of Christ. While for Judaism, the natural human can attain God and fulfillment. In other words, Rahner assumes there needs to be a transformed human by accepting the offer of grace by Christ, while in general, Judaism's repentance is part of the natural human divine relationship not requiring a transformed nature or change of state. Love of neighbor and performing virtuous actions, for Rahner, indicate the acceptance of the potential for transformation within everyone, while for Judaism the ability for virtuous action is natural and universal without any grace.

For Rahner, grace does not mean God's gift of some created or uncreated reality or scholastic potential added to nature, rather God really gives Godself.[43] One experiences Godself in encounter when one acts in grace. At points, Rahner expresses this in terms that we all must be mystics. One finds a resonance in Rabbi Abraham Isaac Kook's view that a Jew can individually realign with their natural self through the keeping of the *mitzvot* or correct the self in one's encounter with God during prayer. In addition, Rahner has resonance with Rabbi A. J. Heschel's view of sympathy with the divine as a prophetic actualization.[44]

From a Jewish perspective, Rahner retains the fundamental Christian dichotomy of not seeing human capabilities as sufficient without God and the need for grace to attain God. Instead of concluding in a Jewish manner of saying that once God engaged in self-communication then humanity has enough power of its own because God is ever present and available to all. Instead, Rahner still focusses on the need for an individual personal acceptance of grace to achieve the needed transformation despite his teaching that divine grace is given naturally to all. Nevertheless, Rahner's emphasis on the person's freedom to accept or reject God's self-communication is closer to Judaism than Augustinian views. The human person has the last word on whether or not he accepts salvation thereby determining his own salvation, hence Rahner has been accused by some of Pelagianism. Rahner rejects this characterization of his thought by claiming that there is a parallel between human freedom, on the one hand, and divine grace on the other. Human knowledge of God and freedom to choose God are only possible due to prior grace; free acceptance of grace is made possible by grace, as an event of grace itself. Salvation ultimately remains God's self-communication, in that, human freedom of choice is already borne by grace, since human freedom itself stands in need of healing and liberation through grace. The difference between the Jewish and Christian versions of salvation returns to the Christian root metaphor of sin as disruptive of natural free will, thereby requiring grace.

A more recent trend developing Rahner's theology further is illustrated in German thinkers such as Thomas Pröpper (1941–2015). Klaus von Stosch (b. 1971), professor for Catholic Theology at the University of Bonn, follows the fruitful ideas of Pröpper in his discussion of Karl Rahner ideas of human freedom and divine love. In von Stosch's formulation, "Only an unconditional being who is nothing else than unconditional free will can realize unconditional love completely." It is only through this unconditional divine love of Christ that "I will know that I can be loved and that I am really loved unconditionally here in this world." In turn, those who acquiesce to this love will be able to trust that they "can respond to this unconditional love adequately—a capacity which is given to humankind by the Holy Spirit." Since the divine love is unconditional, "God's love will forgive every sin without imposing any form of condition before or after love."

Atonement constitutes human fulfillment that is desperately needed by humans because of the misuse of their free will and neglect of human responsibility. Human fulfillment overcomes sin, understood as the misuse of human responsibility. For von Stosch, "Christian anthropology presupposes that all humans suffer in some sense from the condition that they are not in complete union with God. And the basic message of Christianity wants to say that through Christ" in that "through his suffering on the cross, a way to atonement has been opened to all humans." Divine atonement of humans "is the restoration of the union in love between God and human which has overcome all obstacles which make this loving union impossible."[45]

Jewish theologians should take note of current Christian theology moving beyond any remnant of the Augustinian positions on sin, salvation, and atonement. In this Christian anthropology, sin is entirely due to the gift of free will and human negligence, which are ideas dominant in Jewish thinking. But the theological horizons of needing Christ's suffering to atone or even needing Christ to open a way to reunited with God remains foreign.

Finally, Rahner presents death not as a punishment, but as intensifying the relationship between the human person and God, an actualization of grace as God's self-communication. One is called to die every day for the sake of one's neighbor, which is both a selfless act and a powerless submission before the presence of God at the final end of life.

Everyone is asked to model the practice of freedom on the very person of Jesus Christ and die with Christ, a death that fully formed in human freedom. Freedom of the self when used to model Christ conquers the absurdity of death.[46] For Rahner, death is a way to show our submission to the spiritual and to emulate Christ in offering up our lives.

This may sound very foreign to most modern Jews; however, we find similar ideas in the thought of Rabbi Abraham Isaac Kook (1865–1935), modern Jewish mystic. Rabbi Kook writes that only because of the sin of Adam do humans view death as final. Ordinary people are engulfed in a world of materialism, therefore death for them represents the final end of materialism. He writes that "the fear of death is a general sickness of man, a function of sin. Sin created death. Repentance is the sole cure to obliterate death from this world." Kook taught that "death is an illusion" in that "death is actually the epitome of life." Yet, most do not see this because man is plunged by a materialistic superficial vision by following his inclination, therefore the average person mistakenly paints the epitome of life as a dark and dreary picture which he calls death."[47] The religious goal is to realize that the external world shall be indeed secondary in importance, relative to the internal and spiritual, but nonetheless be imbued with importance, with value and mission. Salvation comes from dedication to the observance of Torah.[48]

Moltmann

Our created world—filled with war, massacres, hatred, poverty, sickness, and oppression—for Jürgen Moltmann, is fundamentally a history of suffering needing redemption and salvation. Therefore, Moltmann is convinced that redemption for a Christian must mean a worldly redemption from these political and social calamities. In turn, our world must also be fundamentally a history of God's passionate and compassionate love for the world where Christ offers the needed redemption. Salvation overcomes the fallenness in our political and social lives in which the actual historical, political, and social world becomes transformed.

God's re-entering the godforsaken world to help overcome the alienation is salvation. Moltmann identifies this alienated forsaken world as the vacated space (*halal hapanui*) discussed in Jewish kabbalah and the means to overcome this absence as the presence of the *shekhinah*. The history of salvation is the history of God's reoccupation of the vacated space (*halal hapanui*) of our world in order to transfigure the whole of creation towards participation in the life of God. Overcoming the absence by God becoming present in creation is through the Messiah or messianic redemption, but especially through the *shekhinah* of God's Spirit. The economy of the Trinity is needed for God to enter the space vacated by God and be a dwelling (*shekhinah*) on earth. The ontological gap between Creator and creation is overcome through God's reoccupation of creation, but in a perichoretic way so that creation is not overwhelmed by God's presence.[49]

Moltmann's position constitutes a radical departure from Anselm's understanding of salvation in terms of penal substitution where Christ died on behalf of humanity who has become estranged from God as a result of sin. Moltmann's understanding of suffering contains a version of the theology of redemption of the victorious Christus tradition in which Christ offers victory over the forces of death, liberation from oppression, and an end to suffering. Moltmann completely rejects the spiritualization and eternalization of the experience of salvation in theology where the experience of God is closely identified with the individual soul's experience of purification and salvation. Moltmann rejects a narrowed, spiritualized concept of salvation, arguing that salvation is not about our souls going to heaven when we die, as some timeless concept of "being saved." People were not created to go to heaven, rather we are created for this earth, and our purpose and eternal destiny is on earth. Salvation is all about God's history with the world, which is the biblical understanding of salvation in the Hebrew Bible "understood as *shalom* in the Old Testament sense." "Forgiveness of sins and abolition of godlessness" is integrated with "what was truly meant to be."[50] In other words, salvation correlates with righteousness, defining the latter as "'being in order,' standing in the right relationship; correspondence and harmony. . . ," a victory over the fallenness of the world.[51]

For Moltmann the cross of Jesus Christ constitutes the turning point in the narrative of God's work in terms of the solidarity of God with a suffering creation. God shows vicarious love for the godforsaken world threatened by annihilation providing the protest divine love against the suffering of creation. The cross of Christ is the sign of God's solidarity for all those who live here in the shadow of the cross. The alienating otherness of creation is overcome when such otherness is taken up in God's own being, being abandoned by God becomes something that took place within Godself. Only this one man, Jesus, was raised because through his representative suffering the risen Christ brings righteousness and life to the unrighteous and the dying. Jesus was, therefore, merely the first to be raised and hence all people can live from the expectation of the resurrection of the dead. In this way the "for us and our salvation" of Nicene Christianity provides a response to the theodicy problem. All people can be raised from this event. Because of this solidarity that was made available to humanity through the cross, we are "welcomed into the relation of Father, Son, and Holy Spirit." while at the same time God is experiencing godforsakenness with us. Jesus's life stands as testimony that he always stood with the marginalized, the poor, the prostitutes, and the tax collectors. His death was the result of his life. Christians are called to identify with Christ's suffering and to stand with those whose experience of being forsaken parallels Christ on the cross.[52]

This notion of abandonment reflects Moltmann's deepest intuition that godforsakenness is here not so much a response from God to human corruption, rather abandonment reflects the necessary self-withdrawal (*tzimtzum*) of God, in order to allow creation to be itself. The self-withdrawal leads to suffering and death in creation, to which Moltmann seeks to understand justification from the point of view of the victims, the oppressed, and the suffering. Accordingly, justification is not understood primarily in terms of the forgiveness offered to sinners out of God's grace, but the liberating power impact of such forgiveness; the emphasis is not on pardon in response to wrongdoing, rather God's word of affirmation overcoming, sin, poverty, and war.

Moltmann throughout his works seeks to overcome the separation of a theology of creation and redemption. In his work on creation, he stresses the redemptive thrust of God's acts of creation in the beginning, continuing creation and new creation. Likewise, in his discussion of redemption, he stresses the creative thrust of God's acts of redemption. Here as in Rahner, and unlike Judaism, humanity stands in need of salvation by the work of the indwelling of the second person of the Trinity. For Jews, God alone fulfills that purpose of salvation and ultimate redemption of the unredeemed world.

Moltmann attempts to overcome the tension between a theological understanding of the church as an actualized redemption and the empirical reality of the church mired in the world through the Lutheran notion of the tension between reality and hope. He emphasizes the revolutionary power unleashed by this hope to change the world and its impact on the sanctification of Christian life and on society.[53] The justification of the unrighteous points beyond itself to the lordship of Christ on earth. Moreover, hope points toward the work of the Spirit, namely towards the believer's freedom from sin, liberation from godless powers, the redemption of the body, and the new creation. Justification cannot be narrowly confined to forgiveness, but also includes the notion of new life in righteousness. In line with the rest of his thought, his point here is that an emphasis on forgiveness on the basis of expiation cannot do justice to Christ's resurrection, rather the purpose of justification is for a just world for all created beings.[54]

On the basis of the category of an affirmation of life, those who are being affirmed by God are primarily the social outcasts, those who are not accepted in society, the marginalized, the victims of injustice. Affirmation here implies solidarity with the victims and the affirmation of human dignity—also the dignity of those who are trampled upon—and an affirmation of the value of every life and every form of life. This fusion of natural suffering and human sin as sources of suffering has implications for every aspect of Moltmann's account of God story, a radicalization of the message of redemption. Since the victims are not responsible for their suffering, then no human beings can ultimately be responsible. The only way out is to hold God responsible. For Moltmann, salvation is not dependent on human belief or action; salvation is dependent wholly on God. He writes, "It is not my faith that creates salvation for me; salvation creates for me faith. If salvation and damnation were the results of human faith or unfaith, God would be dispensable."[55] If the case were otherwise, and salvation rested in the human will, "human beings would be their own God."[56] The only way in which God can be declared just in the face of human and other forms of suffering is to proclaim universal salvation. "The true Christian foundation for the hope of universal salvation is the theology of the cross, and the realistic consequence of the theology of the cross can only be the restoration of all things."[57] For Moltmann, any theology centered on the cross must be universalist.[58]

For Moltmann any semblance of hope resides in the cross: "Hope, which is born of the memory of the crucified Lord, therefore leads to hope where there is nothing to hope for."[59] For any theology to be called "Christian," it must take seriously the death of a god-forsaken Christ upon the cross.[60] The suffering Christ, god-forsaken on the cross and subsequent resurrection and redemption by God, offers only hope and love, not despair and judgment.[61]

Comparison

The positions of Rahner and Moltmann have both closed the gap with Judaism, in that, both Rahner and Moltmann disagree with the Augustinian elements and exclusivism of the inherited positions. For Rahner, the particularism of Christ works through all people including Jews in their Judaism, rendering Jews as anonymous Christians since Christ works through them. For Moltmann, the biblical story is a universal story of hope, whose offers apply to anyone taking up the cross of making the world a better place. Salvation is no longer about the spiritual state of the soul accepting Christ. Rahner thinks Christ works through Jews and Moltmann assumes a universal salvation from the forsakenness of this world. Rahner's view of salvation as overcoming fault and sin with one's innate divine soul and the channeling of one's

God given freedom to the love of neighbor is not far from a Jewish position. Once again, Rahner is seemingly closer to a Jewish position from a philosophic perspective. Rahner's emphasis on existential freedom to choose to identify with God is highly similar to Soloveitchik who considered sin as alienation from one true self.[62]

Moltmann, however, offers more points of contact with Biblical and kabbalistic openings for discussion, most notably his viewing of salvation as a need due to our fallen world of alienation and dysfunctionality. Chief Rabbi Jonathan Sacks expresses similar sentiment about the need to be saved from our alienation.

In addition, Moltmann has been criticized by Christians for failing to distinguish between the imperfect fallenness in the natural world and the theological fallenness of the fall of Adam in the original sin.[63] Which may be a criticism from a Christian perspective but actually brings his position closer to Judaism, in that both religions see the fallenness of humanity as a sociopolitical fact. For Judaism, we have to humanly overcome the pain and suffering in the world because we are partners in creation with God. For Moltmann we have Christ-given hope to overcome the brokenness of the world.

The Catholic theologian David Tracy, notes that the Christian understanding of "salvation is always salvation from some state that needs healing (primordially sin and not sins) and salvation for some new, healed state of release promising a new way of authentic freedom." Salvation is about a Christian's central reality and the power for transformation. For Christians, the fundamental state is one of sin and God's self offer of himself, providing a new Christian way of life, "an experience of release from some powerful bondage" or guilt by the forgiveness of sin. "The experience is, at the same time, an experience of releasement to some new way of existing as an authentic human being."[64] For Tracy, "the distinctively Christian understanding of the nature of Ultimate Reality" is "the God who Loves as manifested in Jesus Christ." Salvation is the rubric to understand the entire Christian "symbol system, especially the central doctrines of Christ and God," which cannot "be adequately interpreted save in relationship to the whole." Rahner and Moltmann's this-worldly positions can obscure this basic orientation not shared by Judaism. If a Christian author uses the words "saving covenant" or "salvation" to describe the Jewish concept of "repentance" or "*mitzvot*" then that author is not talking about Judaism. The locution is like saying that Hindus do puja or yoga for salvation, a projection of Christian terms.

Nevertheless, Jews and Christians currently are speaking similar languages, yet the difference remains our sacred narratives. The Jewish narrative arc stretches from Abraham as the start of the Jewish people in Genesis to God redeeming the Jews from slavery in Egypt, the covenant with the Jewish people to observe *mitzvot* and a promise of redemption, while the Christian narrative is a grand dramatic narrative of creation, fall, redemption, and final redemption, starting with creation, spanning to Christ, and culminating in passion, crucifixion, and resurrection. Christian views of atonement and salvation are directly tied to this grand biblical drama. Judaism, in contrast, has a cyclical process of annually repenting of sins and seeking atonement drawing precedent from a host of Biblical and rabbinic characters who serve as paradigms for the internal work of repentance.

Typifying this difference, Cardinal Ratzinger and Lord Chief Rabbi Sacks offer views of salvation with both convergence and divergence. For Cardinal Ratzinger, "The reality of evil and injustice that disfigures the world and at the same time distorts the image of God—this reality exists, through our sin." A Jewish thinker could agree with this. For Chief Rabbi Sacks, "Sin alienates; it distances us from God, and the result is that we are distanced from where we ought to be, where we belong. We become aliens, strangers."[65] In this we have a convergence.

However, Benedict continues: "God himself becomes the locus of reconciliation, and in the person of his Son takes the suffering upon himself. God himself grants his infinite purity to the world. God himself 'drinks the cup' of every horror to the dregs and thereby restores justice through the greatness of his love, which, through suffering, transforms the darkness."[66] In contrast, Sacks's Jewish conclusion focusses on personal behavioral change. "[Repentance] is associated with behavioral change (*teshuvah* as "returning" to the right way) and leads to healing, mercy, forgiveness and restoration . . . atonement relates primarily to individuals." Both theologians share the same formulation of alienation and sin; yet with different liturgical theological settings of salvation—a choice of Christ's redemption or self-mastery to achieve atonement.[67]

Our sacred narratives, liturgy, and religious languages remain different even as we have converged in a late twentieth-century religious language. Liturgical and sacramental imagery of the Eucharist as needed to assure salvation is a sharp divide. "Truly, truly, I say unto you, unless ye eat the flesh of the Son of Man and drink His blood, ye have no life in you" (John 6:53). For Jews, any reference of a paschal victory of Christ as the new Adam allowing for salvation remains foreign. Salvation as requiring the sacrament of Baptism is a different ritual life than Judaism, as are the various Christian penitential traditions and theologies of reconciliation, which are an essential part of the sacramental.

But to be honest, we have new counter trends of theological divergence. For example, Hans Urs von Balthasar (1905–1988), a Swiss theologian and Catholic priest, offers a vision of salvation that has little in common with Jewish repentance and self-perfection, rather salvation is entirely from divine love, to be with all of humanity in their suffering guilt, and shame. In his essay "Tragedy and Christian Faith," he describes Christ as answering the despair of humanity not by dissolving or disregarding it, but by bearing the human condition as it is, in its darkness.[68] For Balthasar, Christ does not refuse human tragedy or awareness of pain. He bears it in love, affirming our tragic human condition, carrying human sorrows to the end, all the way to the heart of God. God's omnipotence made itself known in the Incarnation as powerlessness and unutterable limitation. Christ speaks into human darkness as only one who is acquainted with darkness can. Unlike Moltmann, there is no restoration or repair of the physical world. The suffering and death of Christ gives expression to inexplicable tragedy, unnecessary suffering, and perplexing darkness, yet qualities to which the Son of God willingly submitted himself and thereby heals human tragedy through human integration into divine life.

Jewish Perspectives

Modern Jewish thought on repentance and atonement, as in other topics, has a wide spectrum of opinions. Repentance, unlike some of the other topics in this book, is an ongoing theological concept in contemporary Judaism. The presentation of a contemporary Jewish theology of repentance is usually as a series of lectures over several weeks in which the instructor presents a different theological view each week, rather than a definite dogma. Generally, the focus of repentance in modern Jewish thought is on ethical self-scrutiny, free will, and correcting one's action, not on deliverance and redemption. One popular contemporary book explains repentance as "facing the harm that I caused is an act of profound optimism. It is a choice to grow, to learn, to become someone who is more open and empathetic," through a process of healing, restoration, transformation, and taking responsibility.[69]

Rationalist Jewish thinkers generally only discuss the rabbinic view of repentance and avoid discussing atonement or intercession by the righteous. Other Jewish thinkers with a wider pallet of rabbinic texts accept the extensive gamut of rabbinic statements without a need to organize or systematize them. A naturalist such as Rabbi Mordecai Kaplan (1881–1883), focuses solely on salvation as "deliverance from those evils, external and internal, which prevent man from realizing his maximum potentialities. . . . Stated positively, Salvation means the maximum fulfillment of those human capacities which entitle man to be described as 'made in the image of God'. . ." For Kaplan, salvation "is our duty and within our power to achieve."[70] The neo-Kantian Hermann Cohen (1848–1918) conceptualizes repentance as a sense of personal responsibly with its concurrent sense of sin as more important than any universal ethical categorical. "I therefore am in constant need of God, as the One who forgives sin." We long for nearness to God, and thereby gain God's forgiveness. "Sin alienates me from God; forgiveness brings me near again." The inner process is purifying.[71]

Depicting the back-and-forth dialectics between the human and divine roles in the rabbinic views of repentance, Rabbi Soloveitchik discusses a two-tier form of repentance in which the highest form of repentance is self-perfection by man without God's grace, while the lower repentance out of fear is done by God. He wrote: "absolution obtained as a result of repentance out of fear is granted by God Himself in a transcendent act of grace. The purification accomplished by repentance out of love is accomplished by man himself . . . an act of self-purification, performed by man and only by him . . ." without a divine role.[72] In this presentation, Soloveitchik creates a convergence and difference by alluding to Karl Barth's Christian concept of "a transcendental act of grace" as a lower level before the more Pelagian Maimonidean approach of self-purification as the higher level.[73]

To conclude, for those who still see Christianity as far from Jewish thinking, here is the current Catechism of the Catholic Church. The current catechism presents repentance in terms Maimonides or Soloveitchik would understand with its emphasis on acknowledgment of sin, turning from evil, and resolution to change: "Interior repentance is a radical reorientation of our whole life, a return, a conversion to God with all our heart, an end of sin, a turning away from evil, with repugnance toward the evil actions we have committed. At the same time, it entails the desire and resolution to change one's life, with hope in God's mercy and trust in the help of his grace."[74] In contemporary understanding, to expect salvation without change or repentance would be what the Christian theologian Dietrich Bonhoffer called "cheap grace." At this point, both religions, especially as presented by Rahner and Moltmann, expect inner change and responsibility for outer change of behavior.

CHAPTER FIVE

Messiah

THE ROCK OPERA Jesus Christ Superstar, has as the chorus of its theme song, "Jesus Christ Superstar, / Do you think you're what they say you are?" These lyrics paraphrase Jesus's question, Who do people say that I am? Of which the clear answer given by Peter in the gospels is, "You are the Christ," (Mark 8:27–29). A specific first-century person, Jesus, is the eternal meaning of the biblical promise for the awaited messiah.

Trude Weiss Rosmarin notes that Christians consider Jesus as "not only the incarnation of God but also the Messiah and Redeemer whose future advent is announced in the books of the Hebrew Bible," which she claims forced the Hebrew Bible into the "procrustean bed of the Christian scheme of salvation." She emphasizes that the Christian view of the Messiah did not fulfill Judaic messianic hopes, in that "not one of the Messianic promises was fulfilled through Jesus. He neither established universal peace and social justice for all of mankind nor did he redeem Israel." In her view, Jews see that "their own exile and homelessness and the continuation of war, are conclusive proof of the fact that the Messiah has not yet arrived."[1] The two religions have developed very different starting points. For a Christian following church teaching, the messiah (in Greek *christos*, hence *Christ*) is the suffering servant foretold by Isaiah (7:14) as Emmanuel, who as Jesus becomes incarnate, crucified, and resurrected to bring salvation to the world. In contrast, rabbinic Judaism considers the messiah as "all Biblically inspired Jewish communal hope, spiritual and political, with or without a messiah figure."[2] Judaism's messiah is generally political restoration, this worldly kingdom, or amelioration of the world's problems, which does not need to discuss sin, salvation, or the suffering servant or any specific individual when discussing the messiah. Despite this seeming divergence, the two religions share many messianic sources, conceptions of the Messiah, and forms of messianic hope, with each displaying great diversity. Specifically, this chapter separates the broader concept of messianic hope—both Jewish and Christian—from the specific claim of Christ as the incarnate messianic salvation. In the contemporary convergence, the Christian messianic forms of realized social justice, and the premillennial dispensationalists close some of the gap.

The Messiah

Messiah originally meant in Hebrew "anointed one," initially used to refer to the current reigning monarch as well as priests and some prophets. Over time the word developed the connotation of a future monarchy, specifically, God's promise to David that one of his sons would always sit on the throne in Jerusalem (2 Sam 7). The Babylonian exile ended native kingship in Jerusalem and gave rise to the hope that God will restore the monarchy, bringing a new anointed king, a messiah. Some biblical verses suggest an expected restoration will be at an awaited end of days (Gen 49:1, Num 24:14, Deut 31:29), a broader eschatological leader.[3] The expectation of the Davidic messiah was that the Messiah was supposed to be a warrior who would kill the wicked and drive out the enemies (Isa 11:4). In later centuries, the epithet was also applied to others including the non-Jewish King Cyrus. The awaited messiah was both vaguely defined and political, situated in different dynamic understandings.[4]

Separately, and generative of a new line of thought, Second Temple era Jews start to understand the future king messiah to be the Son of God.[5] In the book of Ezekiel, when Ezekiel is repeatedly addressed as "son of man," the term just means human being. However, in Daniel's apocalyptic visions and bold symbolic images, Son of Man changes from human to divine being; he creates a new category beyond Ezekiel. One of Daniel's symbolic visions depicts "one like a Son of Man coming on the clouds of heaven" (Dan 7:13). In a later chapter in Daniel, that figure is identified as the archangel Michael, who is called the prince of Israel, the leader of the angelic host (Dan 12.1). This text was undoubtedly important in the formation of the ideas of the Trinity and incarnation, but more importantly for this chapter, was interpreted from an early time as the Messiah.[6]

In a Second Temple period non-canonical text, the *Similitudes of Enoch*, a text that is very clearly based on the vision of Daniel, a figure called the Son of Man appears with the Ancient of Days, like in Daniel. However, in this case he is a separate angel above Michael—the second in command in heaven, the heavenly representative of the righteous on Earth. He is also, at least in one case, called the Messiah. This image in Enoch of God, Son of Man, and the angel Michael, plays a role in the imagery that became Jesus as the Son of Man in the New Testament. First century Jews who were followers of Jesus combined the two traditions: the typical belief in a Davidic messiah who would restore the political kingdom of David and the idea that deliverance would come as a heavenly figure, as well as part of a divine hierarchy as an angel, in this, the warrior, the Son of God, and the angel become one.[7]

The Gospel of Matthew connects this vision of Jesus directly with the Isaiah prophecies of a sign from God and Emmanuel as messianic redeemer (Matt 1: 22–23 based on Isa 7:14) and who will appear on the Lord's Dreadful Day (Mal 4:5). He is the promised sapling that bears fruit (Isa 11:1) and the one who will sit on David's throne. (Isa 9:7). The Messiah of the Gospels presents new aspects of the messiah's activities including working miracles, raising the dead, telling parables, and speaking for the Father. In Acts, Stephen says that he has a vision—with imagery from Daniel 7 and Psalm 110—in which he saw the heavens opened, and the Son of Man standing at the right hand of God.

The New Testament literature attests to the culling of proof-texts from the Hebrew Bible to contend for Jesus's status as the Messiah long promised to the Jews. Jesus's triumphant entry into Jerusalem on Palm Sunday was meant to remind people of Zachariah: "Behold your king comes to you, humble and riding on an ass" (Zach 9:9). According to the gospels, his followers got excited because he seemingly was the Messianic King and started shouting, "Hosanna to the Son of David" (Matt 21:9), demonstrating that the apostles considered him the Davidic messiah.

The Romans took him to be a political messianic pretender restoring the kingdom of the Jews.

Paul laments that Jews "demand signs" and receive "Christ crucified" as a "stumbling block" (1 Cor 1:22–23); here, he presumably admits Jesus's lack of fit with acknowledged signs for Israel's Messiah, due foremost to his death by crucifixion (cf. Deut 21:23; Gal 5:11, 6:12) and also to the failure to bring any discernible change to Jewish political circumstances under Roman imperial rule. Isaiah's image of a suffering servant in Isaiah 52–53 bearing sins was applied to Jesus's painful death and the salvation the death offered. The meaning and original context of the passage concerned the people Israel as a national entity.[8]

John C. Collins, scholar of early messianism, presents the prior context for Jesus's followers accepting a martyred messiah and a preexisting Messiah. "In the late-first century CE apocalypses of 4 Ezra and 2 Baruch the messiah dies" showing a broader concept of the messiah than usually assumed for first-century Judaism. But the messiah's death, "does not involve suffering and has no atoning significance." For Collins, "neither scenario bears any similarity to Isaiah 53, the needed context for a messiah offering salvation." In 2 Maccabees, which is part of the Catholic canon but not the Jewish canon, there is a conception of martyrs who suffered vicariously and died because of sin and that their blood was the required price for the nation's salvation.[9] Collins concludes: "There is no evidence that any first century Judaism expected" a suffering martyred figure.[10]

Yet, this became the divide. The early third-century church father Tertullian (d. 220 CE) already concluded that there is no greater dispute between Jews and Christian than the coming of Christ as messiah. However, an important scholar of early messianism notes: "Many Jewish messiah texts bend the messiah myth to accommodate contingent historical developments and persons, while many Christian messiah texts obstinately maintain utopian aspects of the messiah myth despite their nonfulfillment in the career of Jesus." Messianism does not create a fundamental distinction between the two religions, rather, "the enormous popularity of the Jewish Messiah–Christian messiah distinction has always been a result, in large part, of its rhetorical utility for religious self-definition and interreligious dialogue."[11]

Cardinal Kasper (b. 1933) noted the similarity between Second Temple apocryphal works and Jesus regarding the messianic end time. Kasper provides a cultural context, in which the Second Temple books with accounts of Enoch, Elijah, and Baruch described these figures as heavenly observers of the last judgment, while in the New Testament, there was divine heavenly enthronement. In a manner similar to the way Elijah was exalted and expected to return, Jesus has been exalted and will later return as the eschatological Messiah, in which incarnation, messiah, messianic end time, and salvific judgment are intertwined. Kasper admits that the contemporary world finds exaltation of a human into a divine being as bizarre, nevertheless he explains that in Second Temple Judaism, "exaltation (or ecstasy) was the only category available to express the fact that a human being on earth would still play a part in the eschatological events."[12]

An executed messiah, however, was not the kind of messiah that most Jews would have recognized as such. The early followers of Jesus concluded that he is the Messiah, but not the kind of messiah that everybody was expecting. Jesus is a messiah who must die first and then come back. When Simeon Bar Kokhba (Kosibah), a messianic contender a hundred years after Jesus who led a revolt (132–135 CE) against Rome, got killed (in 135 CE), that was the end of him and belief in him. People believed he was the Messiah before he was killed. Once he was killed, that cleared up that question. But in the case of Jesus, his followers believed he was risen from the dead. The first Christians looked through the scriptures to find this new kind of messiah—one who wasn't the political ruler.

In sum, first-century Judaism possesses several distinct views of messianism, some based solely on the political restoration of the monarchy, some expecting a semidivine figure, some expecting a resurrection, or even a redemption from sin, and others, the followers of Christ, accepted him as the awaited Messiah even if he was not in concordance with the prior expectation. By the third century, we have the latter group linking the messiah to the theologies of the Trinity and salvation. According to Larry Hurtado, "the Christology and devotional stance that Paul affirmed, and shared with others in the early Jesus-movement, was not a departure from or a transcending of a supposedly monochrome Jewish messianism, but, instead, a distinctive expression within a variegated body of Jewish messianic hopes." Jesus as the Messiah was an outgrowth of the many and varied Jewish ideas about messianism at the time, but by the fourth century, the Christian idea of the Messiah was a distinctly Christian belief without full parallel in Judaism. For most fourth-century credal Christians, the messiah became defined as a promised incarnate divine figure, the second person of the Trinity, who saves the world from the spiritual burden of sin. Augustine credits Jesus with bringing salvation to all those who accept him as the Messiah and incarnation of God; Christ is the mediator between God and man, as well as divine. The coming of the messiah ushers in a new era of a new covenant in which the prior Jewish law is rendered invalid and belief is Christ is required.

Rabbinic Judaism

For most fourth-century rabbinic Jews, however, the messiah remained a political ruler or worldly teacher who visibly changes the world. The Rabbis, in turn, further dimmed this expectation of a personal Messiah, sometimes as a reaction to Christian ideas. One rabbinic authority, Samuel (third century), declared: "There will be no difference between the current age and the Messianic era except the emancipation from our subjugation to the gentile kingdoms." This view virtually reduces messianic hope to the expectation of an era of peace that Israel will attain without eschatological or salvific meaning. In contrast, Rabbi Eliezer, believed that the next era would be unprecedented, apocalyptic, and qualitatively different.[13]

Many scholars and theologians concluded from Samuel's statement that Judaism is not a messianic religion. Rather, Judaism is about sanctification of life through keeping the scribal-rabbinic way of action, the *mitzvot* in the Torah, as "a way of life."[14] In contrast, Christianity is about salvation and the needed messianic figure to achieve it.

The book of Jewish prayer, the *siddur*, is "saturated through and through" with the "raw hope" of messianic expectation and "simple and compelling petitions." But, as noted by scholars, the messianic speculation in the Jewish prayer book does not stray far from political naturalism in that the appeal is for a general redemption and for a specific Davidic personage as the messiah who is a foretold kingly redeemer, placing greater emphasis on God's redemptive powers than description of the messiah.[15] Within Jewish liturgy, the ebbing of the Sabbath, the liturgy of the festivals and fasting days each have prayers, wishes, and hopes for a messianic redemption, but often leave the terms undefined. And most notably, Jews, since the Middle Ages, end the Passover Seder and the Yom Kippur service by saying "next year in Jerusalem."

But it is not so simple. There were many Jews and many Jewish texts that displayed strong and acute forms of messianism. "Messianic hope is omnipresent in classical Jewish life and literature." A wide variety of messianism and apocalyptic thinking of the early centuries are found in the Talmud, in midrash, and in Jewish liturgical hymns of late antiquity. Many messianic statements in rabbinic literature converge with Christian positions, and many are foreign to Christianity.

The Talmud displays a potpourri of messianic ideas, often cited sequentially on the same page so as to make the rabbinic opinion inconsistent and hard to pin down, leaving the concepts fluid and capacious within Judaism. Among the notable contradictory statements are: there will be no messiah since the messianic promise was only applicable in the era of the First Temple; the messiah will come after six thousand years from creation; and the messiah will come when all Israel are guilty of sin or entirely innocent of sin. The messiah will come when Jews are altogether righteous or altogether guilty and corrupt. Another statement is that brazen open sinning will increase before the messiah arrives. Alternately, the study of Torah and prayer are seen as having messianic redemptive properties. As an important statement for Jewish history, the Talmud states that the messiah will only come through national travail and suffering of the people of Israel, harkening back to suffering servant imagery. The messianic age is a vision of an ideal society in which the wickedness of the world will be eradicated, the Temple will be rebuilt, there will be an ingathering of the exile of Israel, and resurrection of the dead.

In rabbinic texts, there are visions of the destruction of the kingdom of Rome along with a terrible battle, what we call now an Armageddon (parallel to John 16:16) allowing for the destruction of the enemies of the Jewish people followed by an era of material happiness and spiritual bliss. In these apocalyptic visions there are many parallels to Christian apocalypticism and the book of Revelation. The leaders and kings of these battle, however, will be human, not divine.[16]

In addition, there are less well-known rabbinic texts of messianic apocalypse, images of the messiah as divine form, as enthronement, and descriptions of a suffering messiah. A Jewish text, with some of the closest convergences between Judaism and Christianity is the rabbinic Aggadic work *Pesikta Rabbati* (fifth to sixth century), which presents a messiah who, similar to Christian understanding of Jesus, dies and is resurrected and who is the suffering servant spoken of in Isaiah, offering vicarious expiatory suffering. This messiah of *Pesikta Rabbati* had a miraculous birth similar to Jesus, and like Jesus is a teacher, prophet, wonderworker and king offering a new teaching that fulfills the promise for a "new heavens and a new earth" (Isa 65:17). His death as the suffering servant and resurrection brings salvation to the world. This Jewish Aggadic image is clearly modeled on Jesus Christ in order to offer a counter gospel to the Christian story, probably to downplay the uniqueness of Jesus and to offer a Jewish version of those theological ideas. We encounter here a rabbinic re-appropriation of themes usurped by the New Testament Jesus and therefore largely ignored or suppressed by most rabbis, only to make its way back later into the beliefs of certain strands of rabbinic Judaism in the fifth and sixth centuries.

However, the *Pesikta Rabbati* claims this messiah of whom he writes is the Messiah ben Ephraim who precedes the Davidic Messiah.[17] The Messiah ben Ephraim is a rabbinic concept whose idea dates to the Second Temple period and the Dead Sea Scrolls, that there will be two messiahs, a Messiah ben Ephriam (or Messiah ben Joseph) who dies and a later Messiah ben David who ushers in the political era of the messiah.[18] These messianic ideas found in the *Pesikta Rabbati* of a dying and resurrected messiah who suffers as vicarious atonement continue into the writings of medieval Jewry and beyond, producing many later apocalyptic tracts. For example, the *Book of Zerubbabel* (approx. seventh century), which contains much of the *Pesikta Rabbati* narrative with further embellishment, shows that Jews were both deeply attracted to and repulsed by Christian descriptions of a suffering and dying Messiah, his mother Mary, and the figure of Christ, therefore the apocalypse created a Jewish counter-narrative to the gospels.[19]

Turning to the kabbalistic writings, a Zohar apocalypse depicts a messiah waiting in heaven to fight the battles against the nations to avenge the enemies of Israel.[20] In the main body of the Zohar, the protagonist Rabbi Shimon bar Yohai is a messianic figure who repairs the broken cosmos.[21] In later Lurianic kabbalah, human ritual actions repair the fallen divine structure affected by fault in the creation process and human action restores the pristine divine structure. Only after the original fall of the cosmos is repaired the messiah will arrive.[22]

A perusal of the various Jewish apocalyptic texts whose ideas go back to earlier texts show many points of convergence with Christian messianism and millenarianism. The early Church Fathers such as Justin Martyr, Irenaeus, and Tertullian present eschatological views similar to Jewish messianic views. For example, Justin describes a coming kingdom of saints lasting a thousand years in a rebuilt, adorned, heavenly Jerusalem along with the resurrection of the dead and the building of a restored Jerusalem.[23] In these millenarian end of days scenarios we have a close convergence with the contours of Jewish messianism. What the history of Christianity considers general apocalyptic and eschatological visions, Judaism considers messianism. Conversely, what Judaism considers messianism and apocalyptic visions, most Christian would not find a reflection of the incarnate suffering servant bringing salvation.

In addition, many Jewish messianic leaders arose over the millennium, each claiming to be the awaited messiah. Some of them were political leaders and warriors, some of them were magicians and mystics, some teachers of Torah and some charlatans. These messianic figures are important as part of Jewish historical thinking that envisioned this-worldly redemption of the Jewish people but are not directly germane to our theological narrative.[24]

One last Talmudic idea to note is the preexistence of the Messiah and of Torah. The Talmud states that seven things were created before the world was made: Torah, repentance, the garden of Eden, Gehenna, the throne of glory, the house of the sanctuary, and the name of the Messiah" (b. Pes. 54a; cf. b. Ned. 39b). Alternately, "Torah preceded the creation of the world by two thousand years" (Gen. Rab. 8.2). This is parallel to the concept that Christ is preexistent before the creation of the world (Eph 1:4–5, 8–10; 1 Pet 1:1–2, 20; Rev 4:11; Rev 13:8). This commonality between the preexistent Jewish messiah (or Torah) and Christ as preexistent is one of the current starting points for contemporary convergences found in Jewish-Christian dialogue.[25]

Medieval Era

Maimonides

Maimonides (1138–1204), following the third century Samuel, codified rabbinic political naturalism as a political restoration. "In the future, the Messianic king will arise and renew the Davidic dynasty, restoring it to its initial sovereignty. He will build the Temple and gather the dispersed of Israel."[26] Notice that the Jewish messianic vision is national, not individual. At the same time, the vision of restoration is universal. "In that era, there will be neither famine or war, envy or competition, for good will flow in abundance and all the delights will be freely available as dust. The occupation of the entire world will be solely to know God."[27]

Maimonides's messianic realism is further affirmed in his continuation of the passage where the exemplar of a messiah is the mortal second century military leader Bar Kosibah, who lead a rebellion against the Romans.

> One should not presume that the Messianic king must work miracles and wonders, bring about new phenomena in the

> world, resurrect the dead, or perform other similar deeds . . . Proof can be brought from the fact that Rabbi Akiva, one of the greater Sages of the Mishnah, was one of the supporters of King Bar Kozibah and would describe him as the Messianic king. He and all the Sages of his generation considered him to be the Messianic king until he was killed . . . If he did not succeed to this degree or was killed, he surely is not the redeemer promised by the Torah.[28]

Maimonides sums up the Jewish perspective as not expecting a new or changed world. "Do not presume that in the Messianic age any facet of the world's nature will change or there will be innovations in the work of creation. Rather, the world will continue according to its pattern."[29]

Maimonides boldly pushes aside the entire realm of messianic speculation:

> There are some Sages who say that Elijah's coming will precede the coming of the Messiah. All these and similar matters cannot be definitely known by man until they occur for these matters are undefined in the prophets' words and even the wise men have no established tradition regarding these matters except their own interpretation of the verses . . . neither the order of the occurrence of these events or their precise detail are among the fundamental principles of the faith.

The baseline Jewish rationalist position is encapsulated by Maimonides is realistic, political, natural, and generally wary toward messianic thinking.

Nahmanides

The theological divide between Judaism and Christianity was sharpened by Nahmanides (Rabbi Moshe ben Nahman, 1194–1270) in his public dispute with Friar Pablo in Barcelona in 1263. Jewish-Christian intellectual relations during the Middle Ages were often quite bitter, taking the form of polemical disputations about whether the Messiah had come presented together with acrimonious denunciations of Judaism. In this disputation, Nahmanides boldly states that the messianic concept is not a pillar of Judaism because Judaism is not bothered by the idea of an Original Sin that only a supernatural savior could redeem. The coming of the messiah for Nahmanides is akin to a general hope for a better future. He writes: "The Messiah is not fundamental to our religion." In this disputation, Nahmanides may be exaggerating the lack of the messianic concern in Judaism, but his text has shaped Jewish thought, and his basic intuitions are correct. Adding theological hyperbole with a realistic sociology, he declares that the messiah is no different from any other monarch. The King James of Aragon is "worth more to me than the Messiah! You are a king, and he is a king . . . for the Messiah is only a king of flesh and blood like you."[30] Nahmanides's major point is to declare the messiah as in no way divine or bringing salvation. The question of the Messiah had to be a central focus of discussion because the Messiah, or Christ, was important to Christians, not because he was so important to Jews. When Jews explain their religion to non-Christian there were other far more important matters to explain first, such as the covenant on Mount Sinai or Mosaic prophecy.

In addition, Nahmanides told King James that, for a Jew, life in the Exile might have more meaning than life under the Messiah. Nahmanides was not indulging in posturing, but spelling out the saying of the Mishnah, "Better is one hour of repentance and good works in this world than the whole life of the world to come" (M. Avot., 3: 17). In other words, there was more moral excellence in struggling toward a better world than in anticipating an eschatological messianic age. Jospeh Albo, an important fifteenth-century Jewish theologian, even explicitly declared, "the belief in the coming of the Messiah is not a fundamental principle, denial of which would nullify the entire Torah."[31]

Nahmanides was repeatedly asked in different ways if the messiah was both entirely human and truly divine. To which he answered each time, that the messiah is human, a human leader, nothing to do with a hypostatic union or an incarnation into flesh.[32] In this, he is continuing the Jewish philosophic tradition's categorical rejection of God as becoming corporeal.[33]

At the same time as presenting a realistic messianism, Nahmanides, in his biblical commentaries, envisioned the messianic era as a utopian, transformed reality with a change of nature where the leopard will indeed lie with the lamb. A messianic era where all Jews would dwell in the Holy Land in holiness and purity with an ideal paradise of material blessing and spiritual bounty. This era will be a restoration of the Jews from physical exile in the diaspora, a destruction of their enemies, and a return from the religious exile of sin and folly which caused the loss of the original harmony with God.[34] Unlike the Judaism of late antiquity, most of the modern Jewish tradition follows the naturalism of Maimonides and the utopian vision of Nahmanides, or defines the messianic age as social progress.

The Dialectic Theology of Karl Barth and Emil Brunner

To turn to modern theology, Karl Barth focuses on the revelation of God as Christ, the Messiah, as the sole locus of transcendence. Barth's theology of divine revelation eliminates all expectations for the redemption of history or political redeemer, redemption is understood as redemption from history through faith in Christ. For Barth, the meaning of redemption lies in the complete reconfiguration of life through a confrontation with the eternal Word in an eternal now.[35] Barth speaks of the *Parousia*, the second coming, as merely a revelation of what Christ already is. Another dialectic theologian, Emil Brunner (1889–1966) stresses that the messiah has no earthly or historic element. For Brunner, when Christ reveals himself, he is no longer seen as a historical personality, but as the eternal Son of God. Brunner insists that the visible history of the life of Jesus is not to be understood as composing that event. The decisive element in that event is the eternal Word.[36] Here, in the positions of Barth and Brunner, we have a version of the classic position in which Jewish and Christian views of the messiah have no overlap or commonality.

Jürgen Moltmann

After the carnage of World War II and the Holocaust, Jürgen Moltmann acknowledged that we live in a broken, unredeemed world in which any conception of the messianic age needs to accept that our actual world still needs, desperately needs, redemption. This admission, that we are living in an unredeemed world, places his approach within the realm of a Jewish theological understanding. For Moltmann, the message of Christianity is to offer us Christ's redemptive hope in this broken world. The Christian theological axiom that Christ already came means that salvation is already present on some level in our seemingly unredeemed world, giving us hope to redeem the world.

In his hope for a better future, Moltmann was influenced by the secular German-Jewish thinker Ernst Bloch who formulated a Marxist theology of hope, a secularized Jewish messianism. Bloch's philosophy of utopia presents certain inalienable, not-yet-conscious, and not-yet-realized potentialities of the human self, which can provide an alternative to the alienated, reified existence of modern life. For Moltmann, these inalienable and not-yet-discovered potentialities of human existence are not ameliorated through human action but through the cross offering the Christian messianic hope for a utopian future. Moltmann thinks we live in an unredeemed world, yet there is already redemption available as a human potential of messianic hope.[37]

Moltmann recognized the continuing relevance of Jewish messianic expectations for a political realist expectation for a better future, which led him to the rejoining of the separated horizons of realistic eschatological hope and Christological Trinitarian faith. For Moltmann, Christology was unfortunately cut off from its original messianic base and became the domain of metaphysical speculations about the ontological identity of the incarnate God. Christ is usually presented as the second person the Trinity who offered redemption from sin, but that formulation completely ignores the original biblical Jewish messianic meaning of living in a redeemed world.

Moltmann's own definition of the messianic is as the hope for a future political liberation within the present time of political oppression through the presence of an alternative future, the presence of the kingdom of God in the time of history, that the oppressed can have a realistic hope for their coming liberation.[38] God comes from the future, the sphere of redemption, and is anticipatingly present as the future of every moment within time. This latent possibility for Moltmann is the messianic potentiality of each moment. The messianic dimension of the Christian faith is a constant reminder of the incompleteness of the present and of the necessity of hope for the future.[39]

In Moltmann' s opinion, the messianic hope that Judaism and Christianity share is stronger than the obvious differences in the particular characteristics of this hope. For him, the greatest difference between the Jewish and Christian traditions lies in their different evaluations of the identity of Jesus. Christianity identifies Jesus as the Messiah, predicated on certain Second Temple era Jewish messianic expectations of a heavenly figure from Daniel and Enoch. But according to Moltmann, Christianity forfeited this connection to the political aspects of Jewish messianic thinking through elevating the Son within the Trinity to such metaphysical heights that he has no longer any connection to Jesus who preached of the messianic kingdom. For Moltmann, the original "... hope for the messiah links Christians with Jews, and this link is stronger than the division."[40] For him, "Christian Christology is a particular form of Israel's hope for the messiah."[41] He advocates the retrieval of the Jewish messianic base of Christian theology through dialogue with contemporary Jewish messianic thought in order to create a common hope for the kingdom of God, that Judaism and Christianity share. Jewish messianic thinking should inform contemporary Christian theology to be aware of the acutely incomplete nature of present reality, including the harshness of suffering in the world.

As a contrast, Moltmann thinks that because Christianity assumes that Christ fulfilled the messianic expectations of Israel in an absolute sense through the triumph over Sin, the Christian Church dispensed with its initial messianic expectations for a better world, and instead defined itself as faith and doctrine.[42] An incarnate messiah of salvation over original sin bringing divine kingship took precedent over redeeming the world as expected in Jewish messianism. Christian theology has overstressed the Christology, which is cut away from eschatology.

Paradox of Crucifixion and Resurrection

The suffering of the world is removed through the suffering of Christ. Through the messianic sufferings of Jesus and his vicarious death for all things, the world of transience is opened up to the horizon of the future of the new creation. "In the sufferings of Christ the end-time sufferings of the whole world are anticipated and vicariously experienced."[43] Moltmann's messianic Christology contains a paradox, in that, suffering is removed from the world though suffering, Christ's redemptive suffering removes human suffering, a messianic era of a new creation of human life without suffering can only come through a suffering messiah. The paradoxical messiah brings redemption through his own suffering, which anticipates the end of the time of the world that belongs to the new creation.[44] However, through the suffering of the world, people also participate in the suffering of the Messiah, through "the fellowship of suffering."[45] The messianic suffering of the Son becomes comprehensible only through the kenosis—the self emptying—of the Spirit. Though the condescendence of the Spirit in kenosis, Jesus becomes increasingly aware of his messianic identity and could thereby endure his total abandonment by the Father. The presence of the Spirit within the suffering and death of the Son is the presence of new life, the qualitatively new life of the resurrection.

The messianic is the presence of the eschatological future, the kingdom of God, within historical time. "It is already the presence of the future."[46] The eschatological future has become the power that determines the present. By means of hope we can already live in the light of the "new era" in the circumstances of the "old" one. This hope is given the mediating name of "messianic," a mediating category between the life of unfulfillment and the life of fulfillment.[47] There is a confronting of horizons in which the future redeemed kingdom without suffering and the unredeemed suffering of creation meet in the present through hope for the future.[48] Remembering the suffering of the Messiah is the key to understanding the specifically Christian concept of time, in which the time of the present is a time imbued with messianic expectations. Messianic time interrupts the flow of historical time and represents the expectation of a final and conclusive overcoming of the time of history.[49]

Sabbath

Traditionally, the Church Fathers sharply differentiated the earthly Jewish Sabbath from the Lord's Day on Sunday. Moltmann, in contrast, having absorbed the thought of Abraham Joshua Heschel who wrote an entire book on the Sabbath as messianic time, as well as having read other Jewish thinkers on the Jewish concept of the Sabbath, considers the clearest manifestation of messianic time is the time of the Sabbath which is referred to as "messianic intermezzo." The messianic time of the Sabbath anticipates the end and final redemption of history.[50]

For Moltmann, this Jewish expectation of universal redemption gets translated into Trinitarian pneumatology in that redemption becomes the ever-clearer experience of life made possible by the Holy Spirit. Moltmann turns to the Jewish concept of the *Shekhinah* to recover the messianic dimension of Christian Holy Spirit, the same way he turned to the *Shekhinah* to explain the Trinity. He sees the function of the *Shekhinah* as God's presence on earth as functionally similar to the Holy Spirit for several reasons. First, the *Shekhinah* points to the presence of God among the people as a specifically personal presence. Second, the *Shekhinah* points to a self-distinction within God in that the *Shekhinah* is the presence of God who in his sovereignty decides to be present in the history of the suffering of his people.[51] For Moltmann, Israel experiences the presence of God through the *Shekhinah* who suffers with them offering messianic hope for Israel's final deliverance. The messianic hope and the suffering presence of God are dialectically interrelated. In a similar manner, there is a rabbinic story that the Messiah is sitting at the gates of Rome among the poor, the sick, and wretched.

Like them, he changes the bindings of his wounds, but does so one wound at a time, in order to be ready to arrive at a moment's notice."[52]

According to Moltmann, in Judaism the revelation of God finds its meaning within God's promissory history with the people of Israel. For Moltmann, if there is no possibility for experiencing God in human history, then Christian theology abrogates its continuity with the faith of the people of Israel. He wants to close the gap. For him, when eschatology is defined in terms of the absolute eternity of God as the Trinity—as it is for Barth—then the meaning of history is marginalized, separating Christian eschatology from the biblical messianic expectations.[53]

This is where we return to the insights into the Trinity in chapter 1. The *Shekhinah* within Judaism is the lowest element of the divine hierarchy and signifies the exile from the infinite God. The *Shekhinah* is an immanent presence as a fellow refugee in the diasporic wanderings of the Jewish people, a keepsake of the divine in exile. There are passages in the Zoharic corpus where the *Shekhinah* is captive in the demonic realm, herself needing redemption.[54] Jews do not associate the *Shekhinah* with the second person of the Trinity as the messiah. Jews do not say, God as the Shekinah's incarnate presence means we have the messiah, rather a Jewish locution presents her redemption from a fallen state as signifying the redeemed world. The Jewish Friday night Sabbath liturgy of *Lekha Dodi* has this vision of her rising from the dust signifying the redemption of the Sabbath and the ultimate messianic redemption. This dovetails, however, with Moltmann's formulation that without the messianic presence of the *Shekhinah*, as the presence of God among the afflicted people in exile, there would be no messianic mission.[55]

Messianism and Covenant

Messianism, for Moltmann, gives the believer a horizon of expectation within the eschatological new creation. This encourages Christians to practice what Moltmann calls "creative discipleship," a life that transforms the present based on anticipation of the future of God's kingdom.

Material and economic poverty manifests itself in inequalities, deprivation, violence, sickness and ill-health, malnutrition, hunger, and dying. Messianic hope creates a vision for redeeming the world from its poverties. Christian hope takes seriously the possibilities of a new life removing these depravations based on reality of the resurrection of Christ. This new reality is the kingdom of God come to us from the future and making claims upon us now. In Moltmann's view, this vision for the future finds commonality with Judaism in working to create a potential kingdom of God on earth as found in the Jewish liturgy "to found the world on the kingdom of God," thereby creating a convergence of optimism and the potential to transform society. For Moltmann, transforming society brings the fulfilment of the whole history of Christ and his promises.[56] Moltmann finds that the rationale of the incarnation is not in sin, but in perfecting creation to create a kingdom of God here on earth. As we discussed in chapter 2 on original sin, if hope is redemptive then the sin that was, and remains present, is hopelessness, which manifests as sloth, laziness, and giving up.

At this point, Christian thought is not that far from Judaism, we find a similar view articulated by former Chief Rabbi Lord Jonathan Sacks when he describes how we are able to live in the ideal messianic world on the Shabbat. "On Shabbat we engage in a full-dress rehearsal for the Messianic Age when no one will exercise power, political or economic, over anyone else." Similarly, the sabbatical year and the Jubilee year, the seventh and fiftieth years are ideally messianic, "by cancelling debts, releasing slaves, leaving the produce of the land to be enjoyed by everyone equally, and restoring ancestral property to its original owners, we inhabit a world in which the inequities of the market economy have been redressed and, for a year, sometimes two, we suspend the world of competition and live in a world of co-operation and the fellowship of equals."[57] Furthermore, Sacks credits Judaism with the invention of hope as given in the promise of the Jewish covenant.[58] At this point, Sacks and Moltmann can discuss the ideal messianic world and be largely in agreement.

Comparison

After Moltmann, Jews and Christians agree that we are striving for an ideal messianic age where the deprivations of our world will change for the good. Both religions seek to usher in a redeemed world.

We still differ, however, on the Christian theological points of needing a specific person, a paradoxical messiah who is crucified and resurrected. Christians, draw their faith and strength for the messianic change from a personified suffering messiah and an act of remembrance to have fellowship with this messiah in the person of Christ Jesus. We can share theological discussions of the role of memory in bringing redemption or the role of the Sabbath as a foreshadow of the messianic age. But we still diverge on Jesus as the Messiah, and how much the believer in the messianic age is currently already living a new covenant. Jews generally do not seek a new covenant undoing of the old covenant, nor a new temporality undoing the old existence, rather for Jews renewal is a renewing of our days.[59]

The theologian, David Tracy, offers a summary of the changes to Christianity after Moltmann in which the messianic age is no longer spiritualized. "While earlier generations of Christian thinkers tended to stress only the "already here" aspects of the New Testament kerygma, more recent scholarship has sought to reintegrate the eschatological "not yet" into their vision." Therefore, "Christology can and should resist the Christian temptation to so spiritualize the notion of Messiah as to wrench it from real history . . . The always/already/not yet structure of belief pervading Israel's covenant with God and Israel's expectancy of Messianic times remains the fundamental always/already/not yet structure of Christian belief as well. . . ."[60]

Cardinal Ratzinger, in a 2002 preface for the Pontifical Biblical Commission publication stated that "Jewish messianic expectation is not in vain" and therefore that at the end of time both Jews and Christians will recognize the "One who is to come," the eschatological messiah [PBC 2001, §21] and that according to Paul, "all Israel will be saved" (Rom 11:26). For Cardinal Kasper, the first Christians proclaimed Jesus as the eschatological bearer of salvation and fulfillment of Messianic expectations.[61] Kasper treats this common recognition as creating a unity, in that, "Jews and Christians look to the future: they give witness together—in the midst of the many dilemmas and instances of hopelessness in the world—to the hope for the perfect justice and the universal *shalom* that God alone will usher in at the end of time. Thus, they contribute to build a just and humanitarian world in which such a terrible event as the Shoah cannot be repeated."

Tracy and Kasper draw the conclusion that the consistent Jewish "no" to Christian claims concerning Jesus's Messiahship is not necessarily wrong because the Jews do not see the expected messianic realism within history. The Jewish "no," to accepting Jesus, far from being a symptom of "blindness" or "unbelief" on their part, now stands for Christians as a God-given witness to the Church concerning the earthy kingdom of God needing to restore this world. For Moltmann and Kasper, since Jews and Christian together await the fulfillment of God's Reign, it is now possible to envision a sense in which Jew and Christian together can witness to that Reign. For Tracy, the former distinction between the person of the Messiah (whom Christians identify with Jesus as the Christ and Jews do not) and the Messianic Age (in which the biblical promises are made manifest for all humanity) is no longer a crucial one for the Jewish-Christian dialogue.

The traditional Jewish hope for a restored Temple, return to the land of Israel, and an ingathering of the exiles, however, is not part of the discussion for these Christian theologians. In contrast, these aspects are the center of the messianism of many Protestant groups.

Premillennial Dispensation

Millennialism is the concept that the current era has reached the period of the end of days in which there are immanent social changes and awaited utopian transformations. Many Christian forms of millenarianism envision that this change will occur, not when Christ returns, but premillennial, in our own era. In many cases, these visions rely heavily on prior Christian eschatological ideas from the Church Fathers and a millennium of apocryphal works about the end of days.[62]

In the wake of the Reformation, many seventeenth- and eighteenth-century Protestant groups took a renewed interest in the Hebrew Bible with its political understanding of messianic, looking forward to the prospect of Jesus's second coming as a messianic political event.[63] In the mid-seventeenth century, the English Revolution stirred the messianic imagination and gave rise to groups in England that expected the end time to occur imminently. A significant number of Protestant leaders expected the Jews to play an important role in the events of the end time. Jews remain heirs to the covenant between God and Abraham, and the object of biblical prophecies about a restored Davidic kingdom in the Land of Israel. In their eschatological scenarios, the return of the Jews to the Holy Land was one of the first steps in the advancement of the messianic timetable. English Christians adopted for themselves a missional and covenantal calling, which gave England a special mission to restore the Jews to Palestine. At the start of the nineteenth century, in the English-speaking world, restoration of Jews to the Holy Land came to be seen as something that would precede Jewish conversion rather than follow it, as had been the previous restorationist position. Signs of the messianic second coming of Christ including end time miracle are to occur before the actual messianic period due to a premillennial (before the end time) dispensation of end time miracles.[64]

C. I. Scofield (1845–1926) labored to spread the dispensationalist faith in America through publications and conferences. William Blackstone (1841–1935) developed this into a specific end time scenario of the imminent return of the chosen people to Palestine. The Jews will return to their ancient homeland "in unbelief," without accepting Jesus as their Savior, and will establish a political commonwealth there, an instrumental step in the advancement of the messianic timetable. The arrival of Jesus with the true Christians will end the antichrist's rule. Jesus will crush this satanic ruler and his armies and will establish the expected millennial kingdom. Those Jews who survive the turmoil and terror of the Great Tribulation will accept Jesus as their Savior. There will follow a peaceful period marked by the righteous rule of Christ on earth, with the Jews inhabiting David's ancient kingdom and Jerusalem serving as the capital of the entire world. Blackstone's theory is a cornerstone of American Christian Zionists, in which, the United States had a special role and mission in God's plans for humanity: that of a modern Cyrus, to help restore the Jews to Zion. He believed that God has looked favorably upon America on account of its moral superiority over other nations, and that America would be judged, among other things, according to the way it carried out its mission, thereby messianic belief about human history combines with American nationalism.[65]

The excitement of the 1967 Six-Day War fueled Christian premillennialist support for Israel as furthering the unfolding of the messianic age and the establishment of the kingdom of God on earth. The territorial gains of the war strengthened the premillennialists' conviction that Israel was created for a mission in history and was to play an important role in the developments that were to precede the arrival of the Messiah. For evangelical Christians the Israeli takeover of the territory on which the Temple could be rebuilt led to an interest in the specifics of Temple building, its interior plan, and its sacrificial works, as well as in the priestly garments and utensils. In the late 1970s and the 1980s, premillennialist Christians began cooperating with groups of nationalist and Orthodox Jews who were making plans to build the Temple. Similarly, Jewish activists and Israeli leaders have seen in the Christian premillennialist groups unexpected but welcome allies, whose motivation they did not fully comprehend.

In the evangelical Christian bestseller of the 1970s, *The Late Great Planet Earth*, the author, Hal Lindsey, like other premillennialist Christians, was strongly impressed by the Six-Day War and its immediate outcome and placed Israel at the center of the expected eschatological drama. Hal Lindsey also uses Ezekiel 36 and 37 to prove an end-time physical restoration of the Jews to Holy Land before the Great Tribulation. The "physical restoration" is accomplished by unbelieving Jews through their human effort. Great catastrophic events which are to happen to this nation during "the tribulation" are primarily designed to shock the people into believing in their true Messiah.[66]

For example, John Hagee (b. 1940), is the leader of the largest pro-Israel lobby group in the United States, Christians United for Israel (CUFI), who in the early twenty-first century sought to curb the evangelical conversionary mission to the Jews by claiming that Jesus never really meant to save the Jews. "The Jews did not reject Jesus as Messiah; it was Jesus who rejected the Jewish desire for him to be their Messiah," he wrote, seemingly Jews are to be saved through their own covenant with God. Hagee asserts that Jesus was the Messiah to the gentiles and not the Jews, so therefore the Jews did not reject him. Hagee half-jokingly compared the prime minister of Israel to the Messiah, pointing to convergences in messianic thinking.[67]

This emphasis on the new era of messianic signs, especially the Jews returning to the biblical lands, being shown before the actual advent of the messiah bears affinities to the ideas of First Ashkenazi chief rabbi of the return to Zion, Rabbi Abraham Isaac Kook and his spiritual heirs who consider the state of Israel as the dawn of the messianic age that would renew Judaism. After the Six-Day War in 1967, activist messianism, long suppressed by rabbinic Judaism, could reemerge as a powerful expression of Jewish peoplehood. His son, Rabbi Zvi Yehudah Kook was awakened by the Six-Day War and return to the biblical lands. He stressed the glories of war, messianic politics, and nullification of exile. For him, the very building of the life of the nation is a holy edifice; this entire national awakening is in its entirety an absolute divine manifestation. Simply by settling in the Land of Israel, working its soil, and developing its potential for habitation by larger numbers of Jews, the Zionist movement was carrying out the divine plan—a plan to redeem not only the Jewish people, through its restoration in its own land and the coming of the Messiah, but, through them, the gentile nations as well. This redemption will come as the dawn after a period of darkness, and in many small stages, harkening back to the apocalyptic midrashim mentioned earlier in this chapter. Rabbi Tzvi Yehuda went substantially beyond Rav Kook the elder by specifying the political and spiritual stages that the redemptive process would entail, the concrete steps of the twentieth century that had advanced redemption, and the final steps to advance toward its glorious conclusion in the restoration of the messianism Kingdom and the Temple. A Jewish form of premillennial dispensation.[68]

I must point out, however, that much of contemporary Jewish thought focuses on this worldly activity. Rabbi Joseph Soloveitchik (d. 1993) avoided messianism in that messianism is "a foreign branch in his garden" because in a life focused on Jewish law, eschatology does not play a significant role. They are part of the Jewish heritage, but to his way of thinking, these concepts do not have a concrete and practical meaning. There is no importance to the messianic idea from the perspective of his conceptual approach to Talmud study. The Jew dedicated to the keeping of Jewish law (*halakhah)* appeals to earthy reality through conscious categories. The messianic epoch is beyond his horizon because it is beyond this human period.[69]

In contrast, Emmanuel Lévinas does use the image of messianism, but as an ethical aim that is imposed on each person when he responds to the individual call as an ethical demand from the other person. Lévinas sees Messianism as a moral task that is presented to the person from the future that faces him in the other's face. Messianism is not redemption but an ethical response in this world. Lévinas's ideas on the moral self use the thought of the early twentieth century Jewish philosopher Hermann Cohen who explained the concept of messianism as an aspirational ideal that humanity is progressing toward a world of justice, peace, and charity.[70]

Conclusions

The messiah or messianic age can be many ideas, movements, persons, and even personal redemption. Even in the first century there was no one messianic idea among Jews or in Jewish texts. For the scholar Philip Alexander, theologians keep trying to squeeze different concepts of messiahs and messianism into a single rubric. There is no one definition of messianism, Jewish, Christian, or non-Jewish. There are a variety of expectations that are different in their vision with different scopes, different agents, and different scenarios. No religion has a specific form of messianism. Judaism, Christianity, and Islam each have many possible forms of messianism. Some messianism has a person as the messiah as agent or agent of change while other forms of messianism are about an era.[71] In Judaism, studying Torah is messianic, repentance is messianic, procreation is messianic, ecstatic prayer can be messianic, and the righteous can bring the messiah. The Messiah will answer difficult Talmudic questions, alleviate poverty, or everyone will have knowledge of God. Or as stated in many Jewish texts, the messiah is about the instant obliteration of the enemies of the Jewish people, which in many eras meant the Christians. The Jewish idea of the Messiah can vary from between ideal ruler, an era of ideal justice and peace without a personal messiah, or the political state of Israel in its ideal development. In many cases today, the Jewish messianic hopes are similar to those in American popular music in which "redemption" can be a release from slavery, oppression, jail, illness, psychological depression, or disconnection from God.[72]

Similar to the discussion of Jewish God language in chapter 1 on the Trinity, Judaism does not have a need to systematize or concretize its theological ideas. The forest of Jewish messianic ideas remains diverse, while Christianity needs its theology defined. The scholar of religions R. J. Z. Werblowsky aptly characterized Jewish messianism as a "coat of many colors" reflecting the ideal for a change to a happier, better or more perfect situation. Yet, as a result of the false messianic claims of Shabbatai Zvi any attempt at a meaningful enquiry into Jewish messianism is often treated with suspicion.[73]

On the other hand, liturgically, a traditional Jew who affirms daily "I believe with perfect faith in the advent of the messiah, and though he may tarry, I will await his arrival every day" has little in common with the Nicene Creed about Jesus as the second person of the Trinity who "for us men and for our salvation He came down from heaven." There remains in many cases a deep existential and conceptual chasm between the religions despite an overlap of messianic and millenarian language. A Jewish eschatological vision is not the same concept of an incarnate savior of humanity from sin, a human messiah is not the same as a divine messiah. One should not minimize the chasm to a witty, but incorrect, quip that both religions agree on the messiah but only differ whether the messiah will arrive a first or a second time.[74] Jews do not encounter the messiah as a specific divine person offering salvation. Rather, in traditional Judaism, there are prayers concerning "next year in Jerusalem" for an ingathering from the exile, a restored glory of the people, and a rebuilt Temple, or in more modern forms of Judaism, prayers for a redemption of society through human ethical actions.

Moltmann shared a gradualism of perfecting the world socially and economically in a way that most Jews would recognize, and contemporary Christian Zionists share a vision with religious Zionists of restoring the settlement to the land of Israel in order to bring the messiah.[75] However, for any form of Christianity, even when converging with Judaism, we must return to discuss the person of Jesus Christ as the agent bringing about the new era. Moltmann and Christian Zionists converge with Jewish conceptions, but the agency of Jesus remains the divide. For Christians, the messiah is tied to a specific messiah, while for Jews, messianism is a longed-for redemption without being limited to a specific agent, scope, or time frame.

CHAPTER SIX

Covenant

IN MEDIEVAL CHRISTIAN art, Judaism is often depicted as a dejected blinded woman, a personified broken covenant, that has been superseded by the new covenant of Christianity. Basic to traditional Christian theology is that Christianity is the true Israel replacing the old, antiquated covenant with Israel. Trude Weiss Rosmarin encapsulates the Jewish sense of this irreconcilable difference. "The rights and privileges of the Jew under the Old Covenant have been transferred to the Gentile Christians the confessors of Christianity," who are now the chosen true people of the divine covenant. In contrast, Rosmarin states that, "Judaism maintains that the "Covenant with the fathers" as "the true Israel of God" are those, and those alone, who confess the Unity of God as taught by the Torah, the sacred and eternally valid Divine teaching and message to Israel and mankind."[1]

This is generally no longer true; no longer are the Jews the broken staff superseded by Christianity. After Vatican II's *Nostra Aetate: Declaration on the Jews*, as well as the various similar Protestant statements made afterward, rather, the Jewish covenant is recognized as the source and sustenance for Christianity.

> [the] Church, remembers the bond that spiritually ties the people of the New Covenant to Abraham's stock . . . Thus the Church of Christ acknowledges that, according to God's saving design, the beginnings of her faith and her election are found already among the Patriarchs, Moses and the prophets . . . The Church, therefore, cannot forget that she received the revelation of the Old Testament through the people with whom God

> in His inexpressible mercy concluded the Ancient Covenant. Nor can she forget that she draws sustenance from the root of that well-cultivated olive tree onto which have been grafted the wild shoots, the Gentiles.[2]

Nostra Aetate states that there is a bond that ties the people of the "New Covenant" (Christians) to "Abraham's Stock" (Jews) based on Romans 9–11. The document acknowledges that Israel received the revelation first, that Jews remain dear to God, and that Christianity grew out of Judaism. In addition, *Nostra Aetate* rejects the deicide charges and decries all displays of antisemitism made at any time by anyone. Prior to this document, Jews were generally seen as blinded, the devil, and false; and that once the Jews have served their purpose then God has forgotten them. Jesus had nothing in common with his birth religion, according to this now-outdated view.

But the document does not state that the covenant that God made with his people of Israel endures over time and is never invalidated. Three decades later, Pope John Paul II acknowledged Judaism as a living religion with an eternal covenant, recognized the Holocaust, and acknowledged the state of Israel. Further, the era of Pope Benedict XVI and Cardinal Kasper has moved the religions closer in Catholic thought by teaching that Jews and Catholics share one common Abrahamic covenant based on God's covenant with Abraham in Genesis (chapters 15, 17), that the rabbinic tradition is a valid alternate reading of the Bible, and that Jews are saved.

The statement that Judaism has an ongoing covenant was first made for the Catholic Church with full clarity by Pope John Paul II when he said during a meeting with Jewish representatives in Mainz on November 17, 1980 that the old covenant had never been revoked by God: "The first dimension of this dialogue, that is, the meeting between the people of God of the Old Covenant, never revoked by God . . . and that of the New Covenant, is at the same time a dialogue within our Church, that is to say, between the first and the second part of her Bible" (No. 3).[3] The same conviction is stated also in the Catechism of the Catholic Church in 1993: "The Old Covenant has never been revoked" (121).

Speaking at the synagogue of Rome on April 13, 1986, Pope John Paul II made the point: "The Jewish religion is not 'extrinsic' to us, but in a certain way is 'intrinsic' to our own religion. With Judaism, therefore, we have a relationship which we do not have with any other religion. You are our dearly beloved brothers, and, in a certain way, it could be said that you are our elder brothers." In continuity with Vatican II, John Paul II saw the two covenants as intrinsically related. The Old is a preview and promise of the New; the New is the unveiling and fulfillment of the Old. "The New Covenant," he declared, "serves to fulfill all that is rooted in the vocation of Abraham, in God's covenant with Israel at Sinai, and in the whole rich heritage of the inspired Prophets who, hundreds of years before that fulfillment, pointed in the Sacred Scriptures to the One whom God would send in the 'fullness of time.'"

Similarly, many Protestant denominations in subsequent years issued their own statements. The Presbyterian Church (USA) declared in 1987: "The church has not 'replaced' the Jewish people . . . Hence, when speaking with Jews about matters of faith, we must always acknowledge that Jews are already in a covenantal relationship with God." Notably, there were similar statements by Lutheran, Disciples of Christ, World Council of Churches, Episcopalians, and Alliance of Baptists denominations. Much of the Jewish-Christian encounter for several decades focused on these statements.[4]

The current dividing line on covenant is now focused on issues of supersessionalism, which is the Christian theological doctrine that the Christian Church has superseded the nation of Israel.

Covenant

The concept of covenant as a solemn agreement has been of enormous importance in the Hebrew Bible. In the ancient world, a covenant is a promise that is sanctioned by an oath. This promise in turn is accompanied by an appeal to a deity to watch over the behavior of the one who has sworn, and to punish any violation of the covenant by bringing into action the curses stipulated or implied in the swearing of the oath.[5] An exemplary of an ancient covenant from the late Bronze Age (c. 1500 BCE) are the Hittite sources showing the highly developed treaty form with the following structure: preamble, historical prologue, stipulations, provisions for deposit and public reading, witnesses, and curses and blessings formulas.

Scholars noted an astounding similarity between the Hittite treaty structure and the biblical traditions of the Sinai covenant. The giving of the commandments at Mount Sinai by the God of the Israelites yields all the important elements of the Hittite treaty form but in succinct form. God is identified as the covenant giver, and the historical prologue is the announcement that this God was the one who delivered the assembled group from bondage in Egypt (in the thirteenth century BCE). The Sinai covenant marked the kingdom of God; the Holy People as the community of God; and above all, the ethical and legal norms as the essence of divine command. Notable is that the contract was made with God himself.[6]

On Mount Sinai, the giving of the Law, Israel pledged itself to keep His covenant (Exod 19:8). The content of the covenant mainly concerns observance of the commandments and the bond to the land of Canaan. In the Jewish reading of the Bible, covenant became synonymous in Judaism with the Law (Isa 56:6 *et seq.*; Ps 25:10, 14; 1.16; 1 Kings 11:11), later defined as adherence to the Oral Law. The Talmud explicitly states in several places that the Sinai covenant was for the sake of the Oral Law. In fact, rabbinic texts portray Abraham as already fulfilling the Oral Law, keeping not just the law of Moses but as observing all the ordinances of the rabbinic literature as presented in the midrash and Talmud, and as engaged in the study of the Oral Torah.

In Deuteronomy, considered as the "second giving of the Law" the Israelites held a repeat covenant ceremony in the plain of Moab (northeast of the Dead Sea), before entering the Holy Land after having spent forty years in the desert. The covenant at Sinai rested on the ideal of God's Presence dwelling amongst the Jewish people: if the covenant is upheld, God will dwell in the midst of the camp. The covenant of Moab is a worldly focus on the individual and the nation. The covenantal foundation of "that it will be good for you"—personally and nationally—to live a good life before God. Deuteronomy is packed with laws for the entire people of Israel understood as cresting a virtuous society in the land they will inherit, the land of Canaan.

In the fifth century BCE, the time of the prophets Ezra and Nehemiah, another covenant was made that establishes as binding law the complex of traditions that had been preserved and recorded as the "law of God, which was given by Moses, the servant of God" (Neh 10:29) as an enactment by the authorities and representatives of the community. The Sinai covenant had become permanently identified with the accumulation of legal-ritual traditions of the Oral Law, and the community was identified as the ethnic group of those who were heirs of the promise to Abraham in direct lineal descent. The Jewish understanding of Abraham's covenant focuses on his physical descendants as a tribe, family or ethnos, as "everlasting, . . . to be God to you and to your offspring to come" (Gen 17:8). The covenant includes the promise of the Land of Canaan as an everlasting holding. In addition, there is a physical symbol of the covenant, that is, the circumcision of all males on the eighth day after birth.

The rabbinic idea of covenant affirms the idea of a binding relationship between God and a particular chosen people to keep the commandments with a daily affirmation of God's kingship through liturgical recitation of the *shema* and *amidah*. This covenant includes the merit of the patriarchs as the direct ancestors of Israel, which assures Israel that they will be forgiven for their sins. A corollary of this Jewish covenant with God, is that God is also universally available to all other people of the world, without a special covenant or revelation.[7]

In the Jewish understanding, the covenants discussed in the prophets are linked to circumcision, the Sabbath, and the study of the Oral Law. Even when Jeremiah spoke of "the new covenant," which the Lord "will make with the house of Israel and the house of Judah" (Jer 31: 31), Jewish explanation generally understands the verse as fulfilling the law based on the next passage where Jeremiah explains his words by saying that "I will put my law in their inward parts, and write it in their hearts" (Jer 31:33; 33:40). There is no concept of a new mode of religiosity such as shifting from ritual and Temple to inward faith; the Mosaic covenant is eternal. In Jewish readings of this covenant, no matter how much Jews stray from God, He never divorces his people but rather continues to re-offer himself.[8]

Jews are the followers of the Oral Law, a Jewish concept of a dual Torah in that the Torah was revealed to Moses at Mount Sinai in two ways, one written and the other transmitted by oral tradition through the prophets and the sages. The Oral Torah is the tradition collected in the many rabbinic writings known as the *Mishnah*, the *Gemara*, and the midrash. The Jewish covenant is known through the rabbinic reading of the Hebrew Bible, the Oral Law, as taught by the scribal Jews who identified their teachings with the binding covenant made through Moses at Mount Sinai.

E. P. Sanders, (1937–2022) the Protestant New Testament scholar, characterized the rabbinic view as "covenantal nomism." First century Judaism was not legalism as Christians claimed, rather a religion of righteousness from being part of God's covenant people. Sanders does point out that the Jewish covenant was initially God's grace of electing the people, but then staying in God's covenant requires obeying the stipulations of the commandments that come with election, which includes the grace of atonement for inevitable sin.[9] There is no need, at any point for Jews to mention covenant, grace, or salvation. *Mitzvot*, the commandments, are ways of expressing an eternal divine wisdom in the concrete everyday life of the community.

Christianity

The traditional Christian understanding of covenant relates to a salvation history of successive biblical covenants taken to be the chief structural framework for salvation history from Adam to Christ.[10] The Abrahamic covenant is the beginnings of the formal revelation of the covenant of grace, of God's decision to reveal himself to humanity, specifically saving people by offering himself as an act of grace, a gift of divine favor and clemency. The promise to Abraham culminates in the full revelation in Jesus Christ. God's promise that Abraham is going to be a great nation is not limited to his direct descendants. Abraham was declared righteous by faith, (Gal 3:6–9) which is the same way God still responds to anyone who puts their faith in him with his offer of grace.

The covenant in Christian understanding assumes there are two types of covenants, everlasting and conditional. The promise to Abraham and the promise to David are everlasting gratuitous unilateral gifts as well as unconditional and irrevocable. Paul in Romans regards the covenant-law of Sinai as provisional and insufficient, conditional and based on merit. In his letter to the Hebrews, he implied that the prior covenant or covenants were not eternal or definitive, but temporary or preparatory in which the "first covenant" is now "abrogated to make way for the sacrifice and priesthood of Christ." This is the core issue or difference between the religions, between the older Mosaic covenant of Judaism given at Mount Sinai, and the concept of a new covenant in Christianity, contrasting with Judaism.[11] Current scholarship points out that Paul remained Jewish, and his theology was not opposed to Judaism but was another variant in the possibilities of first century Judaism, however the Pauline line of thinking created the division.[12]

The prophet Jeremiah (late seventh century BCE) had predicted a "new covenant" written upon the heart (Jer 31:31). This became the division by Christians of the Bible into the Old and New Testaments, as the old and new covenants, the terms covenant and testament are translations of the same word, which in turn, created two corpuses of books, one for the old covenant and one for the new. The New Testament authors consider Jeremiah as a prediction of the new dispensation, or covenant, that would come about with Christ and the Church (Heb 8:8–13, 10:16; see also 2 Cor 3:3). The New Testament indicates that the Old Law, or the old covenant, has come to an end and been replaced. Paul in 2 Corinthians draws a contrast between the old covenant, carved on stone, which has lost its previous splendor, and the new covenant, written on human hearts by the Spirit, which is permanent and shines brightly as part of a new eschatological age.[13]

The Letter to the Hebrews speaks of "the blood of the eternal covenant" by which Jesus equips the sheep to do God's will. The new covenant included the identification of the bread and the wine of the Last Supper with the body and blood of Christ. The subsequent death of the victim in his blood entails the symbolic death—the ultimate curse for breach of covenant—of all those who were thus identified with the victim and are thereby saved by his body and blood. In the Roman canon of the Mass, the covenant established by the shedding of Christ's blood is described as "new and eternal."[14]

The death of Jesus thus becomes the historical prologue of the covenant leading up to the covenant enactment as an oath to believe in Christ. The oath or the sacramentum, to use the Latin term of the early church, meant primarily the soldier's oath of loyalty to the emperor. The Christian covenant brought about a relationship of the believer to Christ whose unseen glory was identified with that of God himself, whose lordship was operational in history, and whose community of believers was identified with the kingdom of God. The curse was no longer tied to violation of the Sinai covenant but rather to rejection of God's rule in Christ. The community in turn was no longer the lineal descent group of Abraham but the assembly (*ekklēsia*) of those who had through the covenant accepted a relationship to the dominion of Christ.

Already in the early Christian text Epistle of Barnabas (c. 70–135), the Tables of the Law given by Moses are considered as having been broken by him, the testament was to be received anew from the hands of Jesus (Barn. 14); and the Sabbath of Creation points to the millennium after six thousand years, when all life shall have been sanctified by the Messianic advent, whereas the older Jewish Sabbath and holidays have been declared to be unacceptable. Judaism has been superseded by Christianity and even the Bible and their law no longer belongs to them.[15] This trend of transferring everything Jewish to Christianity continued in ideology and polemics for the next centuries.

In the second century CE, Marcion (c. 85–c. 160) of Asia Minor taught that the Old Testament was the work of a strict creator God of justice and wrath, in contrast to Jesus who was a new revelation of a different God of pure love and grace. Any attempt to harmonize Jewish biblical traditions with Christian ones was impossible. They saw no continuity with the Hebrew Bible or any form of Judaism. Christ is neither Jewish nor a Jewish messiah, and Christianity is a different religion than Judaism. Marcion's teachings were strongly condemned by the other Church Fathers including Justin Martyr, Irenaeus, and Tertullian. The other Church Fathers saw the New Testament as the fulfillment of the Hebrew Bible.

Augustine taught that the old covenant has been superseded with the arrival of the new covenant. The law can only give death and needs to be abandoned after Christ; the law is no longer a sign of the covenant. For him, to keep the old covenant law negates the new covenant. Augustine rejects Marcion's approach acknowledging the Jewish covenant, but thinks the old covenant is no longer binding as law, rather as typology for Christ, foreshadowing the new covenant. Christian discussions until the present read the old covenant through Augustine Christological typology. As one scholar notes: "Christian anti-Judaism today is expressed mainly in depreciating law theologically. This kind of Christian anti-Judaism does not need to refer to Jews or Judaism explicitly and thus is especially problematic since it is typically more subtle."[16]

During the Reformation in the sixteenth century, Reformed theology, particularly that of John Calvin (1509–1564) and the later Puritans of the seventeenth century, gave the concept further elaboration. Reformed (Presbyterian) theology often is called "covenant theology" since Calvin's writings stressed a biblical fact of God's covenant of which there were a successive sequence of them—Adamic, Noahite, Abrahamic, Mosaic, Davidic, and new. God's initiative is in making a series of covenantal promises, as being that which undergirds all the biblical narrative, and hence all of creation itself. God's covenant initiative cannot be stymied; God's promise will not be broken. The first covenant is the covenant of works, made with Adam, and continued in the other Old Testament figures, is binding on all of humanity. The other covenant is the covenant of grace, made only with Christ and his church.[17]

It is important to note that the language of covenant is used differently by different religions. For Catholics, a covenant is God's saving gift of revelation, an opening of the accessibility of God to humanity, for Calvinists a covenant is God's plan for this world at a given time, and for rabbinic Judaism, a covenant is the Sinai event and the gifts of Sabbath, Torah, and circumcision. The term covenant is also used in twentieth-century American thought in a broader manner to refer to an existential commitment to a divine mandated religious structure, and structure of one's religious life as a relationship with God and God's word. This has led to a confusion of the twentieth-century definition of covenant as existential decision to affirm a covenant, with the more technical meanings of Jews, Catholics, and Protestants.[18]

Modernity

Nineteenth-century European thinkers, generally, returned to a Marcion position seeing no continuity between the Hebrew Bible and the New Testament. The historian of Christianity Adolf von Harnack (1851–1930) wanted to get rid of the entire old covenant; he agrees with Marcion that the God of Jesus and the God of the old covenant cannot be the same. Judaism was portrayed as a tribal religion, entirely particular without any value to the universalism of Christianity. In this scheme, Judaism has been entirely superseded and was moribund with the coming of Christianity. According to the philosopher Immanuel Kant, Judaism does not count as a religion, but only as a past theocratic cultural formation. The only pure moral religion is Christianity, which owes nothing to Judaism. Fredrich Schleiermacher viewed Judaism as entirely separate and radically different from Christianity, without any continuity. He saw a need to separate Christianity as the spirit that rejects the superstitious mummified Jewish law.[19]

The modern theologians of the twentieth century accomplished a return to a continuity with Judaism. Karl Barth and Hans Urs von Balthasar reclaim the Hebrew Bible. Neither Barth nor Balthasar affirm a covenant theory with Judaism, yet both are credited by later authors as reclaiming Judaism from the nineteenth-century rejection.

Barth

Karl Barth offers the starting point of twentieth-century Christian thinkers who reclaimed the Old Testament as central to the Christian message. Barth states that there is one single divine covenant given from creation that broke into two dispensations, those who accepted the purpose of creation in the incarnation of Christ and those that stuck to the Mosaic law. Jesus Christ was already the God of the Sinai covenant and the Mosaic law itself contains and reflects God's grace. Jews remain elected by God and are a silent witness to the biblical world of Jesus. Barth denies that Christ was the start of a new religion or that the Jews are punished for their rejection. Barth reverses the typical chronology by considering the God of creation as religion of Christ, which had a one-time bound form in the Mosaic law. In his formulation, the gentiles offered the covenant are not joining believing Jews by entering the church, rather Jews who follow Sinai are joining the gentile eternal covenant.

With regard to the Jewish people, Barth states that "it is incontestable that this people as such is the holy people of God: the people with whom God . . . has made his own, and has not ceased to make His own, and will not cease to make His own." Israel's sin is not capable of dissolving its covenant with God, but rather exists within God's indelible election of and commitment to the Jewish people.[20] And there is no active mission to the Jews because they do not need to be saved from idolatry.[21] For Barth, however, the Old Testament law is fulfilled in Christ and only through Christ. Israel's persistence in keeping the law remains a mark of sinfulness. Barth even refers to the Synagogue as "the disobedient, idolatrous Israel of every age," and "with no part now in the fulfilment of the promise given."[22] For Barth,[23] the Synagogue is a "counterfeit Israel".[24] Barth scaringly refers to "the semi-biblical religion of post-Christian Judaism." Judaism no longer worships the true and living God of the patriarchs. the God of the modern Jew is nothing more than the God of the philosophers.[25]

Nonetheless, this same Barth has proved to be the single most significant contributor to twentieth-century Christianity's reaffirmation of Israel's enduring covenant in diverse thinkers such as von Balthasar and Kendall Soulen. In 1967, the theologian Friedrich-Wilhelm Marquardt (1928–2002) first proclaimed Karl Barth's *Church Dogmatics* to be the discovery of Judaism for Christianity, Barth's theology of Jews, Judaism, and Israel has been a matter of increasing interest and contention. According to Jewish theologian Michael Wyschogrod, "Because [Barth] reads Scripture obediently, he becomes aware of the centrality of Israel in God's relation with humanity and with the very message that Christianity proclaims to the world."[26] Barth acknowledges the enduring election of Israel. "Without any doubt, the Jews are to this very day the chosen people of God in the same sense as they have been from the beginning, according to the Old and New Testaments." In sum, Barth provides a basis both for reaffirming Israel's covenant and denigrating it.

Balthasar

Hans Urs von Balthasar (1905–1988) was a Swiss Catholic theologian, who, like Barth and inspired by Barth, reclaims the Hebrew Bible as Israel's covenant after its rejection in the nineteenth century. Catholic theology needs to recognize explicitly and consistently all the church receives from its holy root rather than pretend as if either there is no Judaism after the biblical period or that Judaism's impact on Christianity is marginal at best. For example, he wrote that the church would not have been right to make such wide employment of the Psalms, Israel's hymns of praise, for its own prayers if Israel's Psalms had not been ready to pray. Together with Israel, we pray psalms of penitence, judgment, and confession, thereby knowing and feeling guilt and failure along with Israel.[27] Balthasar thinks that through Israel's covenant God reveals God's virtues. For example, God's relation over time with Israel reveals God first as true or faithful to himself and his promises, especially in liberating Israel from Egypt.

Balthasar singles out for rejection the Marcionite strain of modern Christian thought, which denies the God of Israel's covenant and ongoing relation with Israel. Balthasar rejects prior hard supersessionism, believing that Israel remains God's beloved people. In this, he anticipates the turn of Nostra Aetate of an unbroken covenant based on Romans 9–11. For Balthasar, even though Judaism does not fulfill the biblical form by acknowledging Christ, the form remains standing nevertheless, as the requirement of the law to love God above all things and one's neighbor as oneself.[28] He also rejects a Christian mission to the Jews for the sake of conversion, which, given the continuity of the God's covenant would not quite make sense. According to Balthasar, all people will in the end encounter Christ in his glory. Given that Christians believe this is true and Jews do not, this is a soft supersessionist in which Christians emerge from Israel, without a replacement or rejection of a people. He assumes that the love of God for the Jews is an eternal divine love only available in covenantal mystery.

Balthasar believes that Jews incarnate God's virtues in the world through the details of Torah observance, offering a view of a way to remember God in all details of life in a training for holiness. In this sense, Israel discloses who God is through their own literature, that is, God's personal identity in and through God's actions—righteousness, mercy, truth, justice, and peace (*tzedek*, *hesed*, *emet*, *mispat*, *shalom*). Human hearts now have these divine prophetic virtues of the Hebrew Bible, operative by means of revelation of Christ.[29] Balhtasar's appreciation for Jews, the Hebrew Bible, and for the Jewish commandments moves the discussion far from prior Christian views that thought Judaism is no longer relevant. He also credits the divine presence in the glory (*kavod*) and the tabernacle as forms of the incarnation crediting Judaism with containing much of the Christian sacred promise of incarnate salvation.[30]

Cardinal Walter Kasper

Cardinal Walter Kasper (b. 1933) is a major contemporary Catholic theologian who has written extensively on Judaism's relationship to Catholicism in both theological and doctrinal terms. In 2001, Kasper assessed that covenant is the major point in the Jewish-Catholic encounter, and of fundamental importance for both the Jewish and Christian traditions, although he noted that the covenant idea also defines the differences between us and has often been the object of conflict—in the past as well as in the present.[31] Kasper declared that the view of the Catholic Church is that Judaism is a special religion that springs from divine revelation the way Christianity does. As Kasper noted, "the Church believes that Judaism, i.e. the faithful response of the Jewish people to God's irrevocable covenant, is salvific for them, because God is faithful to his promises." This common revelation applies only to Judaism. Kasper continues "we believe God's infinite grace is surely available to believers of other faiths, it is only about Israel's covenant that the Church can speak with the certainty of the biblical witness. This is because Israel's scriptures form part of our own biblical canon and they have a perpetual value . . . that has not been canceled by the later interpretation of the New Testament."[32] Noticeable, already in 2001, is that Kasper explicitly wrote that Jews are saved through Judaism.

Kasper defines the Hebrew covenant as an agreement between two parties containing "the elementary forms of human life-relations, couple-relations, family-relations, and even power and law relations." He returns to his own understanding of the Hebrew Bible view of covenant clearly stating that "The New Testament is situated in the history of tradition and interpretation of the Old Testament, and, in its own way, takes this history further."[33]

Kasper summarizes his understanding of Nosta Aetate as an unbroken covenant based on the use of Romans 9–11. "In the Second Vatican Council, reference is made to chapters 9–11 of Paul's Letter to the Romans, where we read about the people of Israel: Theirs is the adoption as sons, theirs the divine glory, the covenant, the receiving of the law and the promises . . ." which is an 'unbroken Covenant,' which is uninterrupted because of the unshakeable loyalty of God. Israel has not been replaced by the new Covenant." Rather, "Israel is still God's partner. God is still devoted to his people with love and loyalty, mercy, justice and pardon." Going out on a new limb, he states "God is always with his people especially in the most difficult moments of history. Every Jew, as one of His people, lives in promise."[34]

Since Judaism has an unbroken covenant with a strong connection to Christianity, Kasper asks the obvious question: What is the relation between the old Covenant, which is valid, and the new Covenant, which is described by the New Testament as the eternal Covenant? He reminds his readers that pluralism is not the answer, rather whether there is the one covenant or the two covenants. "Is there only one tradition to which both Jews and Christians belong? Or should we speak of two complementary Covenants?" He notes that "both theories are supported by Catholic as well as Protestant theologians," yet they both have dangers. "The danger in the One Covenant theory is either to 'christianise' Judaism, or to belittle the universalism that Christian faith attributes to Jesus. The danger in the Two Covenant theory is to consider Judaism and Christianity as two independent realities and play down the importance of the Jewish roots of the Church." Kasper was sensitive that this would treat Judaism as another non-Christian group, which downplays Judaism as its own religion.

Kasper outright understands that "Christians and Jews are different. These differences should not be erased." Nevertheless, "Jews and Christians cannot turn away from each other. In their diversity, they are dependent on one another. They are older and younger brothers, who have the same father and the same common root in Abraham." Kasper's surprising answer is that "the relation between Judaism and Christianity is indeed so complex that it cannot be reduced to a concise formula."[35] This was bold in that Cardinal Ratzinger, as head of the magisterium, had pronounced that there is only one covenant and the two-covenant theory is wrong.[36]

From these points, he concludes that "historical theological anti-Judaism has cut off the Church from the supporting and nourishing root of Israel and has therefore impoverished and weakened it. It was also one of the reasons why many Christians did not oppose the Holocaust as would have been expected from them." He concludes that Judaism and Christianity can "recognize and discover each other anew, like Joseph and his brothers after a long search marked by sin and failure. This kind of mutual rediscovery has begun to emerge in the current ecumenical rapprochement."[37]

According to Kasper, Nostra Aetate focused on Romans and did not focus on Hebrews, which would have made the reconciliation more difficult. In Hebrews, Paul speaks of a second, better covenant (8:6–12, etc.) and as the mediator of the new covenant (12:24). Kasper is clear to note that the depiction of the new covenant in Hebrews, creates "an essential discontinuity" between "the New Testament concerning its relation to the Old; one can even speak of renewal and contradiction." Hebrews portrays Christ in a typological manner in which Christ replaces the Old Testament pillars of priest, prophet, and sacrifice, is now found in "Jesus Christ and in his death on the cross." Kasper emphasizes that most first-century Jews rejected this fulfillment scheme of Hebrews, creating "the Christian accusation of unfaith directed against the Jews."

At this point, Christianity acknowledges its difference from Judaism but without the rejection and demonizing of the past, along with an exhortation to learn about each other. For Kasper, "Covenant is also an eschatological one, which, according to both our religious convictions and hopes, will find its full realization only at the end of time. Therefore, our theological knowledge in such issues will always be fragmentary and partial."[38] There is great humility and openness in this admission of the need to avoid until the end of time clear answers or totalizing theological schemes.

The Gifts and Calling of God

In 2015, the Pontifical Commission for Religious Relations with the Jews (CRRJ) published "'The Gifts and the Calling of God are irrevocable' (Rom 11:29): A Reflection on Theological Questions Pertaining to Catholic—Jewish Relations on the Occasion of the 50th Anniversary of 'Nostra Aetate' (No. 4)" [Henceforth: "The Gifts and the Calling"].[39] Cardinal Kasper was its major theoretician and one of its principal authors.[40] Here, Kasper offers more than a decade of further reflection of the Catholic position on the Jewish religion. This document contains a clear statement declaring the ongoing covenant of the Jewish people and that Jews are saved by virtue of their practice of Judaism. Catholic theologies that run counter to this Pauline teaching of irrevocability of the covenant with the Jews such as the theologies of supersessionism, or replacement, are now themselves superseded and replaced.

The document "The Gifts and the Calling" defines covenant in an entirely Christian perspective of God's reveling himself and his salvation plan the humanity. "We find in the Old Testament God's plan of salvation presented for his people (cf. 'Dei verbum,', 14) . . . at the beginning of biblical history in the call to Abraham (Gen 12)." God began his plan of revealing himself "and redeem them from sin God began by choosing the people of Israel through Abraham and setting them apart."[41]

The stated difference between the religions, despite both turning to the same one God, is that "Christians turn to Christ as the fount of new life, and Jews to the teaching of the Torah." In fact, our respective traditions are parallel in that Christian consider Christ as exiting before creation and Jews think Torah existed before creation. The Old and New Testaments and the old and new covenants are two parallel approaches, one of Torah and one of Christ. However, since the official doctrine is one covenant, Kasper reiterates that "the New Covenant does not revoke the earlier covenants, but it brings them to fulfilment. Through the Christ event Christians have understood that all that had gone before was to be interpreted anew." Gentiles follow the new covenant, and Jews continue with the covenant that they were given. The commonality between faiths is "the personal nature of God as revealed in the Old Covenant and establishing it as openness for all who respond faithfully from all the nations (cf. Zech 8:20–23; Ps 87)." And that "each of the two readings serves the purpose of rightly understanding God's will and word."

Nevertheless, for Christians the new covenant has acquired a quality of its own, made in Christ as the culminating point of the promises of salvation of the old covenant, and is to that extent never independent of it. "The New Covenant is grounded in and based on the

Old, because it is ultimately the God of Israel who concludes the Old Covenant with his people Israel and enables the New Covenant in Jesus Christ." Hence, both the old and new covenants are a single covenant. Kasper reiterates that "For the Christian faith it is axiomatic that there can only be one single covenant history of God with humanity." But then returns to difference between the two religions by declaring that "the term covenant, therefore, means a relationship with God that takes effect in different ways for Jews and Christians."[42]

Kasper presents covenants as each one incorporating the prior covenant. "The covenant with Abraham, with circumcision as its sign (cf. Gen 17), and the covenant with Moses restricted to Israel regarding obedience to the law (cf. Exod 19:5; 24:7–8) and in particular the observance of the Sabbath (cf. Exod 31:16–17) had been extended in the covenant with Noah, with the rainbow as its sign (cf. 'Verbum Domini,' 117), to the whole of creation (cf. Gen 9:9ff)." Building on the Jewish focus on the particularity of the Abrahamic and Mosaic covenants, is extended into the universalism of the Noahide covenant. Kasper sees a further covenant in the unique Christian theological framework of a universal eternal new covenant.[43]

The current official Catholic position is that Judaism is the historic origin of the divine covenant to Israel, which Christianity then made universal for all people.

> This recourse to the Abrahamic covenant is so essentially constitutive of the Christian faith that the Church without Israel would be in danger of losing its locus in the history of salvation. By the same token, Jews could with regard to the Abrahamic covenant arrive at the insight that Israel without the Church would be in danger of remaining too particularist and of failing to grasp the universality of its experience of God. In this fundamental sense Israel and the Church remain bound to each other according to the covenant and are interdependent.[44]

According to Kasper, apostle Paul's passionate struggle with the dual fact that the old covenant continues to be in force, even as Israel has not adopted the new covenant. To do justice to this duality Paul coined the expressive image of the root of Israel into which the wild branches of the gentiles have been grafted (Rom 11:16–21). In the end, Judaism and Christianity share one covenant but two understandings, one particular and one universal. "Since God has never revoked his covenant with his people Israel, there cannot be different paths or approaches to God's salvation."[45]

Gavin D'Costa, theologian of the Church's positions on other religions, who specializes in subjecting the Church's documents to razor sharp logic, declared that "The Gifts and the Calling" was a remarkable rejection of the approach of most Christian theologians up until the nineteenth century. For D'Costa, such a frank admission of the need to change a position is bracing and brave.[46]

From a Jewish perspective, despite this covenantal commonality from Catholic teachings, the difference between the religions is that Judaism is not a history of salvation, Abraham is the start of a people, the Jewish people, not of faith. Furthermore, Judaism does not think non-Jews have no access to God without the covenant because God is universal for all people. Kasper's thinking that Christianity brought God to the world is not in line with Jewish thought since Judaism assumes God was always available to all people. God is available to all other people who are not Jews, not just Christians, without a special covenant or revelation.[47]

R. Kendall Soulen

R. Kendall Soulen (b. 1959), an ordained elder in the United Methodist Church, as well as professor at the Candler school of theology, Emory University, is a leading figure in efforts to restore the importance of the Old Testament and identification of God as the God of Israel to Christian theology. Kendall Soulen is explicit that his work belongs to a genre of Christian thought that can be termed "post-Holocaust." Soulen, writing in 1996, sees the current era having been inaugurated by the Holocaust in which Christians have to confess their own complicity, and by the return of the Jewish people to the land promised to Abraham.

For Soulen, not since the New Testament has the church dealt successfully with the Bible's affirmation of God's faithfulness to the Jewish people. Revisiting the teachings of supersessionism after nearly two thousand years, many churches have now publicly confessed that fidelity to the gospel requires the rejection of supersessionism and the affirmation of God's own unbroken fidelity to the Jewish people. Soulen wants to probe deeper into the history of Christian theology to discover how Christianity lost its proper contact with Judaism and the Jewish people and how that contact can be restored in a way that does not derail Christian doctrine of the need for the universal saving grace of Christ. Soulen argues for the plausibility of Christian faith as based on God's promise to Abraham: "in you shall all the families of the earth be blessed" (Gen 12:3).

Soulen recognizes that dismissing the Old Testament's portrayal of God—whether the typology of Augustine or the Marcionism of modern thought—fosters a "double impoverishment for Christian theology." First, ignoring the Old Testament leads to a loss of biblical orientation of Hebrew scriptures for Christian theology. Second, the lack has led to a loss of creative theological engagement with the hard edges of human history as presented in the Hebrew Bible.[48] In Soulen's theology, from the New Testament until modern theology, the Old Testament has been wrongly rejected. Christian theology, as such, is marred by the same "flaw in the heart of the crystal." For him, "the one God, the creator and consummator of all things is the God of the Jews." If Jewish scriptures are not about God then neither is gospel, "if on the other hand, the mystery at the Heart-of-all Things is the I AM who accosted Moses at the bush (Exod 3:13) then the gospel . . . is at least possibly true." Not everything held by the Church is spelled out in the Old Testament. In both classical and modern forms, Christian theology embodies what is in effect an incomplete conversion toward the living God, the God of Abraham, Isaac, and Jacob. The crucial marks of that incomplete conversion are a triumphalist posture toward the Jewish people and a latent assumption that God's engagement in the realm of public history is not part of salvation.[49]

According to Soulen, supersessionism may be best understood when one looks at the way in which Christians interpret the Christian Bible as a narrative unity culminating in the Gospels. When Scripture was expanded to include a second collection of Jewish writings that was to become the New Testament, a canonical narrative or interpretive framework was then needed to enable Christians to read their twofold canon as a theological unity, which determines how Christians read the Bible. Following the Irenaean scheme of covenants as the unfolding of God's successive promises into a single story, he organizes the entire biblical text in the light of two chief ways in which God, the Creator of the world, engages human creation—as consummator and as redeemer. The pattern is four points of biblical history: creation, the fall, the coming of Christ, and the end. Soulen remarks in this respect: "As a result, God's identity as the God of Israel and history with the Jewish people become largely indecisive for the Christian conception of God."[50] What is lost is the story of God of the Israelites who directs kings and prophets, restores Israel, and builds a Temple.

For Christian theology the issue is not about whether Jews are God's chosen people but how. The notion of the "economy of consummation" occupies a central place in Soulen's theological approach. God's great final purpose with his creation is the ultimate worldwide shalom for Israel and the nations, the new heaven and the new earth where God's righteousness will dwell forever. Soulen calls God's great plan to redeem his creation from the consequences of the fall and the power of Satan in the "economy of redemption" by means of two paths: Israel and the nations (similar to Franz Rosenzweig's two paths).[51] God's work as consummator engages the human family in a historically decisive way in God's election of Israel as a blessing to the nations.[52] The resulting distinction and the resulting mutual dependence of Israel and the nations is the fundamental form of the economy of consummation through which God initiates, sustains, and ultimately fulfils the one human family's destiny for life with God.

God's economy of consummation is essentially constituted as an economy of mutual blessing between those who are and who remain different. The mutual blessing of Judaism and Christianity, works the same way as man compliments woman and woman to the man, the parent to the child and the child to the parent, the brother to the sister and the sister to the brother, the Jew to the Greek and the Greek to the Jew, friends to one another etcetera. So, God not only blesses his creation, he also lays down a basic principle of mutual blessing.

Soulen places emphasis on God's role as the consummator of creation, the one who sustains and blesses his creation, with somewhat less emphasis on God as the Redeemer from the original human sin. This theological focus on creation moves his thought closer to Judaism precisely because the focus on question of redemption has been the widest wedge between Judaism and Christianity.

Soulen makes a very rabbinic argument that at the creation of the world the people of Israel are the only nation to receive the commandment to observe the Sabbath, already given from God in Genesis 2. Similar to midrash, for Soulen, creation itself is predicated on Jews keeping the Sabbath. Therefore, already before the fall in Genesis 3, God intended to call Abraham, and to bring forth the people of Israel from his loins as a special election of the Jewish people. The Jews and their commandments are part of the plan of creation, which Christians should acknowledge.

Two Paths of Truth and Covenantal Pluralism

Jewish and Christian truth claims about the function of the Messiah here and now, specific as they are, do come into conflict with each other. Most significantly, the two religions are governed by different norms in their respective relationships with God. In a very real sense, Jews must believe that Christians have missed the point about how to wait for the end, and Christians must believe something quite similar about the Jews. The authenticity of any new Jewish-Christian relationship is energized by this tension as much as it is energized by the rediscovery of much commonality. Once again structurally similar to Franz Rosenzweig.

Soulen's opinion is firm that the crucified messiah must have universal significance. He acknowledges that Christians cannot yield to the view that God's covenant has been annulled for Jews. Paul's conundrum was that he held both views simultaneously: the gospel is for all including Jews who refuse it, but God is faithful to his covenant with them. Later Christians omitted the latter claim while Rosenzweig omitted the former claim. This covenantal pluralism approach asserts that the resurrection had a spin off only for gentiles but not for Jews. Similarly, Christians cannot yield on the idea that the resurrection of the crucified messiah, if true at all, has significance for everyone. "This claim may be puzzling and even offensive to many Jews. But it is tied up with the very notion of resurrection, which by its nature signals the dawn of a new creation."[53] Belief in resurrection means good news for all. The difference that flows from the distinction between creation and resurrection is that Jews become members of the Holy people by birth as descendants of Abraham along with entrance into the covenant of circumcision. But Christians become holy by faith in Jesus as messiah and Lord and baptism into Trinity.[54] The Jewish "no" to Jesus Christ in no way detracts from God's fidelity to his promises to Israel.[55]

Soulen's understanding of the covenant with Abraham draws heavily on the Jewish theologian Michael Wyschogrod, who claims that the mystery of the election of Israel is that it "concerns a natural human family" as a "corporeal election."[56] Jews are about descendants, circumcision, the keeping of physical *mitzvot*, not any theology or philosophy. In contrast, the Christian understanding of Abraham is that the covenant is not about family and lineage, but faith in God. In a Christian reading, the covenant embraced many who were not in any way related to Abraham by blood. For example, the Abrahamic covenant includes all the male members of Abraham's household who were circumcised (Gen 17:12–14), and a household including 318 men of fighting age (Gen 14:14). The covenant is not through the prodigy of Abraham rather a message that was open to all who accepted it.[57]

From a Jewish perspective, Soulen passively perpetuates understanding the Hebrew Bible as a theological work about the God of Israel and faith. The Hebrew scriptures are not solely or even primarily concerned with the antithesis of sin and redemption but much rather with the God of Israel's passionate engagement with the mundane affairs of

Israel, in their kings, kingdoms, and wars. Later Judaism is about the commitment to the scribal study of Torah from Ezra and Nehemiah to the Sages. As noted in chapter 4 on salvation, Judaism is not a religion of salvation but of the scribes teaching Torah for the people to observe. In the Jewish understanding, the Jewish covenant in the Hebrew Bible is not a precursor to another story, it's that the redemptive story continues with the Jewish people until this day. And without assuming that final worldwide shalom requires the saving, reconciling, suffering, and victorious intervention of Jesus, the promised Messiah.

In more recent writings, Soulen extends his argument for the "economy of consummation" by exploring the consequences of a non-supersessionist doctrine of the Trinity based on the shared use of the divine name by the Hebrew Bible and Christianity. Soulen suggests that the Tetragrammaton, YHWH, of Exodus 3 remains the name of the God to whom Jesus prayed. Christians have always affirmed in some fashion that "YHWH is the Triune God," they have interpreted the two parts of this affirmation according to the scheme of Old Testament/New Testament, with the result that God's identity as YHWH is left in the past. In place of this, he proposes that Christians interpret the confession "YHWH is the Triune God" according to the logic of "Jesus is the Christ," with the result that both parts of the affirmation speak to past, present, and future.[58] The singular revelation of the divine, shows that the Jews already had a full covenantal revelation in that God chose the Jews out of love.[59] "God is concerned with sanctifying his name in the eyes of the nations, but the only way God can do that is by honoring the non-fungible status that God accorded" who are the Jews. They remain the primary axis of God's love and activity in the world. For Soulen, this is the same line of reasoning that informs Romans 9–11.[60]

Issues of Supersessionism

Soulen's concern is overcoming the problem of supersessionism, which in one form or another, sees Judaism and the Jewish people as that which the triumph of Christianity over history has left in the irretrievable past. For Soulen there are three types of supersessionism: "economic," whereby the Jews are no longer needed in the divine plan for humankind; "punitive," whereby the Jews are seen as rejected by God because of their rejection of Jesus as the Christ; and "structural," whereby the true relationship is between God and humans and not between God and a singular people. In all three of these views, legitimate Christian teaching is that after Christ came, the special role of the Jewish people came to an end and its place was taken by the church, the new Israel. Soulen sees the Christian struggle with gnosticism and Marcionism lurking behind all forms of supersessionism. Soulen rejects all three.

But many contemporary Christian theologians such as George Husinger and Gavin D'Costa accept the continuous viability of the third approach of a structural supersessionalism. Even the Jewish thinker David Novak recognizes this inevitable mild supersessionism as intrinsic to Christian doctrine. Jesus Christ must be seen as fulfilling the covenant given to Israel in his person—but does not annul it, that he is the savior of the world and thus eschatologically disruptive to all history. But structural supersessionalism keeps these claims free of economic and punitive supersession.[61]

Conclusions

In the other chapters, we looked at a Christian idea seemingly foreign to Judaism, and asked whether we can close the gap between the theology of the two faiths. In this chapter, we looked at a process whereby contemporary Christian thought reconciled with Judaism treating the Jewish covenant as an ongoing covenant. But can Christianity acknowledge the ongoing Sinai law for the Jewish people? If "The Gifts and the Calling" is taken at face value, the document would imply that the ceremonial law of Israel is still valid as an irrevocable gift. "The first Christians were Jews; as a matter of course, they gathered as part of the community in the Synagogue, they observed the dietary laws, the Sabbath and the requirement of circumcision, while at the same time confessing Jesus as the Christ, the Messiah sent by God for the salvation of Israel and the entire human race." But the document does not state that explicitly and may still be a point of contention. However, von

Balthasar and Soulen both acknowledge the ongoing Sinai covenant explicitly.[62]

An opening for even greater recognition was proposed by Robert Jenson (1930–2017) a leading American Lutheran theologian, who explicitly recognized the ongoing validity of the Sinai commandments as explained by Rabbinic Judaism. Teaching, a dual covenant theology, Jenson considers Christianity as an outgrowth of the biblical scripture, in which the Church is an eschatological detour to allow the gentiles to enter the covenant of Israel, while rabbinic Judaism remains another path in which "the synagogue waits by the study of Torah." Therefore, "the study of Torah is indeed worship." The recognition is not just of Sinai but also of the rabbinic understanding of Torah and the Jewish way of life as a response to God.[63]

Jewish theologian Michael Wyschogrod (1928–2015) accepted an understanding of a dual covenant with Christianity as two very different paths both based on Abraham. For Christians, God's promise to Abraham as an opening to God is by means of faith. The Jewish religion, in contrast is a particularism that is tribal and embodied in heredity and ritual. Therefore, he accepts a second path of Jesus bringing a new different covenant of faith to gentiles. This Jewish view of Christianity for Wyschogrod is not just an expanse of Bible monotheism, but a connection of gentiles to the people of Israel as part of the compassion of God. "The Divine promise to Abraham that through his election, or in him, there shall be blessed the families of the earth (Gen 12:3) . . . makes quite clear that the election of Abraham and his seed, while in many ways separating the history of Israel from those of the nations, cannot rest with such a separation." Wyschogrod offers an openness to the broader promise of Abraham to the nations.

Yet on the ongoing significance of the commandments, Wyschogrod preserves the autonomy of Judaism. For him, the purpose of the Jewish commandments has nothing to do with being a sign in a covenantal system. Michael Wyschogrod states that the commandments are not a kerygma or a path of salvation and fulfillment "because they are essentially a set of demands rather than a message of redemption and the forgiveness of sin." In contrast to the Christian covenant of faith, the Jewish commandments are an embodied system of actions that constitute the life of Torah.[64] They are a divine mandated way of life in which one's daily life is surrounded by this system of action. Wyschogrod reminds his reader, that the rabbinic Sages highlighted the patriarch Abraham as keeping all the commandments of the Torah, that is, he kept the covenant of Moses at Sinai, even before the details of the Torah were ostensibly given, typifying a covenant of commandments. For Wyschogrod, Judaism remains an inherent order, an embodied life of practice already kept by Abraham, while Christianity for Wyschogrod is bringing a promise to Abrahm of a religion of faith for the gentiles.

I close this book with the wise words of former Chief Rabbi of the British Empire, Baron Jonathan Sacks (1948–2020). In 2002, Sacks argued that in the modern world there needs to be an acceptance of cultural and religious difference. He wrote that as an Orthodox Jew, he can hear the echoes of the voice of God in a Hindu, Sikh, Christian, or Muslim. There is not one exclusive path to salvation.[65] He argued that we are naturally different, and that we should not seek a universalism, rather we should all work within our own unique covenants. Judaism, Christianity, Islam, Hinduism, Sikhism, are all separate and independent covenants. We must bring our differences as gifts to the common good to build society.[66] For Sacks, a covenant is predicated on difference from other covenants. Difference can compete or difference can cooperate. If we were completely different, we could not communicate. If we are totally the same, we have nothing to say to each other.

At the 2008 Lambeth Conference of Anglican bishops, Rabbi Jonathan Sacks was a guest speaker at one of the plenary sessions. Yet, despite not offering a common Jewish-Christian covenant, Rabbi Sacks answered the following when asked about Jesus: "There is a line we say at the beginning of the prayers on the Holiest of Holy Days: Yom Kippur (*Kol Nidre*) . . . the high priest said on the Day of Atonement: Forgive them father, for they know not what they do. If Jesus said those words on the cross, then Jesus was at his most Jewish. At that moment Jesus was delivering a Jewish message." Globalizing that observation into a bigger statement, Sacks said: "The Christ delivering the message to the world. We did not take it to the world. We are few. You are many. You took it to the world. You have taken that message of one who was a Jew to the world. Take that message as a Jewish message: forgive them Father." We walk side by side in many differences of faith, but with the shared experience of faith. "The world is enlarged by differences."[67] Sacks could hear the Jewish voice and commonality in Jesus's teaching; he could even appreciate Christianity as bringing Jewish teachings to the world. But the two religions remain separate independent covenants.

NOTES

PREFACE

1. Trude Weiss-Rosmarin, *Judaism and Christianity: The Differences* (Jewish Book Club, 1943).
2. James L. Fredericks, *Faith among Faiths: Christian Theology and Non-Christian Religions* (Paulist, 1999), 158–163, 170.
3. Alan Brill, "Recognizing the Other: Sameness and Difference in a Jewish Theology of Religions." Lecture delivered September 21, 2011, printed in *Boston Theological Institute Journal* 11, no. 2 (May 2012): 4–8.
4. Peter Berger, "Judaism and Christianity: Embracing the 'Other?'" *The American Interest* (August 22, 2012).
5. See Alan Brill, *Judaism and World Religions* (Palgrave-Macmillan, 2012), 86–92.
6. Irving Greenberg, *For the Sake of Heaven and Earth: The New Encounter Between Judaism and Christianity* (JPS, 2004), 185, 204.
7. Pinchas Lapide and Jürgen Moltmann, *Jewish Monotheism and Christian Trinitarian Doctrine: A Dialogue*, trans. Leonard Swidler (Fortress Press, 1981); Karl Rahner and Pinchas Lapide, *Encountering Jesus—Encountering Judaism: A Dialogue* trans. Davis Perkins (Crossroad, 1987); Hans Kung and Pinchas Lapide, *Brother or Lord? A Jew and a Christian Talk Together about Jesus* (Fount Paperbacks, 1977).
8. Lapide and Moltmann, *Jewish Monotheism and Christian Trinitarian Doctrine*, 17, 37, 41.
9. Cardinal Kasper, *Christ Jesus and the Jewish People Today: New Explorations of Theological Interrelationships* (Eerdmans, 2011), forward. Available at https://ccjr.us/dialogika-resources/documents-and-statements/roman-catholic/kasper/kasper2011mar20
10. Jacob Neusner, *Jews and Christians: The Myth of a Common Tradition.* (SCM Press and Trinity Press International, 1991), 1.

CHAPTER ONE: TRINITY

1. Trude Weiss-Rosmarin, *Judaism and Christianity: The Differences* (Jewish Book Club, 1943).
2. In this chapter, and throughout the book, I generally follow the contours of Linwood Urban, *A Short History of Christian Thought* (Oxford University Press, 1995). The book is useful for several reasons, first because he is aware of and points out the similarities and differences from Jewish thought, second, because he tries to bridge Catholic and Protestant understandings from an Anglican perspective, and third, his work has been useful as an assigned reading to my classes on comparative theology.
3. *Symbol of Quicunque Virt*, c. sixth century CE. The Athanasian Creed is a gloss on Augustine's *On the Trinity*, not Athanasius; Urban, *A Short History of Christian Thought*, 59, 65.
4. Larry W. Hurtado, *One God, One Lord: Early Christian Devotion and Ancient Jewish Monotheism.* (Fortress Press, 1988); *How on Earth Did Jesus Become a God? Historical Questions about Earliest Devotion to Jesus* (Eerdmans, 2005); *God in New Testament Theology* (Abingdon Press, 2010); *Honoring the Son: Jesus in Earliest Christian Devotional Practice* (Lexham Press, 2018); David B. Capes, April D. DeConick, Helen K. Bond, and Troy Miller, eds. *Israel's God and Rebecca's Children: Christology and Community in Early Judaism and Christianity.* Essays in Honor of Larry W. Hurtado and Alan F. Segal (Baylor University Press, 2007). Peter Schäfer, *The Jewish Jesus: How Judaism and Christianity Shaped Each Other* (Princeton University Press, 2012); *Two Gods in Heaven: Jewish Concepts of God in Antiquity* (Princeton University Press, 2020). Daniel Boyarin, The Gospel of the Memra: Jewish Binitarianism and the Prologue to John," *Harvard Theological Review* 94, vol. 3 (2001): 243–284; Daniel Boyarin, "Two Powers in Heaven; or, The Making of a Heresy," in *The Idea of Biblical Interpretation: Essays in Honor of James L. Kugel*, ed. Hindy Najman and Judith R. Newman (Brill, 2003), 331–370; *The Jewish Gospels: The Story of the Jewish Christ* (The New Press, 2012). There are many other scholars worthy of mention but I point out that a conference volume from twenty-five years ago points out the novelty of considering the Christological monotheism in a Jewish context, *The Jewish Roots of Christological Monotheism: Papers from the St. Andrews Conference on the Historical Origins of the Worship of Jesus*, ed. Carey C. Newman, James R. Davila and Gladys S. Lewis, JSJSup 63 (Brill, 1999.)

5. Daniel Boyarin, *The Jewish Gospels: The Story of the Jewish Christ* (The New Press, 2012), 8.
6. See Ephraim E. Urbach, *The Sages* (Harvard University Press, 1987), 62–63 which notes that a survey of all the passages referring to the Shekhina leaves no doubt that the Shekhina is no "hypostasis" and has no separate existence alongside the Deity. Gershom Scholem also assumed this in order to present kabbalah as a radical break with rabbinic thought. For sources, see Moshe Idel, "Rabbinism Verses Kabbalism: On G. Scholem's Phenomenology of Judaism," *Modern Judaism* 11: (1991), 281–296.
7. In contrast, Michael Fishbane shows continuity between the rabbinic worldview and the medieval kabbalah as does Oded Yisraeli, see Michael Fishbane, *Biblical Myth and Rabbinic Mythmaking* (Oxford University Press, 2003), 9; Michael Fishbane, *The Exegetical Imagination: On Jewish Thought and Theology* (Harvard University Press, 1998), 87–89, 99, 101, 301–304, Oded Yisraeli, *Temple Portals Studies in Aggadah and Midrash in the Zohar* (De Gruyter: 2016). Moshe Idel differentiated between the personalist rabbinic view of God and the kabbalistic impersonal, mechanical divine but nevertheless have a continuity of lower and higher parts of the divine. Also see Yair Lorberbaum, *In God's Image: Myth, Theology, and Law in Classical Judaism* (Cambridge University Press, 2015), 13–45, who explicitly deals with this change of perception of rabbinic thought; also see M. Kister, "Some Early Jewish and Christian Exegetical Problems and the Dynamics of Monotheism" *Journal for the Study of Judaism in the Persian, Hellenistic, and Roman Period* 37, No. 4 (2006), 548–593, and for a broad methodological discussion of the continuity of rabbinic and medieval thought, see Dov Weiss, "The Rabbinic God and Medieval Judaism," *Currents in Biblical Research* 15, no. 3: (2017), 369–390.
8. Daniel Boyarin, *Border Lines: The Partition of Judaeo-Christianity* (University of Pennsylvania Press, 2006), 116–119, 123, and 290 (n. 30). Recently, Tzahi Weiss has argued that there was still Jewish worship of a binitarian divine by Jews in the early thirteenth century, with the doctrine of the *sefirot* emerging as a more acceptable solution to the parts of the divine. Tzahi Weiss, "The Letter of Isaac the Blind to Nahmanides and Jonah Gerondi in Its Historical Context" *Journal of Jewish Studies* 72, no. 2 (Autumn 2021), 327–348; Tzahi Weiss, "Their Heart Was Turned Away from the Uppermost': Rethinking the Boundaries of the 'Kabbalistic Literature' and the Opposition to

'Kabbalah' in the First Half of the 13th Century", *DAAT: Journal for Jewish Philosophy and Kabbalah* 85 (2018), 307–339 [Hebrew].

9. Moshe Idel, *Ben: Sonship and Jewish Mysticism* (Continuum, 2007). Idel even speculates on the connections between the Jewish ideas of Metatron as the true son of God along with the cosmic Adam and the *Shekhinah* are part of as a complex of ideas connected to the Christian concept of incarnation, *Ben*, 119–148. For Platonic common sources, see the idea of the preexistence of the Son. On this point see Harry Austryn Wolfson, "Extradeical and Intradeical Interpretation of Platonic Ideas," in *Religious Philosophy: A Group of Essays* (Belknap Press of Harvard University Press, 1961), 27–68.
10. Anthony J. Saldarini with Joseph A. Kanofsky, "Judaism: God as a Many-sided Ultimate Reality in Traditional Judaism," in *Ultimate Realities: A Volume in the Comparative Religious Ideas Project*, ed. Robert Cummings Neville (SUNY, 2000); Paula Fredriksen, "Philo, Herod, Paul, and the Many Gods of Ancient Jewish Monotheism," *Harvard Theological Review* 115, no. 1 (2022), 23–45; Matthew Novenson, "The Universal Polytheism and the case of the Jews," in *Monotheism and Christology in Greco-Roman Antiquity*. Novum Testamentum, Supplements 180 (Brill, 2020), 32–60.
11. Alon Goshen-Gottstein, "Jewish-Christian Relations and Rabbinic Literature: Shifting Scholarly and Relational Paradigms: The Case of Two Powers," in *Interaction between Judaism and Christianity in History, Religion, Art and Literature*, ed. Marcel Poorthuis, Joshua J. Schwartz, and Joseph Turner (Brill, 2009), 15–44
12. A further line of research would be to investigate the Monarchist Trinitarianism of the Eastern Orthodox theologians, which preserves a monarchist primacy position for the Father but without subordinationism, see John Zizioulas, *Being as Communion* (St Vladimir's Seminary Press, 1985); *Communion as Otherness* (T&T Clark, 2006).
13. Paula Fredriksen, "How Jewish is God?" *Journal of Biblical Literature* 137, no. 1 (2018): 193–212.
14. Wiliam Lane Craig, the philosophic theologian and Christian apologist offers a modern version, in that he argues for the Trinity because a unitarian view of the philosophical God focused only on himself does not give himself away in love for another. For Craig the Christian view has God showing his love to the Son making God essentially loving and active in the world, see J. P. Moreland, and William Lane Craig, *Philosophical Foundations for a Christian Worldview* (IVP Academic, 2003).

15. Saadiah Gaon's discussion of the Trinity and incarnation can be found in Saadia Gaon, *The Book of Beliefs and Opinions*, translated by Samuel Rosenblatt, (Yale University Press, 1948), 101–10; Harry A. Wolfson, "Saadia on the Trinity and the Incarnation," in *Studies and Essays in Honor of Abraham A. Neuman*, ed. M. Ben Horin et al. (Brill, 1962), 547–568.
16. Isaac Albalag, *Sefer Tiqqun haDe'ot*, ed . G. Vajda (Jerusalem, 1973), 69. For the Maimonidean background of these discussions, see Guide I:58 and his rejection of the Trinity in I:50.
17. "Disputation", Cecil Roth (ed.), *Encyclopedia Judaica*, vol. 6 (Keter Publishing, 1972), column 92. If Nahmanides was not sincere in his answers during the polemic, as thought by some scholars, then he would not even have accepted a modalist position, unlike Albalag. Aquinas actually stated clearly that wisdom, will, and power are unified in God (*Summa Theologica* I. 3). Yet for Aquinas the Trinity is much more than just divine attributes, rather the triune God of three persons.
18. Nahmanides on Genesis 18:1; Deuteronomy 11:22; Moshe Halbertal, *Nahmanides: Law and Mysticism*, trans. Daniel Tabak (Yale University Press, 2020), 179. For Nahmanides, the *shekhinah* is not a created entity or angel outside god but a hierarchical manifestation of god. A similar Jewish theological approach is reflected by Justin in the second century CE: see S. Pines, 'God, the Divine Glory, and the Angels According to a Second-Century Theology', in *The Beginnings of Jewish Mysticism in Medieval Europe*, ed. J. Dan (Institute for Jewish Studies, 1987), 1–14 (in Hebrew).
19. Oded Yisraeli, "Monotheism and Dualism in Nahmanides' Kabbalistic Thought: Formation, Volte-face and Evolution," *Journal of Jewish Studies* 70 (2019): 298–317.
20. Generally, the debate among kabbalistic thinkers is whether the *sefirot* are lower created entities made solely for divine manifestation, or divine essences revealed in a hierarchical emanation. The first approach, called vessels (*kelim*), views them as created entities, divine instruments, tools, or vessels of the divine. This enables the vessels or tools to appear to change, while the unknown divine essence remains unchanged.

    The second approach, called essence (*atzmut*), treats these lower entities as divine essence itself, but as intermediaries, the *sefirot* are similar to a Neoplatonic emanation. Moshe Cordovero (1522–1570) accepted both positions by describing them as divine lights invested in vessels. Only the vessels differentiate, while the light, originating from the Ein Sof, is undifferentiated, in the manner water pours into different colored vessels or light streams through different colors of glass. In both positions, there are no separate persons of the divine, one cannot pray to a lower entity, and they do not have independent volition. More importantly, there is no perichoresis, no indwelling of the parts. On the distinction of the *sefirot* as essence (*atzmut)* or vessels (*kelim*), see Moshe Hallamish, *An Introduction to the Kabbalah* (SUNY Press, 1999), 159–164.

21. Cited in Rian Venter, "Reflections on Schleiermacher's God," *HTS Teologiese Studies / Theological Studies* 75, no. 4 (2019): 1–6.
22. Karl Rahner, *The Trinity*, trans. Joseph Donceel (Crossroad, 1998).
23. Rahner, *The Trinity*, 75.
24. Rahner, *The Trinity*, 99–100.
25. Rahner, *The Trinity*, 22, 35.
26. I do acknowledge God's creative vision for the creation of the world, the choice of Israel, divine atonement, divine hesed, and even messianic unfoldings. But the divine itself does not have to unfold as an incarnation for salvation as in the economic Trinity.

    The Jewish equivalent of Christian grace is Torah, or more broadly Torah, *mitzvot*, and prayer, which is the giving of God's presence in revelation at Mount Sinai. There is, however, no need for a prior salvation to engage in these activities because of the lack of original sin. Rahner's formulation of grace as a self-communication of God, makes his position closer to an idea of Torah as God's self-revelation. We would need a separate paper for evaluating salvation, grace, and God's self-communication from a Jewish perspective. In the meantime, see R. J. Zwi Werblowsky, "Tora als Gnade," *Kairos* 15: (1973) [Festschrift Endre von. Ivanka], 156–163.

    I must note that the kabbalists Moshe Chayim Luzzatto (known as Ramchal, 1707–1746) and Shlomo Elyashiv, (known as the Leshem, 1839–1926) both have systems of creation theology where God has to unfold into and through the world, but theologically this is distinct from a divine mission of salvation.
27. Marc Pugliese, "Is Karl Rahner a Modalist?" *Irish Theological Quarterly* 68 (Fall 2003): 229–249.
28. Rahner, *The Trinity*, 112.
29. Rahner, *The Trinity*, 75, 106.
30. Karl Barth, *Church Dogmatics*, vol 1/1 Doctrine of the Word of God. CD I/1, 160–161.
31. Karl Barth, *Church Dogmatics*, vol. 2/I 163, 351; Karl Barth, *Church Dogmatics*, IV/I, 201.

32. Karl Barth, *Church Dogmatics*, IV/I, 201, 314, 335. It is important to note, Barth says all of this against subordination and modalism in the Trinity, yet his critics point out that "missing in Barth's presentation at this point . . . is any account of perichoresis." Paul Molnar criticizes Barth in *Faith, Freedom and the Spirit: The Economic Trinity in Barth, Torrance and Contemporary Theology* (IVP Academic, 2015).
33. While generally not a Jewish view, one serious exception is the Holocaust preacher of the Warsaw Ghetto, Rabbi Kalonymus Kalman Shapira, who combined personalism with a view of God that shares our suffering. Avichai Zur, "'The Lord Hides in Inner Chambers': The Doctrine of Suffering in the Theosophy of Rabbi Kalonymus Kalman Shapira of Piaseczno," *Dapim* (August, 2013): 183–237; Don Seeman, Daniel Reiser, and Ariel Evan Mayse, eds., *Hasidism, Suffering, and Renewal: The Prewar and Holocaust Legacy of Rabbi Kalonymus Kalman Shapira* (SUNY Press, 2021).
34. Jürgen Moltmann, *The Way of Jesus Christ: Christology in Messianic Dimensions* (Fortress Press, 1993), 168.
35. Jürgen Moltmann, *The Trinity and the Kingdom: The Doctrine of God* (Harper & Row, 1980, 1981), 3.
36. A. Roy Eckardt, "Jürgen Moltmann, the Jewish People, and the Holocaust," *Journal of the American Academy of Religion* 44, no. 4 (1976): 675–691.
37. Jürgen Moltmann, "Shekinah: The Home of the Homeless God," in *Longing for Home*, ed. Leroy S. Rouner (Notre Dame University Press, 1996), 178.
38. He relies on the studies of A. M. Goldberg on rabbinic thought and Peter Kuhn's writings on divine self-abasement.
39. Jürgen Moltmann, *The Crucified God: The Cross as the Foundation and Criticism of Christian Theology*, trans. R. A. Wilson and J. Bowden (SCM Press, 1974), 273–274. See Richard Bauchham, *The Theology of Jürgen Moltmann* (T&T Clark, 1995), 1, 3.
40. Lapide and Moltmann, *Jewish Monotheism and Christian Trinitarian Doctrine*, 49; and see, John Jaeger, "Abraham Heschel and the Theology of Jürgen Moltmann," *Perspectives in Religious Studies* 24 (1997): 167–179; Daniel Joslyn-Siemiatkoski, "Divine Suffering and Covenantal Belonging: Considering the Atonement with Heschel and Moltmann," in *Atonement and Comparative Theology: The Cross in Dialogue with Other Religions*, ed. Catherine Cornille (Fordham University Press, 2021), 149–166.

41. Abraham Joshua Heschel, *God in Search of Man: A Philosophy of Judaism* (Farrar, Straus and Giroux, 1983), 21–22. On the topic of Heschel and Moltmann, see Jaeger, "Abraham Heschel and the Theology of Jürgen Moltmann," 167–179.
42. Lapide and Moltmann, *Jewish Monotheism and Christian Trinitarian Doctrine*, 49. Elsewhere Moltmann writes of Heschel's bipolar concept: "In history, God exists in a twofold presence: in heaven and in his exiled people, unlimited and limited, infinite and finite, free from suffering and death, while at the same time suffering and dying with his people." Jurgen Moltmann, "God's Kenosis in the Creation and Consummation of the World," in *The Work of Love: Creation as Kenosis*, ed. John Polkinghorne (Eerdmans, 2001), 143.
43. Donald Wayne Viney, "God as the Most and Best Moved Mover: Hartshorne's Importance for Philosophical Theology," *Midwest Quarterly* 48, no. 1 (2006): 10–28.
44. Jürgen Moltmann, *Sun of Righteousness, Arise! God's Future for Humanity and the. Earth*, trans. Margaret Kohl (SCM Press, 2010), 113.
45. Franz Rosenzweig, *The Star of Redemption*, trans. Barbara E. Galli (University of Wisconsin Press, 2005), 410–411. For God crying in midrash, see *Midrash Eikha Rabba, Petiḥta 24,* (edition Solomon Buber), 25; Alan Mintz, *Ḥurban: Responses to Catastrophe in Hebrew Literature* (Columbia University Press, 1984), 49–83; David Stern, *Parables in Midrash: Narrative and Exegesis in Rabbinic Literature* (Harvard University Press, 1991), 24–34.
46. Moltmann, "Shekinah," 175. For more on Tzimzum in Rosenzweig, see Benjamin Pollock, "The Kabbalistic Problem is Not Specifically Theological": Franz Rosenzweig on Tsimtsum," in *Tsimtsum and Modernity: Lurianic Heritage in Modern Philosophy and Theology*, ed. Agata Bielik-Robson and Daniel H. Weiss (De Gruyter, 2020), 219–246.
47. Rosenzweig, *The Star of Redemption*, 410–411.
48. Moltmann, *The Trinity and The Kingdom*, 108.; Gershom Scholem, *Major Trends in Jewish Mysticism*, (Schocken Publishing House, 1941), 260.
49. Moltmann, *The Trinity and The Kingdom*, 110.
50. Moltmann, *The Trinity and the Kingdom*, 109, 110.
51. Jürgen Moltmann, *The Way of Jesus Christ: Christology in Messianic Dimensions*, (HarperCollins, 1990), 49, 168. Jürgen Moltmann, *The Trinity and the Kingdom*, 76. The connection of *tzimtzum* and kenosis

opens up the theological question of theopaschism, the idea that God suffers, in Moltmann, letting us consider whether the suffering of Christ does not only reveal but constitutes God as a Trinity.

52. Renaissance Christian Kabbalah understood that the emanated light entered into the hollow after the contraction, The tree of life in Christian Kabbalah, is a better analogy to the Trinity than the contraction, See, Maria Rosa Antognazza, *Leibniz on the Trinity and the Incarnation: Reason and Revelation in the Seventeenth Century* (Yale University Press, 2007); Allison P. Coudert, *The Impact of the Kabbalah in the Seventeenth Century: The Life and Thought of Francis Mercury van Helmont (1614–98)* (Brill, 1999); Gershom Scholem, *Kabbalah* (Keter Publishing, 1974), 196–201.
53. Moltmann, "Shekinah," 179.
54. Jürgen Moltmann, *The Church in the Power of the Spirit* (SCM Press, 1975), 58.
55. Geiko Muller-Fahrenholz, *The Kingdom and the Power: The Theology of Jurgen Moltmann* (Fortress Press, 2001).
56. Jürgen Moltmann, *The Spirit of Life: A Universal Affirmation* (Fortress, 1992), 49, 60, 319.
57. Lapide and Moltmann, *Jewish Monotheism and Christian Trinitarian Doctrine*, 38.
58. Here I would suggest that Judaism is actually closer to Hindu imagery rather than Christian theology, see Alan Brill, *Rabbi on the Ganges: A Jewish-Hindu Encounter* (Lexington Books, 2019).
59. "Father" is a metaphor for the relationship of the Jewish people in their relationship with God, not a real relationship within God of Father and Son, parent and child, as in Christianity. Alon Goshen-Gottstein, "God the Father in Rabbinic Judaism and Christianity: Transformed Background or Common Ground?" *Journal of Ecumenical Studies* 38, no. 4 (2001): 470–504.
60. Andrew Louth, "Knowing the Unknowable God: Hesychasm and the Kabbalah," in *Selected Essays*, vol. 1, *Studies in Patristics* (Oxford University Press, 2023).
61. Miroslav Volf, *The Church as the Image of the Trinity* (Eerdmans, 1998), 208–210. I recommend to my readers the influential essay on the trinity by Catherine Mowry LaCugna, who wants to move the entire discussion away from the metaphysics of God's inner life to focusing on the human dimension, "the mystery of God with us, and God for us." She asks the reader to consider the trinity as a pattern of God's redeeming hand in history "made known by Christ and done in the power of the

holy spirit." The trinity is a signpost of the manifestation of God's providence, election, and consummation. This approach can richly be compared to many Jewish thinkers such as Nahmanides. See, Catherine Mowry LaCugna, "The Practical Trinity," *The Christian Century* (July 15–22, 1992), 678–682.

62. Walter Kasper, *The God of Jesus Christ: New Edition* (Continuum, 2012), xviii.

CHAPTER TWO: INCARNATION

1. "Mary, Did You Know?" was written in 1991 by Mark Lowry and Buddy Greene, see https://blog.sheetmusicdirect.com/2017/09/how-well-do-you-know-mary-did-you-know.html
2. Trude Weiss-Rosmarin, *Judaism and Christianity: The Differences* (Jewish Book Club, 1943), 23–24.
3. Linwood Urban, *A Short History of Christian Thought* (Oxford University Press, 1995), 73–100.
4. Bruce L. Shelly, "Fine-Tuning the Incarnation," *Christian History*, vol. 51 (1996), 18–20.
5. Larry W. Hurtado, *Ancient Jewish Monotheism and Early Christian Jesus-Devotion: The Context and Character of Christological Faith* (Baylor University Press, 2017).
6. Khaled Anatolios, *Retrieving Nicaea: The Development and Meaning of Trinitarian Doctrine* (Baker Academic, 2011 & 2018); Linwood Urban, *A Short History of Christian Thought* (Oxford University Press, 1995), 84–90.
7. Walter Kasper, *Jesus the Christ* (Paulist Press, 1976), 225.
8. Samuel Tobias Lachs, "Rabbi Abbahu and the Minim," *Jewish Quarterly Review* 60, no. 3 (Jan. 1970): 197–212.
9. Anselm, *Cur Deus Homo*, (John Grant, 1909). Digitized by University of Minnesota (2013) 1.25.
10. Gary Anderson, *That I May Dwell among Them: Incarnation and Atonement in the Tabernacle Narrative* (Eerdmans, 2023).
11. Hans Hermann Henrix, "Profound Difference and Strong Connection" in *God's Presence in Israel and Incarnation: A Christian-Jewish Dialogue.* Jewish-Christian Relations (June 6, 2008), available online at https://www.jcrelations.net/articles/article/gods-presence-in-israel-and-incarnation-a-christian-jewish-dialogue.html. Reprinted in Leon Klenicki, et al., *Toward the Future: Essays on Catholic-Jewish Relations in Memory of Rabbi León Klenicki,* (Paulist Press, 2013).

12. Jacob Neusner, *The Incarnation of God: The Character of Divinity in Formative Judaism* (Global Publications, 2001), 3–4; Jacob Neusner, *Midrash in Context: Exegesis in Formative Judaism* (Fortress Press, 1983), 137.
13. Yair Lorberbaum, *In God's Image: Myth, Theology, and Law in Classical Judaism* (Cambridge University Press, 2015). He is rejecting Joshua Abelson, *The Immanence of God in Rabbinical Literature* (Macmillan, 1912), 82–97 and Arthur Marmorstein, *The Old Rabbinic Doctrine of God* (Oxford University Press, 1927), 1–157. Ephraim Urbach, *The Sages* (Magnes Press, 1975) rejects the identification of the *shekhinah* with any form of hypostasis or physical light, 79. Morton Smith, "On the Shape of God and the Humanity of Gentiles," in *Religions in Antiquity: Essays in Memory of Erwin Ramsdell Goodenough*, ed. Jacob Neusner (Brill, 1970), 315–326.
14. Alexander Altmann, "'Homo Imago Dei' in Jewish and Christian Theology," *Journal of Religion* 48 (1968): 235–259. A nice survey is offered by José Costa, "The Body of God in Ancient Rabbinic Judaism: Problems of Interpretation," *Revue de l'Histoire des Religions* 227, no. 3 (July 2010): 283–316. Marmorstein and Smith in the works cited in the previous footnote are more circumspect on the issues of anthropomorphism.
15. Christoph Markschies *God's Body: Jewish, Christian, and Pagan Images of God*. Trans. Alexander Johannes Edmonds (Baylor University Press, 2019).
16. Markschies, *God's Body*, 284.
17. Moshe Idel, *Ben: Sonship and Jewish Mysticism*, (London/New York: Continuum, 2007), 2–4, 57–69, 99–101, 585–597. Stefan-Sebastian Maftei, "Sonship" and its Relevance for Jewish and Non-Jewish Mystical Literatures," *Journal for the Study of Religions and Ideologies* 8, no. 23 (2009): 141–153.
18. Richard Bauckham has argued that a Second Temple Jewish monotheism could also allow for a "high Christology" that identified Jesus within the life of God, identifying Jesus directly with the God of Israel, but docetic as a human Jesus, See Bauckham, *God of Israel: God Crucified and Other Studies on the New Testament's Christology of Divine Identity*, (Eerdmans, 1998).
19. Costa "The Body of God in Ancient Rabbinic Judaism."
20. Most contemporary scholars, in contrast to the traditional self-understanding of Judaism, assume that many rabbinic texts assume a corporeality of God. However, it is difficult to determine, based on the texts,

the precise nature of this divine body. Daniel Boyarin thinks that it is the body of the divinity himself, Guy Stroumsa thinks it is only a form of hypostasis. See D. Boyarin "De/Re/constructing Midrash," in *Current Trends in the Study of Midrash*, ed. Carol Bakhos (Brill, 2006). 299–322; Guy Stroumsa, "Polymorphie divine et transformations d'un mythologème: l'Apocryphon de Jean et ses sources," *Vigiliae Christianae* 35, no. 4 (December 1981): 412–434, also see Guy Stroumsa, "Form(s) of God: Some Notes on Metatron and Christ," *Harvard Theological Review* 76, no. 3 (1983): 269–288; Compare, Elliot R. Wolfson, "Judaism and Incarnation: The Imaginal Body of God," in *Christianity in Jewish Terms*, ed. Tivka FrymerKensky et al. (Westview Press, 2000), 239–254.

21. See Idel, *Ben*, 57–69, on the question of the incarnation, see 135–136; Boyarin "De/Re/constructing Midrash," 314. In note 47, Boyarian refers positively to Alon Goshen-Gottstein, "Judaisms and Incarnational Theologies: Mapping out the Parameters of Dialogue," *Journal of Ecumenical Studies* 39, no. 3 (Summer-Fall 2002): 219–247.
22. Alan Brill, *Judaism and Other Religions* (Palgrave-Macmillan, 2010), chapter 8.
23. Hyam Macoby, *Judaism on Trial* (Littman Library, 1982), 19. At the same time, it is important to note that Nahmanides was a kabbalist who accepted various forms of embodied divinity, including the divine embodied as the *shekhinah* available as a sensory apprehension by humans. But in none of Nahmanides's formulations did God take on flesh. Nahmanides had a "pneumatic worldview [that] was crafted in light of several alternate theologies of the spirit and the nature of divine overflow," in which the holy spirit "is the driving force behind his conceptualization of the godhead." For more on the topic see the excellent article by Adam Afterman, "The Mystical Dynamics of the Holy Spirit in Moses Nahmanides' Writings," *Jewish Quarterly Review* 113, no. 4 (2023): 639–668, quote is on 667.
24. Karl Barth, *Church Dogmatics*, ed. G. W. Bromiley and T. F. Torrance (T&T Clark, 1960), I, ii.
25. Karl Barth, *Church Dogmatics*, I, ii, 152; 188
26. Karl Barth, *Church Dogmatics*, IV, i, 389.
27. Karl Barth, *Church Dogmatics*, III, ii, 26.
28. Karl Barth, *Church Dogmatics*, IV, i, 390.
29. Karl Barth, *Church Dogmatics*, I, ii, 156.
30. Karl Barth, *Church Dogmatics*, I, ii, 154.

31. Karl Rahner, "Christology within an Evolutionary View of the World," *Theological Investigations*, vol. 5: 176.
32. Karl Rahner, "The Unity of Spirit and Matter in the Christian Understanding of Faith," *Theological Investigations*, vol. 6: 160.
33. Karl Rahner, "The Body as a Symbol of Man," *Theological Investigations*, vol. 4, 245.
34. Karl Rahner, "On the Theology of the Incarnation," *Theological Investigations*, vol. 4, 105, 120.
35. Karl Rahner, *The Content of Faith*, ed. Karl Lehmann and Albert Raffet, trans. Harvey D. Egan, SJ (Crossroad, 1992), 336.
36. Rahner, *The Content of Faith*, 331.
37. Gerald A. McCool, ed., *A Rahner Reader* (The Seabury Press, 1975), 146.
38. Rahner, "On the Theology of the Incarnation," 105.
39. Rahner, "On the Theology of Incarnation," 107.
40. Paul D. Molnar, *Incarnation and Resurrection: Toward a Contemporary Understanding* (Eerdmans, 2007), 50.
41. Martin Buber, *Two Types of Faith*, trans. N. P. Goldhawk (Macmillan, 1951).
42. Paul Molnar *Incarnation and Resurrection*, 69, citing Colin Gunton, *Yesterday and Today: A Study of Continuities in Christology* (Darton, Longman & Todd, 1983), 16.
43. Moltmann, *Trinity and the Kingdom of God* (Fortress Press, 1993), 116.
44. Moltmann, *Trinity and the Kingdom of God*, 116–117
45. Moltmann, *The Crucified God*. He returns to this theme in *The Trinity and the Kingdom of God* (Ch. 2. "The Passion of God") and in *The Way of Jesus Christ* (Ch. 4. "The Apocalyptic Sufferings of Christ").
46. Moltmann, *The Trinity and the Kingdom of God*, 115–116.
47. Moltmann, *The Trinity and the Kingdom*, 114.
48. Moltmann, *The Way of Jesus Christ*, 319.
49. Moltmann, *The Trinity and the Kingdom*, 114.
50. Elizabeth Johnson, *Creation and the Cross: The Mercy of God for a Planet in Peril* (Orbis Books, 2018), 48. A similar approach had been suggested by David Burrell, "Incarnation and Creation: The Hidden Dimension," *Modern Theology* 12 (1996): 211–220. For a recent contrasting approach, returning to the supralapsarian position, see Edwin Chr. van Driel, "Incarnation and Israel: A Supralapsarian Account of Israel's Chosenness," *Modern Theology* 39, no. 1 (2023): 3–18.
51. Johnson, *Creation and the Cross*, 47–48.

52. Moshe Zvi Neriyah, *Celebration of the Soul: The Holidays in the Life and Thought of Rabbi Avraham Yitzchak Kook,* trans. Pesach Jaffe (Genesis Jerusalem Press, 1992), 36, based on Moadei HaRayah, 60.
53. Elizabeth Johnson, *Creation and the Cross*, 1
54. The Aramaic expression echoes the rabbinic statements explaining God's revealing himself to Moses via a desert shrub as a way of conveying that "there is no place devoid of the *Shekhinah*, not even a shrub" *Midrash Shemot Rabbah* 2:5., similarly, "there is no place of earth devoid of God's presence' (*Pesikta de R. Kahana*, ed. Buber, 2b)

    This widespread concept of divine immanence, is still present in the nineteenth century book, *Nefesh Hahayyim* by Hayyim of Voloshin, who stated that one should concentrate his heart in prayer that God "is the Unified One, the Infinite One, Who fills All of this world, and all of the worlds, and that there is no place devoid of Him."
55. Elizabeth Johnson, *Creation and the Cross*, 190. In a similar manner, Niels Gregersen (b. 1956) calls it "deep incarnation," in which Christ is in all that is. All living things are touched by divine grace—and caught up together in movement toward union with God. Anselm of Canterbury famously asked, "Cur deus homo?" (Why did God become human?) but the New Testament nowhere says that God became human. Rather, it says that "the Word (Logos) became flesh (*sarx*) and lived among us" (John 1:14). Here according to Gregerson, the incarnation in all beings as flesh. For more see, Niels Henrik Gregersen, ed., *Incarnation: On the Scope and Depth of Christology* (Fortress Press, 2015).
56. "Dorothy Sayers To Rev Herbert Kelly Oct 4th 1937," in *Letters of Dorothy Sayers,* vol. 2, ed. Barbara Reynolds (Hodder & Stoughton, 1995), 43.
57. Martin Buber, "The Two Foci of the Jewish Soul," in *Israel and the World Essays in a Time of Crisis* (Schocken Books, 1948), 38.
58. Pinchas Lapide, *The Resurrection of Jesus: A Jewish Perspective* (SPCK, 1984), 28.
59. Lapide, *The Resurrection of Jesus*, 130.
60. Lapide, *The Resurrection of Jesus*, 28.
61. There is a difference between incarnation and various forms of divination, theosis, and incarnational anthropology in which God dwells in the believers or the saint. Theosis is a spiritual or metaphysical journey describing how a person can become more like God, or more united with God. It's also known as deification or divinization in Western Christianity and is rooted in the work of the Holy Spirit. There are

many traditional texts in rabbinics, kabbalah, and Hasidism that depict theosis, but in Christian terms these acts of deification are the work of the Holy Spirit, not the human-divine symbiosis of incarnation as defined by Christian creeds. The Hasidic ideas of self-annihilation are similar to kenosis and theosis, yet these ideas are similar to the workings of the Holy Spirit in Christian saints, not incarnation. For Jewish thinkers, looking in this direction, see Goshen-Gottstein, "Judaisms and Incarnational Theologies"; Shaul Magid, *Hasidism Incarnate: Hasidism, Christianity, and the Construction of Modern Judaism* (Stanford University Press, 2014); Moshe Idel, *Ben: Sonship and Jewish Mysticism*, has an entire chapter on this topic, chapter 8. Jürgen Moltmann defines deification as an emanation of divine powers and energies through the Holy Spirit overcoming the difference but not the distinction between Creator and creature, see Jürgen Moltmann, *The Spirit of Life* (Fortress, 1992), 177. See Afterman, "The Mystical Dynamics of the Holy Spirit in Moses Nahmanides' Writings" which explains clearly a Jewish view of the holy spirit. As noted, in the introduction, I regret not including a chapter on the Holy Spirit in this book.

62. Michael Wyschogrod, "A Jewish Perspective on Incarnation," *New Theology* 12, no. 2 (1996): 195–209. See also, Kendall Soulen, *Abraham's Promise: Judaism and Jewish-Christian Relations* (SCM, 2005), 165–178.
63. Michael Wyschogrod, in Soulen, *Abraham's Promise*, 165–178, especially 174.
64. For example, the Samuel ben Meir (Troyes, c. 1085–c. 1158, known as Rashbam) considers the angels who visited Abraham (Gen 18:1–2) as a manifestation of God, but manifestation is not identical with incarnation, so too Hindus are generally adamant that avatara is not incarnation. For a contemporary understanding of the angelic visitors to Abraham as a divine manifestation, see Benjamin D. Sommer, *The Bodies of God and the World of Ancient Israel* (Cambridge University Press, 2009), 40–41.
65. See Kendall Soulen, *Abraham's Promise*, 1–22. Also, Kendall Soulen, "Michael Wyschogrod and God's First Love," *The Christian Century* (July 2004), 22–27.
66. Henrix, "Profound Difference and Strong Connection."
67. Hans Hermann Henrix points out that the specifically Jewish background of Jesus's teachings had no importance for the noted Catholic theologian Karl Rahner, who had commented that "the Jewish origin

in Jesus is of no interest for Christians today." See Henrix, "Profound Difference and Strong Connection," 119.

68. Pope John Paul II, Address to Members of the Pontifical Biblical Commission—11 April 1997; quoted according to: www.vatican.va/holy_father/john_paul_ii/speeches/1997/april/documents/hf_jp-ii_spe_19970411_pont-com-biblica_en.html.

CHAPTER THREE: ORIGINAL SIN

1. John Donne, "A Hymn to God the Father," also titled "To Christ", published posthumously 1633.
2. Trude Weiss Rosmarin, *Judaism and Christianity*, 48.
3. Samson Raphael Hirsch, *The Pentateuch*, trans. Isaac Levy (Soncino, 1956), Genesis 2:16, 61.
4. Hirsch, *The Pentateuch*, Genesis 3:19, 87.
5. This section of early Christian views relies heavily for its contours on Linwood Urban, *A Short History of Christian Thought*, rev. and exp. ed. (Oxford University Press, 1995), 125–155. Besides presenting the Christian thinkers, Urban takes care to give the Jewish parallels to each section. In addition, Jaroslav Pelikan, *The Christian Tradition: A History of the Development of Doctrine*, vol. 1, *The Emergence of the Catholic Tradition (100–600)* (University of Chicago, 1971) remains a guide.
6. Dov Weiss, "Cyril of Alexandria's Critique of 'Jewish' Parental Sin," *Medieval Encounters* 28 (2022): 221–241; Gerald Bray "Original Sin in Patristic Thought," *Churchman* 108, no. 1 (1994): 37–47; David Weaver, "The Exegesis of Romans 5: 12 among the Greek Fathers and its Implication for the Doctrine of Original Sin: The 5th-12th Centuries," *St Vladimir's Theological Quarterly* 29, no. 2 (1985): 133–159; Justin Martyr, *Dialogue with Typho*, chapters 86, 124, cited in John Toews, *The Story of Original Sin* (Wipf and Stock, 2013) 41–86.
7. Weiss, "Cyril of Alexandria's Critique," 221–224.
8. Augustine, *Confessions*, book one; *The City of God*; *On the Grace of God and On Original Sin*. For a discussion of his doctrine, see Jesse Couenhoven, "St. Augustine's Doctrine of Original Sin," *Augustinian Studies* 36, no. 2 (2005): 359–396; Jesse Cuenhoven, "The Explanatory Power of Original Sin," in *Stricken by Sin, Cured by Christ: Agency, Necessity, and Culpability in Augustinian Theology*, online ed. (Oxford Academic, 2013); Henri Rondet, *Original Sin: The Patristic and*

Theological Background, trans. Cajetan Finnegan OP (Alba House, 1972).

9. L'ubomír Batka, "Luther's Teaching on Sin and Evil," in, *The Oxford Handbook of Martin Luther's Theology*, online ed., ed. Robert Kolb, Irene Dingel, and L'ubomír Batka (Oxford Academic, 2014); N. Vorster, "Calvin's modification of Augustine's doctrine of Original Sin," *In die Skriflig* 44, Supplement 3 (2010): 71–89.
10. For a broader discussion, see Gary Anderson, *Sin: A History* (Yale University Press, 2009).
11. Jeremy Cohen notes that there are many early and late rabbinic sources that point to a notion of inherited sin and corrupted nature. For example, see Pirkei de Rebbe Eliezer, 13 and 21; Genesis Rabbah 12:5; Leviticus Rabbah 21:4; Deuteronomy Rabbah 11:9. But Cohen also notes that Judaism chose the path of personal responsibility for sin through the evil inclination and personal responsibility over the hereditary approaches, or that sin cannot be repaired by human means. Jeremy Cohen, "Original Sin as the Evil Inclination: A Polemicist's Appreciation of Human Nature," *Harvard Theological Review* 73, no. 3–4 (July-October 1980): 495–520.
12. Solomon Schechter, *Aspects of Rabbinic Theology* (Schocken, 1961), 208, 253.
13. Schechter, *Aspects of Rabbinic Theology*, 235–245. Linwood Urban, *A Short History of Christian Thought*, also uses the concept of the good and evil inclinations as a distinction from Christianity.
14. They four who never sinned, therefore only died because of Adam, are: Binyamin the son of Yaakov, Amram the father of Moshe, Yishai the father of David, and Kilav the son of David, *TB Sabbath* 55a-b.
15. *Gen. Rabbah.* 14, *Talmud Yerushalmi, Naz.* 7. 56*b*.
16. Schechter, *Aspects of Rabbinic Theology*, 242–263.
17. Schechter, *Aspects of Rabbinic Theology*, 265. As noted above, rabbinic views overlap with the early Greek Church Fathers such as Justin Martyr. Yet, the concept of an evil inclination is only found in the Christian text *Shepherd of Hermes*.
18. Jacob Neusner, *Classical Christianity and Rabbinical Judaism* (Baker Academic, 2004), 44–47, 143, 184.
19. Jon Levenson, "Did God Forgive Adam? An Exercise in Comparative Midrash," in *Jews and Christians: People of God*, ed. Carl E. Braaten and Robert Jenson (Eerdmans, 2003), 148–70. Compare Joel Kalminsly, "Paradise Regained: Rabbinic Reflections on Original Sin," in *Jews,*

Christians, and the Theology of the Hebrew Scriptures, ed. Alice Bellis and Joel Kaminlsky (Society of Biblical Literature, 2000), 15–43, who broadly applies the Augustinian word "original sin" to a variety of separate ideas including: the stain of sin, inherited sin, the fall of Adam, and the texts presented by Jon Levenson and Jeremy Cohen. For a continuity of some of these themes in the medieval era, see the medieval Jewish thinker Hasdai Crescas. In his polemical work he states that Jews were absolved of the original sin when they were circumcised. *Refutation of the Christian Principles*, trans. with an introduction by D. J. Lasker (SUNY Series in Jewish Philosophy, 1992); Daniel Lasker, "Original Sin and Its Atonement According to Hasdai Crescas," [Hebrew] *Daat* 20 (Winter 1988): 127–135; Joel Renbaum, Medieval Jewish Criticism of the Christian Doctrine of Original Sin, *AJS Review* 7, no. 8 (1982/1983).

20. Later parallels include books of Adam and Eve (chaps. 3, 5 16, 18), the Apocalypse of Moses (24:1–2), 2 Enoch (30:16–18; 31:6), and Targum Pseudo-Jonathan. The common view in the second century BCE was that sin had its beginning in the cohabitation of evil angels with human women (Gen 6 1–4), see 1 Enoch, Jubilees, and the Cairo Damascus Document 11:16–18).
21. On Eve's copulation with the serpent, see b. Shabbat 146a; b. Yevamot 103b; b. Avodah Zarah 22b, *Avot De Rabbi Nathan* B 42, *Pirkei De Rabbi Eliezer* 14, B. Eruvin 100b). For a discussion, see Berel Dov Lerner, "The Ten Curses of Eve," *Women in Judaism: A Multidisciplinary e-Journal* 15, no. 1 (2019): 1–15. A Christian thinker who accepted this fall through Eve was Tertullian (c. 155/160–220 CE), who reminded women that they all share Eve's "ignominy . . . of original sin and the odium of being the cause of the fall of the human race" see, *The Apparel of Women*, Book 1, Chapter. 1.
22. This strand of misogyny continued into some later Jewish pietistic works. One example is the writings of Isaiah Horowitz (known as the Shelah, d. 1630), who writes that women are polluted and polluting. He cautions the reader that in the current era pollution has become more manifest and says the solution is to make more fences and stringencies to the law. For Horowitz, the problem is pollution, not guilt and sin, and as such there is no need for a redeemer. However, it is important to note that in this interpretation the sin was by Eve and not Adam. Further, Christian sinfulness and Jewish pollution are not the same concepts, (see Ricœur on cosmic fall).
23. Maimonides, *Guide* I:2.

24. *Summa Theologiae* 1a2ae, q. 109, a. 8.
25. Macoby, *Judaism on Trial*, 50–52.
26. Macoby, *Judaism on Trial*.
27. Indeed, the "Eve" who gave Adam the fruit was not the woman, rather none other than the divine *shekhinah* herself, helping Adam become a being with free will, see Bezalel Safran, "Rabbi Azriel and Nahmanides: Two Views of the Fall of Man," in *Rabbi Moses ben Nahman: Explorations in His Religious and Literary Virtuosity*, ed. I. Twersky (Harvard University Press, 1983), 86–99.
28. Reinhold Niebuhr, *The Nature and Destiny of Man*, vol. 1 (Scribner's, 1941), 178–260.
29. Karl Rahner, *Foundations of Christian Faith: An Introduction to the Idea of Christianity*, trans. William V. Dych (Seabury Press, 1978).
30. Karl Rahner, *Foundations of Christian Faith*, 111.
31. Rahner, *Foundations of Christian Faith*, 96.
32. Rahner, *Foundations of Christian Faith*, 109–110.
33. Rahner, *Foundations of Christian Faith*, 109–110.
34. Rahner, *Foundations of Christian Faith*, 112–113.
35. Post-Holocaust Jewish thought has thinkers who deemphasize the positive elements of creation in place of a dystopic anger with God, most notably Elie Wiesel, *Night* (Hill & Wang, 1960).
36. The Catholic thinker Piet Schoonenberg understands original sin as the general state of the world, similar to Niebuhr or Tillich, an almost Pelagian or Jewish view, see *Man and Sin: A Theological View* (Sheed and Ward, 1965).
37. Jürgen Moltmann, *An Introduction to Christian Theology*, ed. Douglas Meeks (Duke University Press, 1968), 251–254.
38. Moltmann, *An Introduction to Christian Theology*, 251–254.
39. Moltmann, *An Introduction to Christian Theology*, 251–254.
40. Moltmann, *An Introduction to Christian Theology*, 251–254.
41. Jürgen Moltmann, *Theology of Hope*, trans. James W. Leitch (Harper & Row, 1967), 25.
42. Moshe Halbertal, and Avishai Margalit, *Idolatry* (Harvard University Press, 1992).
43. Emil Brunner, *The Divine Imperative* (Lutterworth Press, 1937).
44. Emil Brunner, *Our Faith* (Scribner's, 1954), ch. 6.
45. Emil Brunner, *Man in Revolt: A Christian Anthropology* (Westminster Press, 1947), 530.
46. Joseph Dov Soloveitchik, *The Emergence of Ethical Man* (Ktav, 2005), 98. This presentation of original sin in Soloveitchik should be limited to

the book *Emergence of Ethical Man*. However, in Soloveitchik's *Lonely Man of Faith* and *Worship of the Heart*, he understands original sin based on Herman Cohen's interpretation of Maimonides as the abandonment of the intellectual-ethical for the aesthetic. (I thank Lawrence Kaplan for this distinction between Soloveitchik's books.)

47. In another place, however, Soloveitchik explains that, "The Biblical account of the original sin is the story of a man of faith who realizes suddenly that faith can be utilized for an acquisition of majesty and glory and who, instead of fostering a covenantal community, prefers to organize a political utilitarian community. . . . The history of organized religion is replete with instances of desecration of the covenant." Joseph B. Soloveitchik, *The Lonely Man of Faith* (Doubleday, 1992), 39–40, in the footnote.
48. It would be worthwhile to compare this chapter to Gabriel Said Reynolds, "Original Sin and the Qur'an," *Islamochristiana* 46 (2020), who shows that Islam has a fall of Adam, a sin of Adam, and sees humanity as susceptible to evil and desires, but that there is no original sin in Augustinian sense, humanity is not culpable for Adam's sin and there is no drama of redemption.
49. Paul Ricœur, "The 'Adamic' Myth and the 'Eschatological' Vision of History," in *The Symbolism of Evil* (Beacon Press, 1967), 269–286, and "Original Sin: A Study of its Meaning," in *The Conflict of Interpretations: Essays in Hermeneutics* (Northwestern University Press, 1974), 269–286. For further development of Ricoeur's perspectives, see Stephen J. Duffy, "Our Hearts of Darkness: Original Sin Revisited," *Theological Studies* 49 (1988): 597–622.
50. For a breakdown of components, see Linwood Urban, *A Short History of Christian Thought* (Oxford University Press, 1995).
51. We also encounter this idea in thinkers such as Rabbi Tzadok Hakohen of Lublin (1823–1900), who taught that the psychic energy of sin leads to a more fervent and intense repentance, see Alan Brill, *Thinking God: The Mysticism of Rabbi Zadok of Lublin* (YU Press, 2002).
52. Steven Kepnes, "'Turn Us to You and We Shall Return': Original Sin, Atonement, and Redemption in Jewish Terms," in *Christianity in Jewish Terms*, ed. Tikva Frymer-Kensky, et. al. (Westview, 2000), 293–304.
53. For an introduction to Lurianic kabbalah, see Lawrence Fine, *Physician of the Soul, Healer of the Cosmos: Isaac Luria and His Kabbalistic Fellowship* (Stanford University Press, 2003). These ideas also exist in the circa 1300 text *Tikkune Zohar* where after the fall of cosmic Adam,

humans have a mixture of good and evil, do not have direct access to divinity, and divinity itself is shattered, see *Tikkune Zohar*, 97b, 102a.

54. Isaac Luria, *Shaar Hapesukim,* Bereshit 2.
55. Luria's student Chaim Vital claims that to regather the cosmic sparks one needs to engage in the commandment of procreation sex in order to bring souls into the world. Such engagement requires no degradation of human sexuality, or propagating the sin via intercourse. For Vital, sexuality redeems Adam's sin by bringing souls into the world, see *Gate of Reincarnations*, chapter 11, section 9.
56. For example, Simon D. Podmore, "'Abyss Calls Unto Abyss': Tsimtsum and Kenosis in the Rupture of God-forsakenness," in *Tsimtsum and Modernity: Lurianic Heritage in Modern Philosophy and Theology*, ed. Agata Bielik-Robson and Daniel H. Weiss (De Gruyter, 2020), 311–338.

CHAPTER FOUR: SALVATION AND ATONEMENT

1. Trude Weiss-Rosmarin, *Judaism and Christianity: The Differences* (Jewish Book Club, 1943), 54.
2. https://www.britannica.com/topic/salvation-religion/Judaism
3. Urban, *A Short History of Christian Thought*, ch. 4; https://www.britannica.com/topic/salvation-religion/Christianity
4. The idea that one figure is both the priest and the sacrifice as well as being a cultic item has its antecedents in the Second Temple era work The Apocalypse of Abraham, which influenced the Epistle to the Hebrews. On this topic, see Andrei Orlov, *Heavenly Priesthood in the Apocalypse of Abrham* (Cambridge University Press, 2013).
5. *The Letter of the Church of Rome to the Church of Corinth* (commonly known as *Clement's First Letter*). One recent book described early Jewish and Christian texts as a "vast marketplace of atonement theologies" with "highly flexible" logic. See, Max Botner, Justin Harrison Duff, and Simon Dürr, eds. *Atonement: Jewish and Christian Origins* (Eerdmans, 2020), introduction.
6. Augustine, *Confessions*, Book I 5, 11; Augustine, *Faith and Works.*
7. B. R. Rees and Pelagius, *Pelagius: Life and Letters* (Boydell Press, 1998), 221–222; Burton L. Visotzky, "Will and Grace: Aspects of Judaising in Pelagianism in Light of Rabbinic and Patristic Exegesis of Genesis," in *The Exegetical Encounter Between Jews and Christians in Late Antiquity*, ed. Emmanouela Grypeou and Helen Spurling (Brill, 2009), 43–62.

8. Francis A. Sullivan, *Salvation Outside the Church: Tracing the History of the Catholic Response* (Paulist Press, 1992), 5. In contrast, in a Talmud story, Roman Emperor Antoninus worries that as a descendant of Esau, he will not be saved to enter the world to come. Antoninus said to Rabbi Yehudah HaNasi: "Will I enter the World-to-Come?" Rabbi Yehudah HaNasi gave to him an emphatic "Yes!" because you do not behave in a sinful manner like Esau (b. Avodah Zarah 10b). Here is a clear story that salvation is not limited to Jews but is available to all who behave in a virtuous manner, including pagans. Cf. Maimonides, Laws of Kings, *Mishnah Torah* 8:11. Or as defined by Chief Rabbi Sacks: "Judaism . . . believes in one God but not in one exclusive path to salvation. The God of the Israelites is the God of all humankind, but the demands made of the Israelites are not asked of all humankind. There is no equivalent in Judaism to the doctrine that *extra ecclesiam non est salus* (outside the Church there is no salvation). To the contrary, Judaism's ancient sages maintained that "the pious of the nations have a share in the world to come." Jonathan Sacks, *Dignity of Difference: How to Avoid the Clash of Civilizations* (Continuum, 2002), 52–53.
9. Schechter, *Aspects of Rabbinic Theology* , 313–343.
10. TB Pesahim 54a; TY Pe'ah 17:1; *Genesis Rabbah* 1:4, 12; *Lamentations Rabbah* 3:5; Midrash on Psalm 57:90; cf. *Pesikta Rabbati* 158b.
11. Gary Anderson, *Sin A History* (Yale University Press, 2010), 96.
12. George F. Moore, *Judaism*, vol. 1 (Harvard University Press, 1966), 500.
13. Ilaria Ramelli, "Forgiveness in Patristic Philosophy: The Importance of Repentance and the Centrality of Grace," in *Ancient Forgiveness: Classical, Judaic, and Christian*, ed. Charles L. Griswold and David Konstan (Cambridge University Press, 2012), 195–215. On tears in Judaism, see Moshe Idel, *Kabbalah: New Perspectives* (Yale University Press, 1989), 75–88, 197–199.
14. Danya Ruttenberg, *On Repentance and Repair: Making Amends in an Unrepentant World* (Beacon Press, 2022), 27, 46, 52, 56, 122, 152, 196.
15. Ruttenberg, *On Repentance and Repair.*
16. Jonah of Gerondi, *The Gates of Repentance* (Feldheim, 1976).
17. Nahmanides, "Commentary on Lev 16."
18. Kaufman Kohler, *Jewish Theology Systematically and Historically Considered* (Macmillan, 1918), 247–255. For an emphasize on these convergences as a common spiritual neighborhood, see John Lyden, "Atonement in Judaism and Christianity: Toward a Rapprochement," *Journal of Ecumenical Studies* 29 (1992): 47–54. Lyden points out the

importance of vicarious atonement, sacrifice, and the role of the suffering servant in both religions. He places the difference in the role of Christ. He does not mention later developments in the Jewish tradition after early rabbinic midrash, and the author explicitly rejects as non-rabbinic Hermann Cohen and by extension Maimonides.

19. Maimonides, "Introduction to Helek"; Abraham Isaac Kook, *Midbar Shor* (Jerusalem, 1999), 36.
20. Mekilta., Yitro, 10; Sifre, Deut. 32; Ber. 5a.
21. Pesiḳta. xxv. 165a.
22. TB Sanh. 37b, Gen. R. xlii.; Ex. R. xxxi.:10; Lev. R. xi.
23. Sifre, Num. 112; Mek., Yitro, 7.
24. TB Berakhot 55a; Tanhuma Vayishlach 6.
25. R. H. 18a; Yeb. 105a; Lev. R. xxv.
26. Berel Wein, *The Triumph of Survival: The Story of the Jews in the Modern Era 1650–1990* (Shaar, 1990), 14.
27. Schechter, *Aspects of Rabbinic Theology*, 310–311.
28. TB. Sotah 14a; TB Berakhot 32a.
29. Leviticus Rabbah 20:12; *Sifre Deut.* §333 (140a).
30. On the image of father in Jewish and Christian texts, see Alon Goshen-Gottstein, "God the Father in Rabbinic Judaism and Christianity: Transformed Background or Common Ground?" *Journal of Ecumenical Studies* 38, no. 4 (Fall 2001).
31. In Talmud tractate Rosh Hashanah 17b, there is an opinion that after the twelve months, the wicked just cease to exist. Dov Weiss, "Gehinnom's Punishments in Classical Rabbinic Literature," in *Jewish Culture and Creativity: Essays in Honor of Michael Fishbane* (Academic Studies Press, 2023), 77–90; John J. Collins, "The Afterlife in Apocalyptic Literature," in *Judaism in Late Antiquity 4: Death, Life-After-Death, Resurrection and The World-to-Come in the Judaisms of Antiquity*, ed. Jacob Neusner and Alan J. Avery-Peck (Brill, 2000), 117–139. In general, Second Temple and Christian literature places angels, demons, and Satan in charge of the afterlife realms, but Jewish texts place God in charge.
32. "The Rebbe's Promise" at https://breslov.org/the-rebbes-promise/
33. See Moses Mendelssohn, *Jerusalem, or On Religious Power and Judaism*, trans. Allan Arkush, ed. Alexander Altmann (University Press of New England, 1983), 97, 248; *Moses Mendelssohn: Writings on Judaism, Christianity, and the Bible* , trans. Curtis Bowman,Elias Sacks, and Allan Arkush, ed. Michah Gottlieb (University Press of New England, 2011), 16–27.

34. Maxie D. Dunnam, *Going on to Salvation: A Study of Wesleyan Beliefs* (Abingdon Press, 2008), 38–39. Jeff Wells, "A Movement on Fire: Salvation—It's Not What You Think!" at https://www.churchofthevillage.org/salvation-its-not-what-you-think
35. Joseph Ringel, "'There but for the Grace of God Go I': A Theological Contrast Between Jean Calvin and Maharal," *Brandeis Graduate Journal* 3 (2005), 1–7.
36. Owen Strachan, "Carl F. H. Henry's Doctrine of the Atonement: A Synthesis and Brief Analysis," *Themelios* 38, no. 2 (2013).
37. Karl Rahner, *Foundation of Christian Faith: An Introduction to the Idea of Christianity* (Crossroad, 2005), 218–223.
38. Rahner, "Concerning the Relationship between Nature and Grace," in *Theological Investigations* 1 (Crossroad, 1961), 297–317.
39. For a full discussion on the role of the cross in Rahner's theory of atonement, see Brandon R. Peterson, "Rahner and the Cross: What Kind of Atoning Story Does He Tell?" *Philosophy & Theology* (2021): 113–137.
40. Karl Rahner, *Experience of the Spirit: Source of Theology, Theological Investigations*, vol. 16 (Crossroad, 1983), 55; Rahner, *Foundations of Christian Faith*, 143.
41. Peter C. Phan, "Mystery of Grace and Salvation: Karl Rahner's theology of the Trinity," in *The Cambridge Companion to the Trinity*, ed. Peter Phan (Cambridge University Press, 2011), 192–207.
42. Rahner, *Foundations of Christian Faith*, 284.
43. Karl Rahner, "Some Implications of the Scholastic Concept of Uncreated Grace," in *Theological Investigations*, vol. 1, 319–346. Scholastic theology distinguished between uncreated grace being God's gift of Godself whereas created grace is the transformation of human nature which either precedes or accompanies this gift.
44. Abraham Joshua Heschel, *God in Search of Man* (J. P. S., 1955), especially 75–90.
45. Klaus von Stosch, "How Q 5:75 Can Help Christians Conceptualize Atonement." In *Atonement and Comparative Theology: The Cross in Dialogue with Other Religions*, edited by Catherine Cornille, (Fordham University Press, 2021), 61–77. Von Stosch based his ideas on Thomas Pröpper, *Theologische Anthropologie* (Herder, 2011).
46. "Death," in Karl Rahner, ed., *Encyclopedia of Theology: The Concise Sacramentum Mundi* (Seabury, 1975), 329–330; Karl Rahner, *On the Theology of Death* (Herder and Herder, 1961), 35.
47. Abraham Isaac Kook, "The Vitality of the World" *Orot Ha-Kodesh* [Heb.], (Mosad ha-Rav Ḳuḳ, 1963) ch. 40, 2.

48. Kook, "The Vitality of the World" *Orot Ha-Kodesh*. For Kook, "Before the sin in the Garden of Eden man lived on the supreme level of the unity of body and soul. The taste of the tree was like the taste of the fruit. Then, man's sin separated the body from the soul and man lived the life of the body. The goal is to reunite the body and soul by seeing a death to the material life." In contrast, for Soloveitchik, unlike Rahner and Kook, death is feared and reviled. Through learning the laws of mourning, we attempt to give death objectivity and life meaning, in order to free ourselves from the fear of death. See, Gerald J. Blidstein, "Death in the Writings of Rabbi Joseph Dov Soloveitchik," *Tradition* 44, no. 1, (2011), 7–18.
49. Moltmann, *The Trinity and the Kingdom of God: The Doctrine of God* (SCM,1981), 87–88.
50. Jürgen Moltmann, *Theology of Hope*, trans. James W. Leitch (Harper & Row, 1967), 329, 216.
51. Moltmann, *Theology of Hope*, 203, 224.
52. Jürgen Moltmann, *The Crucified God* (Fortress, 1993), 276.
53. Jürgen Moltmann, *The Church in the Power of the Spirit* (SCM Press, 1975), 66.
54. Jürgen Moltmann, *The Way of Jesus Christ: Christology in Messianic Dimensions* (SCM Press, 1990).
55. Jürgen Moltmann, *The Coming of God: Christian Eschatology* (Fortress Press, 1996), 245.
56. Moltmann, *The Coming of God*, 245.
57. Moltmann, *The Coming of God*, 251.
58. Moltmann, *The Crucified God*, 195.
59. Jürgen Moltmann, *Man: Christian Anthropology in the Conflicts of the Present* (Fortress Press, 1974), 117.
60. Moltmann writes, "I saw the God-forsaken cry with which Christ dies on the cross as the criterion for all theology which claims to be Christian." See Moltmann, *The Way of Jesus Christ*, 152, as well as, "The death of Jesus on the cross is the *centre* of all Christian theology . . . All Christian statements about God, about creation, about sin and death have their focal point in the crucified Christ." See Moltmann, *The Crucified God*, 204.
61. Nicholas Ansell, *Annihilation of Hell: Universal Salvation and the Redemption of Time in the Eschatology of Jürgen Moltmann* (Milton Keynes: Paternoster, 2013), 49.
62. Jospeh Dov Soloveitchik, *Before HaShem You Shall Be Purified: Rabbi Joseph B. Soloveitchik on the Days of Awe*. Summarized and annotated by Arnold Lustiger (Ohr Publishing, 1998), 8–10, 28–29, 135.

63. Ernst M. Conradie, "The Justification of God? The Story of God's Work according to Jürgen Moltmann: Part 1 & 2," *Scriptura* 97 (2008): 76–105
64. David Tracy, "The Christian Understanding of Salvation-Liberation," *Buddhist-Christian Studies* 7 (1987): 129–138.
65. Jonathan Sacks, "Two Concepts of Teshuvah" Nitzavim, 5767 [2007] accessed at https://rabbisacks.org/covenant-conversation/nitzavim/two-concepts-of-teshuvah/
66. Cardinal Ratzinger, *Jesus of Nazareth, Part 2, Holy Week: From the Entrance into Jerusalem to the Resurrection* (Ignatius Press, 2011), 232.
67. Sacks, "Two Concepts of Teshuvah."
68. Hans Urs von Balthasar, "Tragedy and Christian Faith," in *Explorations in Theology*, vol. 3, *Spiritus Creator*, trans. Brian McNeil (Ignatius Press, 1993), 391–411.
69. Danya Ruttenberg, *On Repentance and Repair*, 58.
70. Mordecai Kaplan, *Questions Jews Ask* (Reconstructionist Press, 1956), 128.
71. Lawrence Kaplan, "Hermann Cohen and Rabbi Joseph Soloveitchik on Repentance," *Journal of Jewish Thought and Philosophy* 13, no. 1–3 (2004): 213–258.
72. Kaplan, "Hermann Cohen and Rabbi Joseph Soloveitchik on Repentance," 228.
73. Karl Barth, *Church Dogmatics* IV, 665.
74. *Catechism of The Catholic Church*, 1431.

CHAPTER FIVE: MESSIAH

1. Weiss-Rosmarin, *Judaism and Christianity*, 118, 129.
2. William Horbury, "Introduction to the Second Edition," *Messianism among Jews and Christians: Biblical and Historic Studies* (Bloomsbury T&T Clark, 2016), 1.
3. Sigmund Mowinckel, *He That Cometh: The Messiah Concept in the Old Testament and Later Judaism*, forward John Collins (Eerdmans, 2005); Adela Yarbro Collins, and John J. Collins, *King and Messiah as Son of God: Divine, Human, and Angelic Messianic Figures in Biblical and Related Literature* (Eerdmans, 2008); Magnus Zetterholm, *The Messiah: In Early Judaism and Christianity* (Fortress Press, 2007); Urban, *A Short History of Christian Thought*, 18–23, 34.
4. Horbury, *Messianism among Jews and Christians*.

5. For example, Psalm 22 discusses the Lord and his messiah. On Psalm 22 in the context of messianism, see Peter Schäfer, *The Jewish Jesus: How Judaism and Christianity Shaped Each Other* (Princeton University Press, 2012). Jewish commentators assume the verse is about David as King, see the traditional commentaries cited in Rivka Ulmer, "Psalm 22 in Pesiqta Rabbati: The Suffering of the Jewish Messiah and Jesus," in *The Jewish Jesus: Revelation, Reflection, Reclamation*, ed. Zev Garber (Purdue University Press, 2011), 106–128.
6. The relevant pre-Christian Jewish sources of the divine messiah are presented in Martin Hengel, *The Son of God: The Origin of Christology and the History of Jewish-Hellenistic Religion* (SCM Press, 1976). The lines between divine and human become complex in which the messiah can be divine.
7. John Collins, "Why Do We Call Jesus the Messiah?" *U.S. Catholic* 82, no. 12 (Dec. 2017): 34–37.
8. Walter Brueggemann, *Isaiah 40–66* (Westminster John Knox, 1998), 143, states: "There is no doubt that Isaiah 53 is to be understood in the context of the Isaiah tradition. Insofar as the servant is Israel—a common assumption of Jewish interpretation." The passage, however, had already been connected to the messiah by Zachariah 13, and possibly also in the book of Daniel, see Israel Knohl, *The Messiah before Jesus: The Suffering Servant of the Dead Sea Scrolls*, trans. David Maisel (University of California Press, 2002). On later Jewish interpretation of the passage, as a selection from the extensive literature, see Adolf D. Neubauer and Samuel R. Driver, *The Fifty-Third Chapter of Isaiah according to the Jewish Interpreters*, 2 vols. (Oxford University Press, :1877); Joel Rembaum, "The Development of a Jewish Exegetical Tradition Regarding Isaiah 53," *HTR* 75 (1982): 289–311.
9. 2 Macc 7:18, 32–38; 12:39–42; 4 Macc 4:21, 28–29; 17:21–22.
10. Collins, "Why Do We Call Jesus the Messiah?" 3. In contrast to Collins, Daniel Boyarin makes a broad sweeping generalization that that idea of the Suffering Messiah has been "part and parcel of Jewish tradition from antiquity to modernity," For him, ancient Jews read Isaiah 52–53 as referring to the Messiah and that they also expected a divine-human Messiah. Daniel Boyarin, *The Jewish Gospels: The Story of the Jewish Christ* (The New Press, 2012), 152.
11. Matthew V. Novenson, *The Grammar of Messianism: An Ancient Jewish Political Idiom and Its Users* (Oxford University Press, 2017), ch. 6, author's abstract. A similar conclusion was reached in Michael Morgen

and Steven Weitzman, eds., *Rethinking the Messianic Idea in Judaism* (Indiana University Press, 2015).

12. Walter Kasper. *Jesus the Christ* (Paulist Press, 1981), 149.
13. TB Shabbat 63a.
14. Jacob Neusner, *Messiah in Context: Israel's History and Destiny in Formative Judaism* (Fortress Press, 1984), 1, 17–18, 231. Ephraim E. Urbach, *The Sages* (Harvard University Press, 1987), 308–314, 659–689.
15. Neusner, *Messiah in Context,* 235; Michael Fishbane, "5 Midrashic Theologies of Messianic Suffering," in *The Exegetical Imagination: On Jewish Thought and Theology* (Harvard University Press, 1998), 73–85. Reuven Kimelman, "The Messiah of the Amidah: A Study in Comparative Messianism," *Journal of Biblical Literature* 116, no. 2 (Summer 1997), 313–320.
16. Schechter, *Aspects of Rabbinic Theology*, 101–103.
17. Rivka Ulmer, "The Contours of the Messiah in Pesiqta Rabbati," *Harvard Theological Review* 106, no. 2 (2013): 115–144; Rivka Ulmer, "Psalm 22 in Pesiqta Rabbati: The Suffering of the Jewish Messiah and Jesus," in *The Jewish Jesus: Revelation, Reflection, Reclamation*, ed. Zev Garber (Purdue University Press, 2011), 106–128.
18. Sukkah 52a has a narrative with the Messiah ben Joseph who is killed.
19. Martha Himmelfarb. *Jewish Messiahs in a Christian Empire: A History of the Book of Zerubbabel,* (Cambridge: Harvard University Press, 2017).
20. Zohar II:7a–9a.
21. Yehuda Liebes, "The Messiah of the Zohar: On R. Simeon bar Yohai as a Messianic Figure," in *Studies in the Zohar* (SUNY Press, 1993), 1–84; Liebes, "Sabbatian Messianism," in *Studies in Jewish Myth and Jewish Messianism* (SUNY Press: 1992), 93–106.
22. Moshe Idel, *Messianic Mystics* (Yale University Press, 1998), 226
23. James D. Tabor, "Ancient Jewish and Early Christian Millennialism," in *The Oxford Handbook of Millennialism*, ed. Catherine Wessinger (Oxford University Press, 2011), 252–266; Brian E. Daley, *The Hope of the Early Church: A Handbook of Patristic Eschatology* (Cambridge University Press, 1999); Adela Yarbro Collins, "The Book of Revelation," in *The Continuum History of Apocalypticism*, ed. Bernard J. McGinn, John J. Collins, and Stephen J. Stein(Continuum, 2003), 195–220.
24. On Jewish messianic movements, see Harris Lenowitz, *The Jewish Messiahs: From the Galilee to Crown Heights* (Oxford University Press,

1998); Raphael Patai, *The Messiah Texts* (Wayne State University Press, 1979); Michael Morgen and Steven Weitzman, eds., *Rethinking the Messianic Idea in Judaism* (Indiana University Press, 2015). It is important to note that some of these messianic movements arose under Islam and use Shia and general Quranic models of an eschatological leader or Mahdi. For an overview of these movements, see Bat-Zion Eraqi Klorman, *The Jews of Yemen in the 19th Century: A Portrait of a Messianic Community* (Brill, 1993). These Jewish apocalyptic depictions of the end times are weak on a personal messiah or specific agent, rather they envisioned great battles, destruction of enemies, a period of anarchy, and then a leader to lead the people in the correct ways of justice. They also lack a concept of salvation. If the messianic vision includes the destruction of the Christian empires, then the division of Jews and Christians is clearly not just a question of the messiah's first or second arrival.

25. Messiah created by God before the creation of the world—Pesikta 33:33–37, 36:3–4, Pesachim 54a–b, Nedarim 39a based on 4 Ezra 7:26, 1 Enoch 46:1–2, Seder Gan Eden 3:132.
26. Maimonides, *Mishneh Torah,* ch. 11 Halacha 1.
27. Maimonides, *Mishneh Torah,* ch. 11, Halacha 5.
28. Maimonides, *Mishneh Torah,* ch. 11, Halacha 3.
29. Maimonides, ch. 12, Halacha 1.
30. Hyam Macoby, *Judaism on Trial: Jewish-Christian Disputations in the Middle Ages* (The Littman Library of Jewish Civilization, 1982), 52–53.
31. Joseph Albo, *Sefer ha-'Ikkarim* [Book of Principles], trans. and ed. I. Husik (The Jewish Publication Society of America, 1929), 4, 42:1. "Every adherent of the Law of Moses is obliged to believe in the coming of the Messiah, as we explained above. The Torah expressly commands us to believe the words of the prophet: 'Unto him ye shall hearken.' The prophets announced the coming of the Messiah, hence it is clear that any one who does not believe in the coming of the Messiah denies the words of the prophets and transgresses a mandatory precept. But the belief in the coming of the Messiah is not a fundamental principle, denial of which would nullify the entire Torah."
32. Hyam Macoby, *Judaism on Trial*, 53–54.
33. Saadiah, *Book of Belief and Opinions*, 2; Maimonides, *Mishneh Torah,* Teshuvah 3:7.
34. Nahmanides, Sefer Geulah, *Writings and Discourses* 1:280. And see Jeremy Philip Brown, "What Does the Messiah Know? A Prelude to Kabbalah's Trinity Complex," *Maimonides Review of Philosophy*

and Religion 2 (2023): 1–49; Oded Yisraeli, "The 'Messianic Idea' in Nahmanides' Writings," *Jewish Studies Quarterly* 29, no. 1 (2022): 22–45. Nahmanides in his biblical commentary (Deut. 30:6) envisioned that in the days of the Messiah, the choice of the good will be natural without improper desires, as he was before the primordial sin of Adam.

35. Karl Barth, *Church Dogmatics*, II.2, 94–99.
36. Emil Brunner, *The Mediator: A Study of the Central Doctrine of the Christian Faith* (Lutterworth Press, 1934), 338–345.
37. Jürgen Moltmann, *Theology of Hope: On the Ground and the Implications of a Christian Eschatology*, (SCM, 1967), 54; *The Coming of God: Christian Eschatology* (Fortress, 1996), 14.
38. Jürgen Moltmann, *The Way of Jesus Christ* (SCM, 1990), 21; *The Trinity and the Kingdom* (Fortress Press, 1993), 49.
39. Jürgen Moltmann, *The Spirit of Life: A Universal Affirmation* (SCM, 1992), 130.
40. Moltmann, *The Way of Jesus Christ*, 132.
41. Moltmann, *The Way of Jesus Christ*, 133–4.
42. Jürgen Moltmann, *Church in the Power of the Spirit* (Fortress Press, 1993), 136.
43. Moltmann, *The Way of Jesus Christ*, 155.
44. Moltmann, *The Way of Jesus Christ*, 135–136, 153, 164.
45. Moltmann, *The Way of Jesus Christ*, 147, 156.
46. Moltmann, *Church in the Power of the Spirit*, 193. In *The Trinity and the Kingdom*, 75–83, Moltmann first makes the crucial distinction between active and passive suffering, in which Jesus's suffering "is no unwilling, fortuitous suffering; it is *passio activa*" (75); See Paul Fiddes, *The Creative Suffering of God* (Oxford University Press, 1988).
47. See Moltmann, *The Church in the Power of the Spirit*, 192.
48. Compare to Franz Rosenzweig, who sees the Jewish liturgy has bring the past and the messianic future into the present. See Rosenzweig, *Star of Redemption* (Rinehart and Winston, 1971), 308, 313, 323 on Shabbat. Steve Kepnes makes the argument of past and future in present in Jewish liturgy connecting Rosenzweig and Augustine, see Steven Kepnes, *Jewish Liturgical Reasoning* (Oxford University Press, 2007), 98–99.
49. Moltmann, *The Church in the Power of the Spirit*, 233. For some Jewish parallels of the messianic as a force found in the present that overcomes the suffering of the world, see Elliot Wolfson, "Suffering Time: Maharal's Influence on Ḥasidic Perspectives on Temporality,"

Kabbalah: Journal for the Study of Jewish Mystical Texts 44 (2019): 7–73.

50. Moltmann, *The Way of Jesus Christ*, 27; Abraham Joshua Heschel, *The Sabbath* (Farrar, Straus and Giroux, 1951). Moltmann himself wants to directly engage in Jewish-Christian reconciliation in that very chapter by comparing his messianic view to those of Martin Buber, Schalom Ben-Chorin, and Gershom Scholem. He clearly disagrees with their characterization of Christian messianism as limited to the salvation of the soul.
51. See Moltmann, *The Spirit of Life*, 48
52. *Sanhedrin*, 98a. The story concludes, that when asked when he will come to the world, the messiah answers "Today!" explained as "Today, if you will hear his voice." The point of the Talmudic story is that the messianic age relies on human activity to alleviate suffering. A message less about hope and more about responsibility.
53. See Moltmann, *Theology of Hope*, 84–94.
54. Ruth Kara-Ivanov Kaniel, *The Feminine Messiah: King David in the Image of the Shekhinah in Kabbalistic Literature* (Brill, 2021) contains a wealth of material of the messianic role of King David and the *Shekhinah* including his feminization and his need for a transgressive path with a subsequent repair. She also notes the Jewish polemics against Christianity in some of these presentations. In a recent article, she further develops these themes: see "The Stillborn Messiah and the Non-Viable Redeemer: Gender and Judeo-Christian Entanglement," in *Constructions of Gender in Religious Traditions of Late Antiquity*, ed. K. Ehrensperger, Sh. Sheinfeld, J. Hoppe (Lexington Books, 2024), 323–344.The need for the messiah to be transgressive and outside of expectations is developed for the twentieth century in Joseph Dov Soloveitchik, *Abraham's Journey*, (KTAV, 2008), 177–182.
55. Moltmann, *Life of the Spirit*, 62–63.
56. Moltmann, *Way of Jesus Christ*, 319.
57. Jonathan Sacks, "The Chronological Imagination," at https://rabbisacks.org/covenant-conversation/behar/the-chronological-imagination/
58. Jonathan Sacks, *Future Tense: A Vision for Jews and Judaism in the Global Culture* (Hodder & Stoughton, 2011), 231–252.
59. Jewish apocalyptic texts, some kabbalistic texts, and messianic figures such as Shabbati Zevi did seek a new temporality.
60. David Tracy, "Religious Values after the Holocaust: A Catholic View," in *Jews and Christians After the Holocaust*, ed, A. Peck (Fortress Press, 1982), 99–100.

61. Kasper, *The God of Jesus Christ*, 163.
62. Norman Cohn, *The Pursuit of the Millennium: Revolutionary Millenarians and Mystical Anarchists of the Middle Ages* (Oxford University Press, 1970); Bernard McGinn, *Visions of the End: Apocalyptic Traditions in the Middle Ages*, 2nd ed. (Columbia University Press, 1998); James D. Baghos, "Nuancing the 'Millennium' in the Writings of Norman Cohn," *Literature & Aesthetics* 33, no. 1 (2023): 37–54.
63. Yaakov Ariel, "Messianic Hopes and Middle East Politics: The Influence of Millennial Faith on American Middle East Policies," *Revue LISA/LISA e-journal* [Online], vol. 9, no.1 (2011): document 13, http://journals.openedition.org/lisa/4165, accessed April 17, 2023.
64. See Andrew Crome, *Christian Zionism and English National Identity, 1600–1850* (Palgrave Macmillan, 2018), 227. For a Jewish parallel, see the writings of Menashe ben Israel who states that the Messiah will only come if the Jews settle and resettle in all corners of the world.
65. Ariel, "Messianic Hopes and Middle East Politics."
66. Yaakov Ariel, "How are Jews and Israel Portrayed in the Left Behind Series?" in *Rapture, Revelation and the End Times*, ed. Bruce Forbes and Jeanne Kilde (Palgrave Macmillan, 2004), 131–166; Ariel, "Biblical Imagery, the End Times, and Political Action: The Roots of Christian support for Zionism and Israel," in *The Bible in the Public Square: Its Enduring Influence in American Life*, ed. Mark A. Chamey, Carol Meyers, and Eric M. Meyers (SBL Press, 2014), 37–64.
67. John Hagee, *In Defense of Israel* (Frontline Books, 2007); Maayan Jaffe-Hoffman, "For Evangelicals, is Benjamin Netanyahu the Fallen Messiah?" *Jerusalem Post* (June 6, 2021).
68. Faydra L. Shapiro, *Christian Zionism: Navigating the Jewish-Christian Border* (Cascade Books, 2015). For more on Tzvi Yehudah Kook's messianism, see Motti Inbari, *Messianic Religious Zionism Confronts Israeli Territorial Compromises* (Cambridge University Press, 2012).
69. Joseph Soloveitchik, "On Love of Torah and the Redemption of the Soul of the Generation," In *Aloneness and Togetherness, BeSod HaYachid VehaYachad* (Orot, 1976), 403–432 [Heb.], quotation from 404.
70. Emmanuel Levinas, "Revelation in the Jewish Tradition," in *Beyond the Verse,* trans. G. D. Mole (Indiana University Press, 1994), 139–140. Hermann Cohen, *Religion of Reason Out of the Sources of Judaism*, trans. Simon Kaplan (Oxford University Press, 1972).
71. Philips Alexander, "The King Messiah in Rabbinic Judaism," in *King and Messiah in Israel and the Ancient Near East 1998 Proceedings of*

the Oxford Old Testament Seminar, ed. John Day. (Sheffield Academic Press, 1998), 456–473; "The Rabbis and Messianism," in *Redemption and Resistance: The Messianic Hopes of Jews and Christians in Antiquity* (T&T Clark, 2009), 227–244. Alexander gives a typology of four types of messianisms: catastrophe, gradualist, single event, and mystical. For a similar approach to consider messianism a diverse phenomenon, see Idel, *Messianic Mystics*.

72. I relegate the following to a footnote in order not to veer from the discussion of Moltmann and premillennial dispensation. Menachem Mendel Schneerson (d. 1994), developed a full-blown messianic movement around him as a messiah and saint with devotion to his grave as a source of blessing after he died. This would need to be analysed in the context of Holy Spirit, divination, and saints. However, I must point out that, despite popular perceptions, his personal messianic theology teaches about an interiority of the heart from the spark of divinity in each soul. The messianic goal is to liberate the heart from the lowest earthly state to an expansive spiritual state; a state of consciousness above knowledge reaching a selfless life of active service in the concrete physical world. His doctrines still use traditional messianism of the Davidic Messiah, the resurrection of the dead, and the building of the third Temple, but the innovation is that the redemption is available in the here and now to be called to a meaningful life. For him, the function of the Jewish people is to reveal Torah to the world, bringing light to darkness. This American messianism offered a vision of meaningful lives, a good marriage, building a Jewish home, creating community, educating one's children, or having second chances in life after jail or illness. On his messianic theology, see Elliot R. Wolfson, *Open Secret: Postmessianic Messianism and the Mystical Revision of Menahem Mendel Schneerson* (Columbia University Press, 2009); For a summary of his conclusions, see Elliot R. Wolfson, "Open Secret in the Rearview Mirror," *AJS Review* 35, no. 2 (2011): 393–400. On the messianic social theory, see Sue Fishkoff, *The Rebbe's Army: Inside the World of Chabad-Lubavitch* (Schocken Books, 2013). Philip Wexler, *Social Vision: The Lubavitcher Rebbe's Transformative Paradigm for the World* (Herder and Herder, July 2019).

73. R. J. Zwi Werblowsky, "Messianism in Jewish History," in *Essential Papers on Messianic Movements and Personalities in Jewish History*, ed. Marc Saperstein (New York University Press, 1992), 35–52.

74. Reinhold Niebuhr presented the difference between the religions on messianism as only one "of emphasis, but there is no radical contrast" in

Pious and Secular America (Scribner's, 1958), 101. For a Jewish variant, see the covenantal pluralism and partnership of Irving Greenberg, *For the Sake of Heaven and Earth: The New Encounter between Judaism and Christianity* (Jewish Publication Society, 2004), throughout, but especially, 176, 197, 230–233.

75. Gershom Scholem famously reduced Jewish messianism to liberal political amelioration of the human condition on one side, and on the other side kabbalistic apocalyptic messianism. Scholem contrasted these to a Christian pietistic messianism of salvation of the soul. However, Moltmann's political realism and the Christian Zionist correspond well to these allegedly two Jewish poles, while there are many pietistic Jewish messianisms of the soul. Alexander points out that all Scholem's characterizations in this essay are historically incorrect generalizations. Scholem's essay is found in Gershom Scholem, *The Messianic Idea in Judaism: And Other Essays on Jewish Spirituality* (Schocken Books, 1978).

CHAPTER SIX: COVENANT

1. Weiss-Rosmarin, *Judaism and Christianity*, 101, 108.
2. https://www.vatican.va/archive/hist_councils/ii_vatican_council/documents/vat-ii_decl_19651028_nostra-aetate_en.html, section 4, paragraphs 1, 2.
3. Address to representatives of the Jewish community in Mainz, West Germany November 17, 1980. This document was given in the Vatican document "Notes on the Correct Way to Present the Jews and Judaism in Preaching and Catechesis in the Roman Catholic Church" (June 24, 1985).
4. "A Theological Understanding of the Relationship between Christians and Jews," Office of the General Assembly of the Presbyterian Church (1987) issued by the Presbyterian Church (USA). https://www.pcusa.org/resource/theological-understanding-relationship-between-christians-and-jews. Compare with "A Statement on Relations between Jews and Christians" issued by the Disciples of Christ Church *Received by the General Assembly, St. Louis, MO in 1993 (No 9313)* a detailed document affirming the continued election and covenant of the Jewish people and that Christianity is in continuity with Judaism and an affirmation of Judaism. https://www.disciplescuim.org/publications/a-statement-on-relations-between-jews-and-christians/. Also compare with the 2019 statement of the Anglican Church about the ongoing Jewish covenant, *God's Unfailing*

Word Theological and Practical Perspectives on Christian-Jewish Relations The Faith and Order Commission (Church House Publishing, 2019). For a broad article presenting Anglican discussions of the ongoing covenant and prayer book revisions, see Daniel Joslyn-Siemiatkoski, "Talking about Jews: Principles, Problems, and Proposals for Prayer Book Revision," *Anglican and Episcopal History* 92, no. 2 (2023): 245–266. For a through history on the topic of covenant and Jewish-Christian relations in the twentieth century, see Eugene J. Fisher, "Covenant Theology and Jewish-Christian Dialogue," *Journal of Theology & Philosophy* 9, no. 1–2 (January–May, 1988): 5–40.

5. George Emery Mendenhall, "Covenant," *Encyclopedia Britannica*, August 25, 2022, a summary of his classic work *Law and Covenant in Israel and the Ancient Near East* (The Biblical Colloquium, 1955). https://www.britannica.com/topic/covenant-religion. Accessed March 13, 2024.
6. Mendenhall, "Covenant"; Moshe Weinfeld, "Covenant" in *Encyclopedia Judaica* 5: 1012–1022.
7. Schechter, *Aspects of Rabbinic Theology*; Reuven Kimelman, "The Shema Liturgy: From Covenant Ceremony to Coronation," in *Kenishta: Studies of the Synagogue World*, ed. J. Tabory (Bar Ilan University Press, 2001), 9–105; and Jon Levenson, *Sinai and Zion: An Entry into the Jewish Bible* (Winston Press, 1985), 82–86.
8. For an excellent article on the Jewish readings of the verses in Jeremiah, see Richard Sarason, "The Interpretation of Jeremiah 31:31–34 in Judaism," in *When Jews and Christians Meet*, ed. Jakob Petuchowski (SUNY Press, 1988), 99–123
9. E. P. Sanders comes from *Paul and Palestinian Judaism* (Fortress Press, 1977) 84–107 "Lawrence Schiffman, The Rabbinic Understanding of Covenant," *The New Testament and Judaism, Review and Expositor* 84 (1987), 289–298. Lawrence Schiffman, "The Concept of Covenant in the Qumran Scrolls and Rabbinic Literature," in *The Idea of Biblical Interpretation: Essays in Honor of James L. Kugel,* Supplements to the Journal for the Study of Judaism, ed. Hindy Najman and Judith H. Newman (Brill, 2004), 257–278.
10. Beyond our scope are the differences between the Calvinist, Catholic, and patristic versions of covenantal history.
11. For those who see covenant as not a major category for Paul, see Stanley Porter, "The Concept of the Covenant in Paul," in *The Concept of the Covenant in the Second Temple Period*, ed. S. Porter and J. De Roo (Brill, 2003), 269–286; and in the same volume James Dunn, "Did Paul

Have a Covenant Theology? Reflections on Romans 9:4 and 11:27," 287–307.

12. Matthew Thiessen, *A Jewish Paul: The Messiah's Herald to the Gentiles* (Baker Academic, 2023).
13. On the development of the idea of a new covenant in Qumran, see Shemaryahu Talmon, "The Community of the Renewed Covenant: Between Judaism and Christianity," in *The Community of the Renewed Covenant: The Notre Dame Symposium on the Dead Sea Scrolls*, ed. Eugene Ulrich and James VanderKam (Notre Dame University Press, 1994), 43–110.
14. Robert Eisenman, "An Esoteric Relation between Qumran's 'New Covenant in the Land of Damascus' and the New Testament's 'Cup of the New Covenant in (His) Blood?'" *Revue de Qumran* 21 (2004): 439–456.
15. Epistle of Barnabas 4:7–8; 13:1, from *Early Christian Writings* https://www.earlychristianwritings.com/text/barnabas-lightfoot.html
16. Barbara Meyer, *Jesus the Jew in Christian Memory: Theological and Philosophical Explorations* (Cambridge University Press, 2022), 51.
17. For a recent work explaining the meaning of covenant for contemporary Evangelicals, see Harison Perkins, *Reformed Covenant Theology: A Systematic Introduction* (Lexham Press, 2024). The covenant of God finds its home in the political commonwealth following God's law. This Calvinist or Reformed concept was invoked by many in the United States from the pilgrims to today to refer the aspirational Christian political community.
18. The term covenant was used extensively in late twentieth-century Jewish thought to mean an existential commitment to a singular commanding covenantal relationship with God. This concept of covenant theology was coined in 1961 by Eugene Borowitz and then picked up by David Hartman, David Novak, Irving Greenberg, Emil Fackneheim and many of their followers. In a later work, Borowitz defined covenant as follows: "The covenantal approach is meant as an alternative to the approaches of Jewish peoplehood, or tribalism, or abstract ethical monotheism. Following Rosenzweig on personally hearing God's commanding voice, the covenantal encounter yields communal commandments. The intimate covenantal relationship that God previously established with Abraham is personally renewed as both a dialogue between God and the Jewish people and a dialogue between individual Jews, a relationship of personal autonomy and God's voice." See, Eugene Borowitz, *Renewing the Covenant: A Theology for the Postmodern Jew*

(JPS, 1991), 222. A prominent Protestant version was Paul Ramsey, *Patient as Person* (Yale University Press, 1970). For both Jewish and Protestant versions, see Paul Tillich, *Dynamics of Faith* (Yale University Press, 1970), 67. I have given attention to this detour because much of the current literature blurs this existential definition with the theological definitions.

19. Amy Newman, "The Death of Judaism in German Protestant Thought from Luther to Hegel," *Journal of the American Academy of Religion* 61, no. 3 (Autumn, 1993): 455–484; Joseph W. Pickel, "Schleiermacher on Judaism," *The Journal of Religion* 60 (1980): 115–137; Christian Wiese, *Challenging Colonial Discourse: Jewish Studies and Protestant Theology in Wilhelmine Germany*, trans. Barbara Harshav and Christian Wiese (Brill, 2005), Samuel J, Loncar, "Christianity's Shadow Founder Marcion, Anti-Judaism, and the Birth of Protestant Liberalism," *Marginalia Review of Books*, November 19, 2021, https://themarginaliareview.com/christianitys-shadow-founder-marcion-anti-judaismand-the-birth-of-liberal-protestantism/
20. Karl Barth, *Church Dogmatics*, trans. G. W. Bromily, T. F. Torrance, et al. (T&T Clark, 1936–69) II/2, 287 as cited in Eberhard Busch, *Karl Barth and the Jews: The History of a Relationship in Karl Barth, the Jews, and Judaism*, ed. George Hunsinger (Eerdmans, 2018).
21. George Hunsinger, "After Barth: A Christian Appreciation of Jews and Judaism," *Pro Ecclesia*, 24, no. 3 (2015): 390–402.
22. Karl Barth, *Church Dogmatics*, trans. G. W. Bromily, T. F. Torrance, et al. (T&T Clark, 1936–69) §34.2, 210/231 II.2.p.234 Karl Barth, "The Jewish Problem and the Christian Answer," in *Against the Stream: Shorter Post-War Writings 1946–52* (Philosophical Library, 1954), 200.
23. This paragraph is based on Derek Woodard-Lehman, "Saying 'Yes' to Israel's 'No': Barth's Dialectical Supersessionism and the Witness of Carnal Israel," in *Karl Barth Post-Holocaust Theologian?* ed. George Hunsinger (Bloomsbury T&T Clark, 2018), 67–68; See Eugene Rogers, "Supplementing Barth on Jews and Gender: Identifying God by Analogy and Spirit," *Modern Theology* 14, no. 1 (January 1998): 55, 62.
24. Derek Woodard-Lehman, "Saying 'Yes' to Israel's 'No,'" 73 citing CD II/2., 294–295/324, he revised the translation since the "English translation perhaps overreaches with "debased Israel."
25. Derek Woodard-Lehman, "Saying 'Yes' to Israel's 'No,'" 73 Karl Barth, Church Dogmatics, III/3, §48.1, 28/31 similarly

unreasonable when he discusses "the History of the Jews" at CD III/3, §49.3 (238–57/175–271).

26. Michael Wyschogrod, "Review of Friedrich-Wilhelm Marquardt, *Das Christliche Bekenntnis zu Jesus, dem Juden. Eine Christologie*," *Journal of Ecumenical Studies* 29, no. 2 (1992): 275–276.; Wyschogrod, "A Jewish Perspective on Karl Barth," in *How Karl Barth Changed My Mind*, ed. Donald K. McKim (Eerdmans, 1986), 156–161; "Why Was and Is the Theology of Karl Barth of Interest to a Jewish Theologian?" in *Footnotes to a Theology: The Karl Barth Colloquium of 1972*, ed. M. Rumscheidt (SR Supplements, 1972), 95–111.
27. Hans Urs von Balthasar, *The Glory of the Lord: A Theological Aesthetics* (T&T Clark, 1983), 409. Balthasar was deeply touched by Martin Buber, *Two Types of Faith*, trans. N. P. Goldhawk (Macmillan, 1951) confessing that for two thousand years Christians did not feel addressed by Jews and assumed that the Jews were done having fulfilled their mission. For Balthasar, Buber offer Christians something to learn, that the church failed to recognize itself in the heart of Israel; Israel's innermost nature implies a Christology. See Hans Urs von. Balthasar *Martin Buber & Christianity: A Dialogue between Israel and the Church* (Macmillan, 1960), 15, 21.
28. Hans Urs von Balthasar, *Glory of the Lord VI*, 403.
29. Kevin Mongrain, *The Systematic Thought of Hans Urs von Balthasar: An Irenaean Retrieval* (Crossroad, 2002), 89–101.
30. Anthony C. Sciglitano, *Marcion and Prometheus: Balthasar against the Expulsion of Jewish Origins in Modern Religious Thought* (Crossroad, 2014).
31. Walter Cardinal Kasper, *The Theology of the Covenant as Central Issue in the Jewish-Christian Dialogue* delivered at Sacred Heart University in Fairfield, Connecticut December 4, 2001 accessed at https://www.ccjr.us/dialogika-resources/documents-and-statements/roman-catholic/kasper/wk01dec4
32. Walter Cardinal Kasper, "Dominus Iesus." Address delivered at the 17th meeting of the International Catholic-Jewish Liaison Committee, New York, May 1, 2001, accessed at https://www.ccjr.us/dialogika-resources/documents-and-statements/roman-catholic/kasper/kasper01may1-1
33. Cardinal Ratzinger, *Jesus of Nazareth: From the Baptism in the Jordan to the Transfiguration* (Ignatius Press, 2007) reiterates this point by repudiating the Marcionism of Harnack and presenting a continuity of many religious ideas between the Hebrew Bible and the Gospel,

albeit in a Christological reading of prophet, priest, kingship, and sacrifice.

34. Kasper, *The Theology of the Covenant*.
35. During the oral presentation of this talk, Kasper said this was his main thesis and the online version has a note: "Webmaster's note: During the dialogue, the author stated that this sentence was a main thesis."
36. Kasper, *The Theology of the Covenant*.
37. Kasper, *The Theology of the Covenant*.
38. Kasper, *The Theology of the Covenant*.
39. The document is available on many websites including the Vatican's at http://www.christianunity.va/content/unitacristiani/en/commissione-per-i-rapporti-religiosi-con-l-ebraismo/commissione-per-i-rapporti-religiosi-con-l-ebraismo-crre/documenti-della-commissione/en.html and the CCJR's at https://ccjr.us/dialogika-resources/documents-and-statements/roman-catholic/vatican-curia/crrj-2015dec10.
40. For a sense of the influences on the document including Cardinal Kasper and Cardinal Koch, see Philip A. Cunningham, "The Sources Behind 'The Gifts and the Calling of God Are Irrevocable' (Rom 11:29): A Reflection on Theological Questions Pertaining to Catholic-Jewish Relations on the Occasion of the 50th Anniversary of Nostra Aetate (No. 4)," *Studies in Christian-Jewish Relations* 12, no. 1 (Mar. 2017).
41. "Gifts and the Calling," para. 21.
42. "Gifts and the Calling," para. 27.
43. "Gifts and the Calling," para. 32.
44. "Gifts and the Calling," para. 33.
45. "Gifts and the Calling," para. 35.
46. Gavin D'Costa. "Supersessionism: Harsh, Mild or Gone for Good?" *European Judaism* 50, no. 1 (2017): 99–107
47. See the Jewish Reflection by the Synagogue Council of America issued as part of the "Reflections on Covenant and Mission" (2002), https://www.usccb.org/resources/reflections-covenant-and-mission
48. R. Kendall Soulen, *The God of Israel and Christian Theology* (Augsburg Fortress, 1996).
49. R. Kendall Soulen, "Israel and the Church: A Christian Response to Irving Greenberg's Covenantal Pluralism," in *Christianity in Jewish Terms*, ed. Tikva Frymer-Kensky, David Novak, Peter Ochs, David Fox Sandmel, and Michael A. Singer (Westview Press, 2000), 167.
50. R. Kendall Soulen, *The God of Israel and Christian Theology*, 33.

51. The literature on the two path approach of Franz Rosenzweig is large, a philosophic presentation is Stéphane Mosès's "Judaism and Christianity in Franz Rosenzweig: Two Forms of Eternity," in *Displacements: Selected Essays on German-Jewish Literature and Modernity* (De Gruyter, 2024), 249–264; The introduction of Rosenzweig's two path approach to the English speaking audience was Will Herberg, "Rosenzweig's 'Judaism of Personal Existence': A Third Way Between Orthodoxy and Modernism," *Commentary Magazine* (Dec. 1950), 541–549.
52. Soulen, *The God of Israel and Christian Theology*, 111
53. Soulen, "Israel and the Church" 167–174.
54. Soulen, "Israel and the Church," 172.
55. Soulen, "Israel and the Church," 174. Compare with Cardinal Kasper who has similar views. The first to take this approach of seeing the Jewish "no" as positive was Wilhelm Marquardt, *Theological Audacities: Selected Essays*, ed. Andreas Pangritz and Paul S. Chung (Wipf & Stock, 2010). Marquardt wrote: "We will not have Christian Anti-Judaism behind us until we are theologically able to do something positive with the Jewish No to Jesus," (3).
56. It is important to note that according to Soulen, Christians are to avoid overt proselytizing of Jews, but they can certainly encourage and welcome Jews who want to become Christians. In the same way, Jews have to encourage and welcome Christians who want to become Jews.
57. Peter Leithart, "Anti Anti-Supercessionism," *Theopolis* (May 13, 2013) https://theopolisinstitute.com/anti-anti-supercessionism/
58. R. Kendall Soulen, "Hallowed be Thy name! The Tetragrammaton and the Name of the Trinity," in *Jews & Christians, People of God*, ed. C. Braaten and R. Wilken (Eerdmans, 2003), 14–20.
59. R. Kendall Soulen, *Irrevocable: The Name of God and the Unity of the Christian Bible* (Fortress, 2022), 72. For Soulen, similar to Maimonides, Abraham uniquely recognized God, while the other nations rejected the Torah. In contrast, Wyschogrod and Novak both agree that the election was solely due to God's choice.
60. R. Kendall Soulen, *Irrevocable*, 89.
61. D'Costa, "Supersessionism: Harsh, Mild or Gone for Good?"
62. "The Gifts and the Calling," para. 15. This was a rapid change from 2000, when Cardinal Avery Dulles, "The Covenant with Israel," *First Things* (November 2000) affirmed that there is only one covenant that excludes salvation of the Jews. By 2015, the question was answered by

Cardinal Ratzinger and Cardinal Kasper that there is one common covenant but two approaches.

63. On his dual covenant approach, see Robert Jensen, *Systematic Theology*, vol 2, *The Works of God* (Oxford University Press, 2001), 171. On his appreciation of Torah study and Rabbinic Judaism see Andrew W. Nicol, *Exodus and Resurrection: The God of Israel in the Theology of Robert W. Jenson* (Fortress Press, 2016), 194. A refreshing Christian theological appreciation of a rabbinic text is Daniel Joslyn-Siemiatkoski, *The More Torah, the More Life: A Christian Commentary on Mishnah Avot* (Peeters, 2018).
64. Michael Wyschogrod, "The Torah as Law in Judaism," in *"Your World Is a Lamp To My Feet and a Light To My Path" (Ps 119: 105) SIDIC Periodical* 35, no. 2–3 (2002): 18–23.
65. Jonathan Sacks, *The Dignity of Difference: How to Avoid the Clash of Civilizations* (Continuum, 2002). This quote remained in the 2003 second edition.
66. This is the opening caption to Jonathan Sacks, *The Home We Build Together* (Bloomsbury Continuum, 2006).
67. "Rabbi Sir Jonathan Sacks Answers Questions on Covenants, Jesus and Peace," ed. Chris Sugden and Cherie Wetzel, July 30, 2008 press conference on Monday at the Lambeth Conference. https://virtueonline.org/rabbi-sir-jonathan-sachs-answers-questions-covenants-jesus-and-peace

BIBLIOGRAPHY

Abelson, Joshua. *The Immanence of God in Rabbinical Literature.* Macmillan, 1912.

Albalag, Isaac. *Sefer Tiqqun haDe'ot.* Edited by G. Vajda. Jerusalem, 1973.

Albo, Joseph. *Book of Principles.* Translated and edited by I. Husik. The Jewish Publication Society of America, 1929.

Alexander, Phillips. "The King Messiah in Rabbinic Judaism." In *King and Messiah in Israel and the Ancient Near East: Proceedings of the Oxford Old Testament Seminar,* edited by John Day. Sheffield Academic Press, 1998.

Alexander, Phillips. "The Rabbis and Messianism." In *Redemption and Resistance: The Messianic Hopes of Jews and Christians.* T&T Clark, 2009.

Altmann, Alexander. "'Homo Imago Dei' in Jewish and Christian Theology." *Journal of Religion* 48 (1968): 235–259.

Anatolios, Khaled. *Retrieving Nicaea: The Development and Meaning of Trinitarian Doctrine.* Baker Academic, 2018.

Anderson, Gary. *Sin: A History.* Yale University Press, 2010.

Anderson, Gary, *That I May Dwell Among Them: Incarnation and Atonement in the Tabernacle Narrative.* Eerdmans, 2023.

Ansell, Nicholas. *Annihilation of Hell: Universal Salvation and the Redemption of Time in the Eschatology of Jürgen Moltmann.* Paternoster, 2013.

Ariel, Yaakov. "Biblical Imagery, the End Times, and Political Action: The Roots of Christian Support for Zionism and Israel." In *The Bible in the Public Square: Its Enduring Influence in American Life,* edited by Mark A. Chamey, Carol Meyers, and Eric M. Meyers. SBL Press, 2014.

Ariel, Yaakov. "How Are Jews and Israel Portrayed in the *Left Behind* Series?" In *Rapture, Revelation, and the End Times,* edited by Bruce Forbes and Jeanne Kilde. Palgrave Macmillan, 2004.

Ariel, Yaakov. "Messianic Hopes and Middle East Politics: The Influence of Millennial Faith on American Middle East Policies." *Revue LISA/LISA e-journal* [Online], vol. 9, no. 1 (2011), document 13. Online since April 1, 2011. Accessed April 17, 2023. http://journals.openedition.org/lisa/4165.

Balthasar, Hans Urs von. *The Glory of the Lord: A Theological Aesthetics*. T&T Clark, 1983; Ignatius Press, 1991.

Balthasar, Hans Urs von. *Martin Buber & Christianity: A Dialogue between Israel and the Church*. Macmillan, 1960.

Barth, Karl. *Church Dogmatics*. Translated by G. W. Bromily and T. F. Torrance. T&T Clark, 1936–1969.

Barth, Karl. "The Jewish Problem and the Christian Answer." In *Against the Stream*. Philosophic Library, 1954.

Bauckham, Richard. *God of Israel: God Crucified and Other Studies on the New Testament's Christology of Divine Identity*. Eerdmans, 1998.

Bauckham, Richard. *The Theology of Jürgen Moltmann*. T&T Clark, 1995.

Batka, L'ubomír. "Luther's Teaching on Sin and Evil." In *The Oxford Handbook of Martin Luther's Theology*, edited by Robert Kolb, Irene Dingel, and L'ubomír Batka. Online edition, Oxford Academic, June 2, 2014.

Benin, Stephen D. "The Mutability of an Immutable God: Exegesis and Individual Capacity in the *Zohar* and Several Christian Sources." *Jerusalem Studies in Jewish Thought* 8 (1989): 67–86.

Berger, Peter. "Judaism and Christianity: Embracing the 'Other'?" *The American Interest*, August 22, 2012.

Blidstein, Gerald J. "Death in the Writings of Rabbi Joseph Dov Soloveitchik." *Tradition* 44, no. 1 (2011): 7–18.

Boyarin, Daniel. "De/Re/constructing Midrash." In *Current Trends in the Study of Midrash*, edited by Carol Bakhos. Brill, 2006.

Boyarin, Daniel. "The Gospel of the Memra: Jewish Binitarianism and the Prologue to John." *Harvard Theological Review* 94, no. 3 (2001): 243–284.

Boyarin, Daniel. *The Jewish Gospels: The Story of the Jewish Christ*. The New Press, 2012.

Boyarin, Daniel. "Two Powers in Heaven; or, The Making of a Heresy." In *The Idea of Biblical Interpretation: Essays in Honor of James L. Kugel*. Brill, 2003.

Brey, Gerald. "Original Sin in Patristic Thought." *Churchman* 108, no. 1 (1994).

Brill, Alan. "Elements of Dialectic Theology in Rabbi Soloveitchik's View of Torah Study." In *Study and Knowledge in Jewish Thought*, vol. 1, edited by Howard Kreisel. Ben-Gurion University of the Negev Press, 2006.

Brill, Alan. *Judaism and Other Religions*. Palgrave Macmillan, 2010.

Brill, Alan. *Judaism and World Religions*. Palgrave Macmillan, 2012.

Brill, Alan. *Rabbi on the Ganges: A Jewish-Hindu Encounter*. Lexington Books, 2019.

Brill, Alan. "Recognizing the Other: Sameness and Difference in a Jewish Theology of Religions." *Boston Theological Institute Journal* 11, no. 2 (May 2012): 4–8.

Brill, Alan. *Thinking God: The Mysticism of Rabbi Zadok of Lublin.* YU Press, 2002.

Brill, Alan. "Triumph without Battle: The Dialectic Approach to Culture in the Thought of Rabbi J. B. Soloveitchik." In *Rabbi in the New World: The Influence of Rabbi J. B. Soloveitchik on Culture, Education and Jewish Thought*, edited by Avinoam Rosenak and Naftali Rothenberg. Magnes, 2010.

Brown, Jeremy Philip. "What Does the Messiah Know? A Prelude to Kabbalah's Trinity Complex." *Maimonides Review of Philosophy and Religion* 2 (2023): 1–49.

Brueggemann, Walter. *Isaiah 40–66.* Westminster John Knox Press, 1998.

Brunner, Emil. *The Divine Imperative.* Lutterworth Press, 1937.

Brunner, Emil. *Man in Revolt: A Christian Anthropology.* Westminster Press, 1947.

Brunner, Emil. *The Mediator: A Study of the Central Doctrine of the Christian Faith.* Lutterworth Press, 1934.

Brunner, Emil. *Our Faith.* Charles Scribner's, 1954.

Buber, Martin. "The Two Foci of the Jewish Soul." In *Israel and the World: Essays in a Time of Crisis.* Schocken Books, 1948.

Buber, Martin. *Two Types of Faith.* Translated by N. P. Goldhawk. Macmillan, 1951.

Burrell, David. "Incarnation and Creation: The Hidden Dimension." *Modern Theology* 12 (1996): 211–20.

Busch, Eberhard. "Karl Barth and the Jews: The History of a Relationship." In *Karl Barth, the Jews, and Judaism*, edited by George Hunsinger. Eerdmans, 2018.

Cohen, Jeremy. "Original Sin as the Evil Inclination: A Polemicist's Appreciation of Human Nature." *Harvard Theological Review* 73, no. 3–4 (July–October 1980): 495–520.

Costa, José. "The Body of God in Ancient Rabbinic Judaism: Problems of Interpretation." *Revue de l'Histoire des Religions* 227, no. 3 (July 2010): 283–316.

Collins, John. "Why Do We Call Jesus the Messiah?" *U.S. Catholic* 82, no. 12 (December 2017): 34–37.

Conradie, Ernst M. "The Justification of God? The Story of God's Work According to Jürgen Moltmann: Part 1 & 2." *Scriptura* 97 (2008): 76–105.

Couenhoven, Jesse. "St. Augustine's Doctrine of Original Sin." *Augustinian Studies* 36, no. 2 (2005): 359–396.

Couenhoven, Jesse. "The Explanatory Power of Original Sin." In *Stricken by Sin, Cured by Christ: Agency, Necessity, and Culpability in Augustinian Theology*. Oxford Academic, 2013.

Crescas, Hasdai. *Refutation of the Christian Principles*. Translated with an introduction by D. J. Lasker. SUNY Series in Jewish Philosophy, 1992.

Crome, Andrew. *Christian Zionism and English National Identity, 1600–1850*. Palgrave Macmillan, 2018.

Cunningham, Philip A. "The Sources Behind 'The Gifts and the Calling of God Are Irrevocable' (Rom 11:29): A Reflection on Theological Questions Pertaining to Catholic-Jewish Relations on the Occasion of the 50th Anniversary of *Nostra Aetate* (No. 4)." *Studies in Christian-Jewish Relations* 12, no. 1 (March 2017): 1–39.

D'Costa, Gavin. "Supersessionism: Harsh, Mild or Gone for Good?" *European Judaism* 50, no. 1 (2017): 99–107.

Duffy, Stephen J. "Our Hearts of Darkness: Original Sin Revisited." *Theological Studies* 49 (1988): 597–622.

Dulles, Avery. "The Covenant with Israel." *First Things*, November 2000.

Eckardt, A. Roy. "Jürgen Moltmann, the Jewish People, and the Holocaust." *Journal of the American Academy of Religion* 44, no. 4 (1976): 675–691.

Fiddes, Paul. *The Creative Suffering of God*. Oxford University Press, 1988.

Fishbane, Michael. *Biblical Myth and Rabbinic Mythmaking*. Oxford University Press, 2003.

Fishbane, Michael. *The Exegetical Imagination: On Jewish Thought and Theology*. Harvard University Press, 1998.

Fredericks, James L. *Faith among Faiths: Christian Theology and Non-Christian Religions*. Paulist, 1999.

Fredrickson, Paula. "How Jewish Is God?" *Journal of Biblical Literature* 137 (2018): 193–212.

Goshen-Gottstein, Alon. "God the Father in Rabbinic Judaism and Christianity: Transformed Background or Common Ground?" *Journal of Ecumenical Studies* 38, no. 4 (Fall 2001): 470–504.

Goshen-Gottstein, Alon. "Jewish-Christian Relations and Rabbinic Literature: Shifting Scholarly and Relational Paradigms: The Case of Two Powers." In *Interaction between Judaism and Christianity in History, Religion, Art and Literature*, edited by Marcel Poorthuis et al., 15–44. Brill, 2009.

Goshen-Gottstein, Alon. "Judaisms and Incarnational Theologies: Mapping out the Parameters of Dialogue." *Journal of Ecumenical Studies* 39, no. 3 (Summer–Fall 2002): 219–47.

Greenberg, Irving. *For the Sake of Heaven and Earth: The New Encounter Between Judaism and Christianity*. JPS, 2004.

Gregersen, Niels Henrik, ed. *Incarnation: On the Scope and Depth of Christology*. Fortress Press, 2015.

Halbertal, Moshe. *Nahmanides: Law and Mysticism*. Translated by Daniel Tabak. Yale University Press, 2020.

Halbertal, Moshe, and Avishai Margalit. *Idolatry*. Harvard University Press, 1992.

Hengel, Martin. *The Son of God: The Origin of Christology and the History of Jewish-Hellenistic Religion*. SCM Press, 1976.

Henrix, Hans Hermann, and Eduard Kessler. "God's Presence in Israel and Incarnation: A Christian-Jewish Dialogue." *Jewish Christian Relations* (2008). Accessed online at https://www.jcrelations.net/articles/article/gods-presence-in-israel-and-incarnation-a-christian-jewish-dialogue.html.

Heschel, Abraham Joshua. *God in Search of Man: A Philosophy of Judaism*. Farrar, Straus and Giroux, 1983.

Heschel, Abraham Joshua. *The Sabbath*. Farrar, Straus and Giroux, 1951.

Himmelfarb, Martha. *Jewish Messiahs in a Christian Empire: A History of the Book of Zerubbabel*. Harvard University Press, 2017.

Hirsch, Samson Raphael. *The Pentateuch*. Translated and explained by Samson Raphael Hirsch. English translation by Isaac Levy. Soncino, 1956.

Horbury, William. *Messianism among Jews and Christians: Biblical and Historic Studies*. Bloomsbury T&T Clark, 2016.

Hunsinger, George. "After Barth: A Christian Appreciation of Jews and Judaism." *Pro Ecclesia* 24, no. 3 (2015): 390–402.

Hurtado, Larry W. *Ancient Jewish Monotheism and Early Christian Jesus-Devotion: The Context and Character of Christological Faith*. Baylor University Press, 2017.

Hurtado, Larry W. *God in New Testament Theology*. Abingdon Press, 2010.

Hurtado, Larry W. *Honoring the Son: Jesus in Earliest Christian Devotional Practice*. Lexham Press, 2018.

Hurtado, Larry W. *How on Earth Did Jesus Become a God? Historical Questions about Earliest Devotion to Jesus*. Eerdmans, 2005.

Hurtado, Larry W. *One God, One Lord: Early Christian Devotion and Ancient Jewish Monotheism*. Fortress Press, 1988.

Idel, Moshe. *Ben: Sonship and Jewish Mysticism*. Continuum, 2007.

Idel, Moshe. *Messianic Mystics*. Yale University Press, 1998.

Inbari, Motti. *Messianic Religious Zionism Confronts Israeli Territorial Compromises*. Cambridge University Press, 2012.

Jaeger, John. "Abraham Heschel and the Theology of Jürgen Moltmann." *Perspectives in Religious Studies* 24 (1997): 167–179.

Jaffe-Hoffman, Maayan. "For Evangelicals, Is Benjamin Netanyahu the Fallen Messiah?" *Jerusalem Post*, June 6, 2021.

Johnson, Elizabeth. *Creation and the Cross: The Mercy of God for a Planet in Peril*. Orbis Books, 2018.

Joslyn-Siemiatkoski, Daniel. "Divine Suffering and Covenantal Belonging: Considering the Atonement with Heschel and Moltmann." In *Atonement and Comparative Theology: The Cross in Dialogue with Other Religions*, edited by Catherine Cornille. Fordham University Press, 2021.

Kalminsky, Joel. "Paradise Regained: Rabbinic Reflections on Original Sin." In *Jews, Christians, and the Theology of the Hebrew Scriptures*, edited by Alice Bellis and Joel Kalminsky. Society of Biblical Literature, 2000.

Kaplan, Lawrence. "Hermann Cohen and Rabbi Joseph Soloveitchik on Repentance." *Journal of Jewish Thought and Philosophy* 13, no. 1–3 (2004): 213–258.

Kimelman, Reuven. "The Messiah of the Amidah: A Study in Comparative Messianism." *Journal of Biblical Literature* 116, no. 2 (1997): 313–320.

Kimelman, Reuven. "The Shema Liturgy: From Covenant Ceremony to Coronation." In *Kenishta: Studies of the Synagogue World*, edited by J. Tabory. Bar Ilan University Press, 2001.

Kister, M. "Some Early Jewish and Christian Exegetical Problems and the Dynamics of Monotheism." *Journal for the Study of Judaism in the Persian, Hellenistic, and Roman Period* 37, no. 4 (2006): 548–593.

Lasker, Daniel. "Original Sin and Its Atonement According to Hasdai Crescas." [Hebrew] *Daat* 20 (Winter 1988): 127–135.

Leithart, Peter. "Anti Anti-Supercessionism." *Theopolis*, May 13, 2013. https://theopolisinstitute.com/anti-anti-supercessionism/.

Lerner, Berel Dov. "The Ten Curses of Eve." *Women in Judaism: A Multidisciplinary e-Journal* 15, no. 1 (March 9, 2019). Accessed at https://wjudaism.library.utoronto.ca/index.php/wjudaism/article/view/32359.

Levenson, Jon. *The Death and Resurrection of the Beloved Son*. Yale University Press, 1993.

Levenson, Jon. "Did God Forgive Adam? An Exercise in Comparative Midrash." In *Jews and Christians: People of God*, edited by Carl E. Braaten and Robert Jenson. Eerdmans, 2003.

Levenson, Jon. *Sinai and Zion: An Entry into the Jewish Bible.* Winston Press, 1985.

Kaniel, Ruth Kara-Ivanov. *The Feminine Messiah: King David in the Image of the Shekhinah in Kabbalistic Literature.* Brill, 2021.

Kasper, Walter. *Christ Jesus and the Jewish People Today: New Explorations of Theological Interrelationships.* Eerdmans, 2011. Available at https://ccjr.us/dialogika-resources/documents-and-statements/roman-catholic/kasper/kasper2011mar20.

Kasper Walter. "Dominus Iesus." Address delivered at the 17th meeting of the International Catholic-Jewish Liaison Committee, New York, May 1, 2001. Accessed at https://www.ccjr.us/dialogika-resources/documents-and-statements/roman-catholic/kasper/kasper01may1-1.

Kasper, Walter. *The God of Jesus Christ: New Edition.* Continuum, 2012.

Kasper, Walter. *Jesus the Christ.* Paulist Press, 1981.

Kasper, Walter. "The Theology of the Covenant as Central Issue in the Jewish-Christian Dialogue." Delivered at Sacred Heart University, Fairfield, Connecticut, December 4, 2001. Accessed at https://www.ccjr.us/dialogika-resources/documents-and-statements/roman-catholic/kasper/wk01dec4.

Kepnes, Steven. *Jewish Liturgical Reasoning.* Oxford University Press, 2007.

Knohl, Israel. *The Messiah before Jesus: The Suffering Servant of the Dead Sea Scrolls.* Translated by David Maisel. University of California Press, 2002.

Kohler, Kaufman. *Jewish Theology Systematically and Historically Considered.* Macmillan, 1918.

Lachs, Samuel Tobias. "Rabbi Abbahu and the Minim." *The Jewish Quarterly Review* 60, no. 3 (January 1970): 197–212.

Lapide, Pinhas, and Jürgen Moltmann. *Jewish Monotheism and Christian Trinitarian Doctrine: A Dialogue.* Translated by Leonard Swidler. Fortress Press, 1981.

Lapide, Pinchas, and Karl Rahner. *Encountering Jesus—Encountering Judaism: A Dialogue.* Translated by Davis Perkins. Crossroad, 1987.

Lapide, Pinchas, and Hans Kung. *Brother or Lord: A Jew and a Christian Talk Together about Jesus.* Translated by Edward Quinn. Fount Paperbacks, 1977.

Lenowitz, Harris. *The Jewish Messiahs: From the Galilee to Crown Heights.* Oxford University Press, 1998.

Liebes, Yehuda. "The Messiah of the Zohar: On R. Simeon bar Yohai as a Messianic Figure." In *Studies in the Zohar.* SUNY Press, 1993.

Liebes, Yehuda, "Sabbatian Messianism." In *Studies in Jewish Myth and Jewish Messianism.* SUNY Press, 1992.

Lorberbaum, Yair. *In God's Image: Myth, Theology, and Law in Classical Judaism*. Cambridge University Press, 2015.

Lyden, John. "Atonement in Judaism and Christianity: Toward a Rapprochement." *Journal of Ecumenical Studies* 29 (1992): 47–54.

Macoby, Hyam. *Judaism on Trial: Jewish-Christian Disputations in the Middle Ages*. The Littman Library of Jewish Civilization, 1982.

Magid, Shaul. *Hasidism Incarnate: Hasidism, Christianity, and the Construction of Modern Judaism*. Stanford University Press, 2014.

Markschies, Christoph. *God's Body: Jewish, Christian, and Pagan Images of God*. Translated by Alexander Johannes Edmonds. Baylor University Press, 2019.

Marmorstein, Arthur. *The Old Rabbinic Doctrine of God*. Oxford University Press, 1927.

Marquardt, Wilhelm. *Theological Audacities: Selected Essays*. Edited by Andreas Pangritz and Paul S. Chung. Wipf & Stock, 2010.

McCool, Gerald A., ed. *A Rahner Reader*. Seabury Press, 1975.

Meyer, Barbara. *Jesus the Jew in Christian Memory: Theological and Philosophical Explorations*. Cambridge University Press, 2022.

Mendelssohn, Moses. *Jerusalem, or On Religious Power and Judaism*. Translated by Allan Arkush, edited by Alexander Altmann. University Press of New England, 1983.

Mendelssohn, Moses. *Writings on Judaism, Christianity, and the Bible*. Translated by Curtis Bowman, Elias Sacks, and Allan Arkush. Edited by Michah Gottlieb. University Press of New England, 2011.

Molnar, Paul D. *Incarnation and Resurrection: Toward a Contemporary Understanding*. Eerdmans, 2007.

Moltmann, Jürgen. *The Church in the Power of the Spirit*. SCM Press, 1975.

Moltmann, Jürgen. *The Coming of God: Christian Eschatology*. Fortress Press, 1996.

Moltmann, Jürgen. *The Crucified God: The Cross as the Foundation and Criticism of Christian Theology*. Translated by R. A. Wilson and J. Bowden. SCM Press, 1974.

Moltmann, Jürgen. "God's Kenosis in the Creation and Consummation of the World." In *The Work of Love: Creation as Kenosis*, edited by John Polkinghorne. Eerdmans, 2001.

Moltmann, Jürgen. *An Introduction to Christian Theology*. Edited by Douglas Meeks. Duke University Press, 1968.

Moltmann, Jürgen. *Man: Christian Anthropology in the Conflicts of the Present*. Fortress Press, 1974.

Moltmann, Jürgen. "Shekinah: The Home of the Homeless God." In *Longing for Home*, edited by Leroy S. Rouner. Notre Dame University Press, 1996.

Moltmann, Jürgen. *The Spirit of Life: A Universal Affirmation*. SCM Press, 1992.

Moltmann, Jürgen. *Sun of Righteousness, Arise! God's Future for Humanity and the Earth*. Translated by Margaret Kohl. SCM Press, 2010.

Moltmann, Jürgen. *Theology of Hope*. Translated by James W. Leitch. Harper & Row, 1967.

Moltmann, Jürgen. *The Trinity and the Kingdom: The Doctrine of God* Harper & Row, 1980.

Moltmann, Jürgen. *The Way of Jesus Christ: Christology in Messianic Dimensions*. SCM Press, 1990.

Mongrain, Kevin. *The Systematic Thought of Hans Urs von Balthasar: An Irenaean Retrieval*. Crossroad, 2002.

Moore, George F. *Judaism*. Harvard University Press, 1966.

Morgen, Michael, and Steven Weitzman, eds. *Rethinking the Messianic Idea in Judaism*. Indiana University Press, 2015.

Mowinckel, Sigmund. *He That Cometh: The Messiah Concept in the Old Testament and Later Judaism*. With a foreword by John Collins. Eerdmans, 2005. Originally published by Abingdon Press in 1956.

Muller-Fahrenholz, Geiko. *The Kingdom and the Power: The Theology of Jurgen Moltmann*. Fortress Press, 2001.

Nahmanides. *Commentary on the Torah*. 5 vols. Translated by Charles B. Chavel. Shilo, 1971.

Nahmanides. *Writings & Discourses*. 2 vols. Translated by Charles B. Chavel. Shilo, 1978.

Neriyah, Moshe Zvi. *Celebration of the Soul: The Holidays in the Life and Thought of Rabbi Avraham Yitzchak Kook*. Translated by Pesach Jaffe. Genesis Jerusalem Press, 1992.

Neusner, Jacob. *Classical Christianity and Rabbinical Judaism*. Baker Academic, 2004.

Neusner, Jacob. *Jews and Christians: The Myth of a Common Tradition*. SCM Press and Trinity Press International, 1991.

Neusner, Jacob. *The Incarnation of God: The Character of Divinity in Formative Judaism*. Global Publications, 2001.

Neusner, Jacob. *Midrash in Context: Exegesis in Formative Judaism*. Fortress Press, 1983.

Niebuhr, Reinhold. *The Nature and Destiny of Man*. Scribner's, 1941.

Niebuhr, Reinhold. *Pious and Secular America*. Scribner's, 1958.

Novenson, Matthew V. *The Grammar of Messianism: An Ancient Jewish Political Idiom and Its Users*. Oxford University Press, 2017.

Patai, Raphael. *The Messiah Texts*. Wayne State University Press, 1979.

Pines, Shlomo. "God, the Divine Glory, and the Angels According to a Second-Century Theology." In *The Beginnings of Jewish Mysticism in Medieval Europe*, edited by J. Dan. Institute for Jewish Studies, 1987.

Podmore, Simon D. "Abyss Calls Unto Abyss': Tsimtsum and Kenosis in the Rupture of God-forsakenness." In *Tsimtsum and Modernity: Lurianic Heritage in Modern Philosophy and Theology*, edited by Agata Bielik-Robson and Daniel H. Weiss. De Gruyter, 2020.

Pollack, Benjamin. "The Kabbalistic Problem Is Not Specifically Theological: Franz Rosenzweig on Tsimtsum." In *Tsimtsum and Modernity: Lurianic Heritage in Modern Philosophy and Theology*, edited by Agata Bielik-Robson and Daniel H. Weiss. De Gruyter, 2020.

Pugliese, Marc. "Is Karl Rahner a Modalist?" *Irish Theological Quarterly* 68 (Fall 2003): 229–49.

Rahner, Karl. "Concerning the Relationship between Nature and Grace." In *Theological Investigations*, vol. 1. Helicon Press, 1961.

Rahner, Karl. *The Content of Faith*. Edited by Karl Lehmann and Albert Raffelt. Translated and edited by Harvey D. Egan, SJ. Crossroad, 1992.

Rahner, Karl. "Christology within an Evolutionary View of the World." In *Theological Investigations*, vol. 5. Helicon Press, 1961.

Rahner, Karl. "Death." In *Encyclopedia of Theology: The Concise Sacramentum Mundi*, edited by Karl Rahner. Seabury, 1975.

Rahner, Karl. *Foundations of Christian Faith: An Introduction to the Idea of Christianity*. Translated by William V. Dych. Seabury Press, 1978.

Rahner, Karl. "On the Theology of the Incarnation," In *Theological Investigations*, vol. 4. Helicon Press, 1961.

Rahner, Karl. "Some Implications of the Scholastic Concept of Uncreated Grace." In *Theological Investigations*, vol. 1. Helicon Press, 1961.

Rahner, Karl. *The Theology of Death*. Herder and Herder, 1961.

Rahner, Karl. *The Trinity*. Translated by Joseph Donceel. Crossroad, 1998.

Rahner, Karl. "The Unity of Spirit and Matter in the Christian Understanding of Faith." In *Theological Investigations*, vol. 6, *On the Theology of the Incarnation*. Helicon Press, 1961.

Ramelli, Ilaria. "Forgiveness in Patristic Philosophy: The Importance of Repentance and the Centrality of Grace." In *Ancient Forgiveness: Classical, Judaic, and Christian*, edited by Charles L. Griswold and David Konstan. Cambridge University Press, 2012.

Ratzinger, Joseph. *Jesus of Nazareth: From the Baptism in the Jordan to the Transfiguration*. Ignatius Press, 2007.

Ratzinger, Joseph, *Jesus of Nazareth: Part Two: Holy Week: From the Entrance into Jerusalem to the Resurrection*. Ignatius Press, 2011.

Rees, B. R. *Pelagius: Life and Letters*. Boydell Press, 1998.

Renbaum, Joel. "Medieval Jewish Criticism of the Christian Doctrine of Original Sin." *AJS Review* 7–8 (1982–83): 353–382.

Reynolds, Gabriel Said. "Original Sin and the Qur'an." *Islamochristiana* 46 (2020): 197–218.

Ricœur, Paul. "Original Sin: A Study of Its Meaning." In *The Conflict of Interpretations: Essays in Hermeneutics*. Northwestern University Press, 1974.

Ricœur, Paul. *The Symbolism of Evil*. Beacon Press, 1967.

Ringel, Joseph. "'There but for the Grace of God Go I': A Theological Contrast Between Jean Calvin and Maharal." *Brandeis Graduate Journal* 3 (2005): 1–7.

Rogers, Eugene. "Supplementing Barth on Jews and Gender: Identifying God by Analogy and Spirit." *Modern Theology* 14, no. 1 (January 1998): 43–82.

Rondet, Henri. *Original Sin: The Patristic and Theological Background*. Translated by Cajetan Finnegan, OP. Alba House, 1972. Originally published 1967.

Rosenzweig, Franz. *The Star of Redemption*. Translated by Barbara E. Galli. University of Wisconsin Press, 2005.

Rosenzweig, Franz, *The Star of Redemption*. Translated by William H. Hallo. Holt, Rinehart and Winston, 1971.

Ruttenberg, Danya. *On Repentance and Repair: Making Amends in an Unrepentant World*. Beacon Press, 2022.

Saadia Gaon. *The Book of Beliefs and Opinions*. Translated by Samuel Rosenblatt. Yale University Press, 1948.

Sacks, Jonathan. "Covenant and Conversation: The Chronological Imagination – Behar-Bechukotai 5767, 5770, 5773." Accessed at https://rabbisacks.org/covenant-conversation/behar/the-chronological-imagination/.

Sacks, Jonathan. *The Dignity of Difference: How to Avoid the Clash of Civilizations*. 1st ed. Continuum, 2002; 2nd ed., 2003.

Sacks, Jonathan. *The Home We Build Together*. Bloomsbury Continuum, 2006.

Sacks, Jonathan, "Rabbi Sir Jonathan Sacks Answers Questions on Covenants, Jesus and Peace." Press conference at the Lambeth Conference, July 30, 2008. Edited by Chris Sugden and Cherie Wetzel. https://virtueonline.org/rabbi-sir-jonathan-sachs-answers-questions-covenants-jesus-and-peace.

Sacks, Jonathan. "Two Concepts of Teshuvah." *Nitzavim*, 5767 [2007]. Accessed at https://rabbisacks.org/covenant-conversation/nitzavim/two-concepts-of-teshuvah/.

Safran, Bezalel. "Rabbi Azriel and Nahmanides: Two Views of the Fall of Man." In *Rabbi Moses ben Nahman: Explorations in His Religious and Literary Virtuosity*, edited by I. Twersky, 86–99. Harvard University Press, 1983.

Saldarini, Anthony J., with Joseph A. Kanofsky. "Judaism: God as a Many-sided Ultimate Reality in Traditional Judaism." In *Ultimate Realities: A Volume in the Comparative Religious Ideas Project*, edited by Robert Cummings Neville. SUNY Press, 2000.

Sanders, E. P. *Paul and Palestinian Judaism*. Fortress Press, 1977.

Sarason, Richard. "The Interpretation of Jeremiah 31:31-34 in Judaism." In *When Jews and Christians Meet*, edited by Jakob Petuchowski. SUNY Press, 1988.

Schäfer, Peter. *The Jewish Jesus: How Judaism and Christianity Shaped Each Other*. Princeton University Press, 2012.

Schäfer, Peter. *Two Gods in Heaven: Jewish Concepts of God in Antiquity*. Princeton University Press, 2020.

Schechter, Solomon. *Aspects of Rabbinic Theology*. Schocken, 1961.

Schiffman, Lawrence. "The Rabbinic Understanding of Covenant." *The New Testament and Judaism, Review and Expositor* 84 (1987): 289–298.

Sciglitano, Anthony C. *Marcion and Prometheus: Balthasar against the Expulsion of Jewish Origins in Modern Religious Thought*. Crossroad, 2014.

Scholem, Gershom. *The Messianic Idea in Judaism: And Other Essays on Jewish Spirituality*. Schocken Books, 1978.

Shapiro, Faydra L. *Christian Zionism: Navigating the Jewish-Christian Border*. Cascade Books, 2015.

Shelly, Bruce L. "Fine-Tuning the Incarnation." *Christian History* 51 (1996): 18–20.

Smith, Morton. "On the Shape of God and the Humanity of Gentiles." In *Religions in Antiquity: Essays in Memory of Erwin Ramsdell Goodenough*, edited by Jacob Neusner. Brill, 1970.

Soloveitchik, Joseph Dov. *The Emergence of Ethical Man*. Ktav, 2005.

Soloveitchik, Joseph Dov. *The Lonely Man of Faith*. Doubleday, 1992.

Soulen, R. Kendall. *Divine Name(s) and the Holy Trinity*, vol. 1, *Distinguishing the Voices*. Westminster John Knox Press, 2011.

Soulen, R. Kendall. *The God of Israel and Christian Theology*. Augsburg Fortress, 1996.

Soulen, R. Kendall. "Hallowed Be Thy Name! The Tetragrammaton and the Name of the Trinity." In *Jews & Christians, People of God*, edited by C. Braaten and R. Wilken. Eerdmans, 2003.

Soulen, R. Kendall. *Irrevocable: The Name of God and the Unity of the Christian Bible* Fortress Press, 2022.

Soulen, R. Kendall. "Israel and the Church: A Christian Response to Irving Greenberg's Covenantal Pluralism." In *Christianity in Jewish Terms*, edited by Tikva Frymer-Kensky. Westview Press, 2000.

Soulen, R. Kendall. "Michael Wyschogrod and God's First Love." *The Christian Century* (July 2004): 22–27.

Sullivan, Francis A. *Salvation Outside the Church: Tracing the History of the Catholic Response.* Paulist Press, 1992.

Strachan, Owen. "Carl F. H. Henry's Doctrine of the Atonement: A Synthesis and Brief Analysis." *Themelios* 38, no. 2 (2013): 43–54.

Stroumsa, Guy. "Form(s) of God: Some Notes on Metatron and Christ." *Harvard Theological Review* 76, no. 3 (1983): 269–288.

Stroumsa, Guy. "Polymorphie divine et transformations d'un mythologème: l'Apocryphon de Jean et ses sources." *Vigiliae Christianae* 35, no. 4 (December 1981): 412–434.

Talmon, Shemaryahu. "The Community of the Renewed Covenant: Between Judaism and Christianity." In *The Community of the Renewed Covenant: The Notre Dame Symposium on the Dead Sea Scrolls*, edited by Eugene Ulrich and James VanderKam. Notre Dame University Press, 1994.

Thiessen, Matthew. *A Jewish Paul: The Messiah's Herald to the Gentiles.* Baker Academic, 2023.

Tracy, David. "The Christian Understanding of Salvation-Liberation." *Buddhist-Christian Studies* 7 (1987): 129–138.

Tracy, David. "Religious Values After the Holocaust: A Catholic View." In *Jews and Christians After the Holocaust*, edited by A. Peck. Philadelphia: Fortress, 1982.

Ulmer, Rivka. "The Contours of the Messiah in Pesiqta Rabbati." *Harvard Theological Review* 106, no. 2 (2013): 115–144.

Ulmer, Rivka. "Psalm 22 in Pesiqta Rabbati: The Suffering of the Jewish Messiah and Jesus." In *The Jewish Jesus: Revelation, Reflection, Reclamation*, edited by Zev Garber. Purdue University Press, 2011.

Urban, Linwood. *A Short History of Christian Thought.* Oxford University Press, 1995.

Urbach, Ephraim. *The Sages: Their Concepts and Beliefs.* Magnes Press, 1975.

Visotzky, Burton L. "Will and Grace: Aspects of Judaising in Pelagianism in Light of Rabbinic and Patristic Exegesis of Genesis." In *The Exegetical*

Encounter Between Jews and Christians in Late Antiquity, edited by Emmanouela Grypeou and Helen Spurling. Brill, 2009.

Volf, Miroslav. *The Church as the Image of the Trinity*. Eerdmans, 1998.

Vorster, N. "Calvin's Modification of Augustine's Doctrine of Original Sin." *In die Skriflig* 44, supplement 3 (2010): 71–89.

Weaver, David. "The Exegesis of Romans 5:12 among the Greek Fathers and Its Implication for the Doctrine of Original Sin: The 5th–12th Centuries." *St. Vladimir's Theological Quarterly* 29, no. 2 (1985): 133–159.

Weiss, Dov. "Cyril of Alexandria's Critique of 'Jewish' Parental Sin." *Medieval Encounters* 28 (2022): 221–241.

Weiss, Dov. "Gehinnom's Punishments in Classical Rabbinic Literature." In *Jewish Culture and Creativity: Essays in Honor of Michael Fishbane*. Academic Studies Press, 2023.

Weiss, Dov, "The Rabbinic God and Medieval Judaism." *Currents in Biblical Research* 15, no. 3 (2017): 369–390.

Weiss Tsaḥi. "The Letter of Isaac the Blind to Nahmanides and Jonah Gerondi in Its Historical Context." *Journal of Jewish Studies* 72, no. 2 (2021): 327–348.

Weiss, Tzahi. "'Their Heart Was Turned Away from the Uppermost': Rethinking the Boundaries of the 'Kabbalistic Literature' and the Opposition to 'Kabbalah' in the First Half of the 13th Century." *DAAT: Journal for Jewish Philosophy and Kabbalah* 85 (2018): 307–339 [Hebrew].

Weiss-Rosmarin, Trude. *Judaism and Christianity: The Differences*. Jewish Book Club, 1943.

Werblowsky, R. J. Zwi. "Messianism in Jewish History." In *Essential Papers on Messianic Movements and Personalities in Jewish History*, edited by Marc Saperstein. New York University Press, 1992.

Werblowsky, R. J. Zwi. "Tora als Gnade." *Kairos* 15 (1973): 156–163.

Wolfson, Elliot R. "Judaism and Incarnation: The Imaginal Body of God." In *Christianity in Jewish Terms*, edited by Tikva Frymer-Kensky, et al. Westview Press, 2000.

Wolfson, Elliot R. *Open Secret: Postmessianic Messianism and the Mystical Revision of Menahem Mendel Schneerson*. Columbia University Press, 2009.

Wolfson, Elliot R. "Open Secret in the Rearview Mirror." *AJS Review* 35, no. 2 (2011): 393–400.

Wolfson, Elliot R. "Suffering Time: Maharal's Influence on Hasidic Perspectives on Temporality." *Kabbalah: Journal for the Study of Jewish Mystical Texts* 44 (2019): 7–73.

Wolfson, Harry Austryn. "Extradeical and Intradeical Interpretation of Platonic Ideas." In *Religious Philosophy: A Group of Essays*. Belknap Press of Harvard University Press, 1961.

Wolfson, Harry A. "Saadia on the Trinity and the Incarnation." In *Studies and Essays in Honor of Abraham A. Neuman*, edited by M. Ben Horin, et al. Brill, 1962.

Woodard-Lehman, Derek. "Saying 'Yes' to Israel's 'No': Barth's Dialectical Supersessionism and the Witness of Carnal Israel." In *Karl Barth: Post-Holocaust Theologian?*, edited by George Hunsinger. Bloomsbury T&T Clark, 2018.

Wyschogrod, Michael. "Incarnation and God's Indwelling in Israel." In *Abraham's Promise: Judaism and Jewish-Christian Relations*, edited by R. Kendall Soulen. Eerdmans, 2004.

Wyschogrod, Michael. "A Jewish Perspective on Incarnation." *New Theology* 12, no. 2 (1996): 195–209.

Wyschogrod, Michael. "A Jewish Perspective on Karl Barth." In *How Karl Barth Changed My Mind*, edited by Donald K. McKim. Eerdmans, 1986.

Wyschogrod, Michael. "Review of Friedrich-Wilhelm Marquardt, *Das Christliche Bekenntnis zu Jesus, dem Juden. Eine Christologie*." *Journal of Ecumenical Studies* 29, no. 2 (1992): 275–276.

Wyschogrod, Michael. "The Torah as Law in Judaism." In *"Your World Is a Lamp to My Feet and a Light to My Path" (Ps 119:105). SIDIC Periodical* 35, no. 2–3 (2002): 18–23.

Wyschogrod, Michael. "Why Was and Is the Theology of Karl Barth of Interest to a Jewish Theologian?" In *Footnotes to a Theology: The Karl Barth Colloquium of 1972*, edited by M. Rumscheidt. SR Supplements, 1972.

Yisraeli, Oded. "The 'Messianic Idea' in Nahmanides' Writings." *Jewish Studies Quarterly* 29, no. 1 (2022): 22–45.

Yisraeli, Oded. "Monotheism and Dualism in Nahmanides' Kabbalistic Thought." *Journal of Jewish Studies* 70, no. 2 (2019): 298–317.

Yisraeli, Oded. *Temple Portals: Studies in Aggadah and Midrash in the Zohar*. De Gruyter, 2016.

Zetterholm, Magnus. *The Messiah: In Early Judaism and Christianity*. Fortress Press, 2007.

INDEX